Gothic Dreams

Necronomicon

Dark Fantasy, Digital Art & H.P. Lovecraft

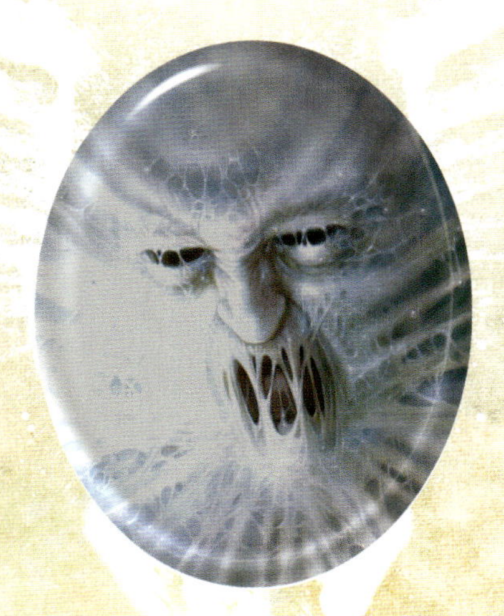

SAMMY MAINE

Foreword by S.T. Joshi

FLAME TREE
PUBLISHING

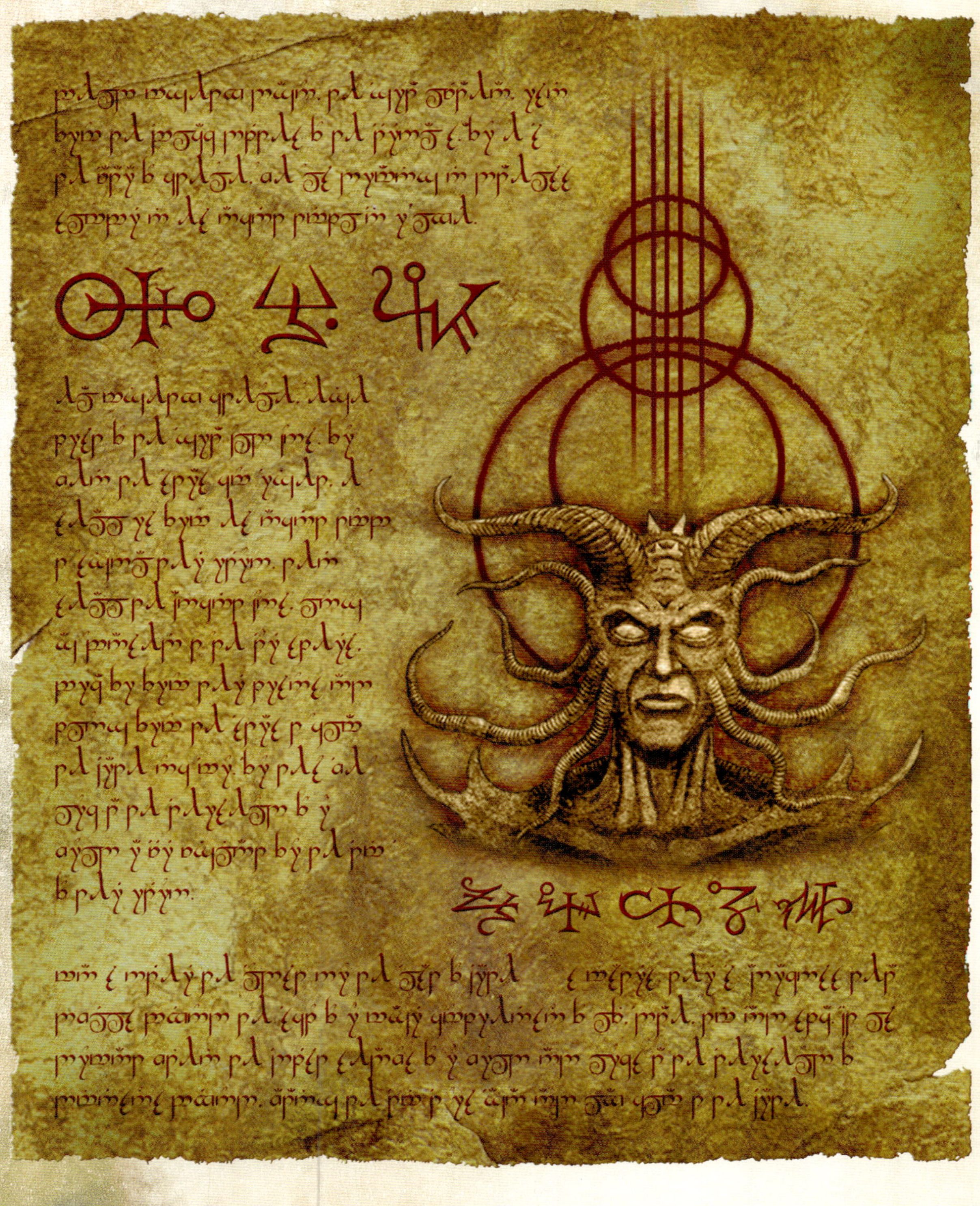

Gothic Dreams

Necronomicon

Dark Fantasy, Digital Art & H.P. Lovecraft

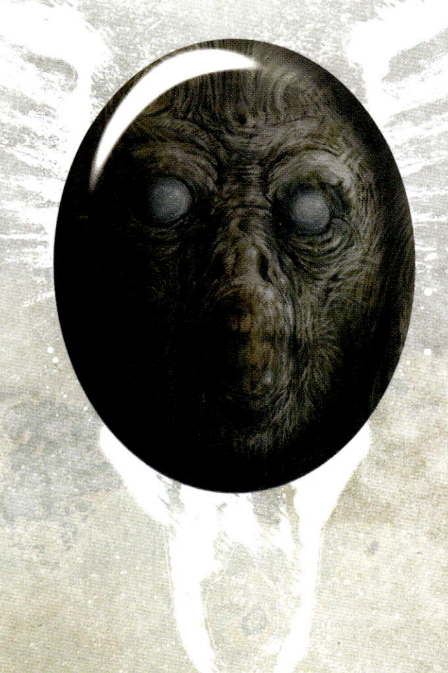

Publisher and Creative Director: Nick Wells
Project Editor: Laura Bulbeck
Picture Research: Laura Bulbeck and Katie Hewett
Art Director: Mike Spender
Copy Editor: Ramona Lamport
Proofreader: Amanda Crook

Special thanks to: Fraces Bodiam, Helen Crust and the artists who allowed us to reproduce their fantastic artwork

FLAME TREE PUBLISHING
Crabtree Hall, Crabtree Lane
Fulham, London SW6 6TY
United Kingdom

www.flametreepublishing.com

First published 2015

15 17 19 18 16
1 3 5 7 9 10 8 6 4 2

A CIP record for this book is available from the British Library upon request.

ISBN 978-1-78361-320-5

Printed in China

Contents

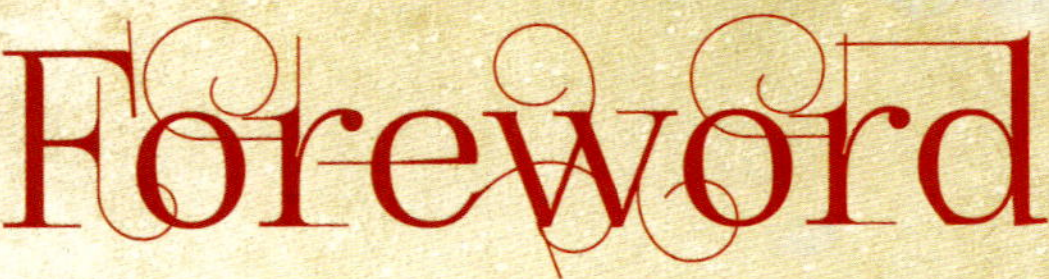

Foreword

H. P. Lovecraft was a lover of words. In his youth he successively discovered the worlds of wonder and terror opened up to him by Grimm's fairy tales, classical and Arabian myth, and the writings of a long line of weird authors from Edgar Allan Poe to Arthur Machen to Lord Dunsany and many others.

It is, therefore, understandable that he would devise the notion of the 'forbidden book' – a book that contains such unholy knowledge that the mere act of reading it could cause death or madness. Hence the ***Necronomicon*** was eventually born, along with an entire library of other tomes that are kept locked away in the world's great libraries to protect the world's sanity. The cleverness of Lovecraft's prodigal invention of imaginary occult titles is that he deftly cited real books in the midst of his fictitious ones – whether they be sober anthropological treatises such as Margaret Murray's ***The Witch-Cult in Western Europe*** or centuries-old volumes of strange lore such as Remigius's ***Daemonolatreia***. Readers can be forgiven for not knowing which books are real and which are invented.

Lovecraft once provided a derivation for the word ***Necronomicon***: 'An Image [or Picture] of the Law of the Dead'. Unfortunately, Lovecraft's knowledge of Greek (and specifically of the rules of etymology) was negligible, and his derivation is almost entirely erroneous. Later writers have provided still more erroneous derivations, such as 'Book of the Names of the Dead'. The proper derivation is a bit more prosaic: 'A Book Classifying the Dead'. And yet, there is some use in knowing what Lovecraft ***thought*** the title meant. And it is fascinating to trace the development of the tome throughout his fiction, where it seems to progress from a work that warns against the cosmic monsters it is writing about to one that actively fosters their imminent return to the Earth by means of spells and incantations.

The ***Necronomicon*** has, as this book splendidly demonstrates, taken on a life of its own both in literature and in popular culture. Lovecraft himself, a keen devotee of weird art, would have been fascinated by both the text and the vivid images this book contains. It is as vital a tribute to Lovecraft's imagination as any I have seen.

S.T. Joshi

www.stjoshi.org

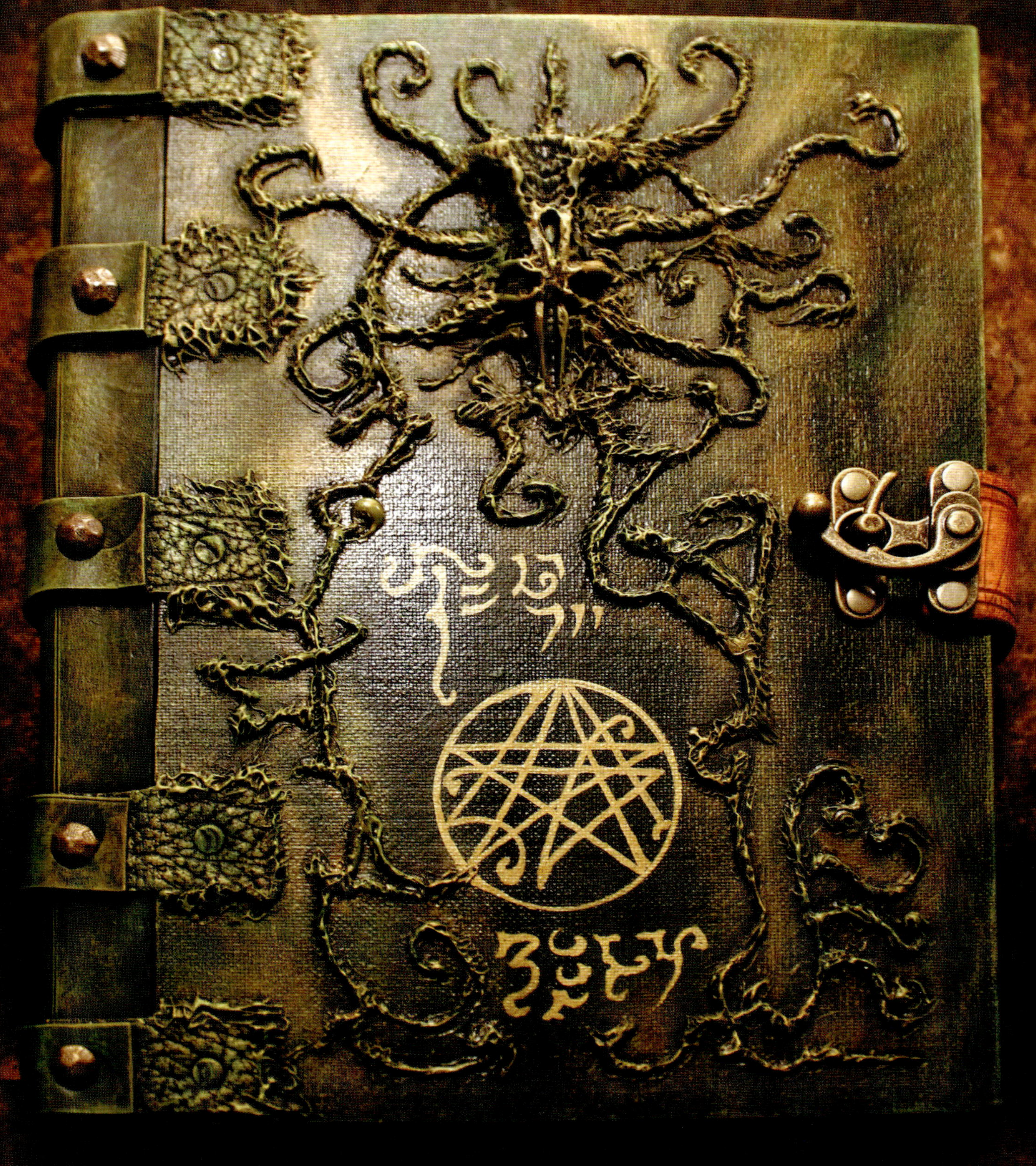

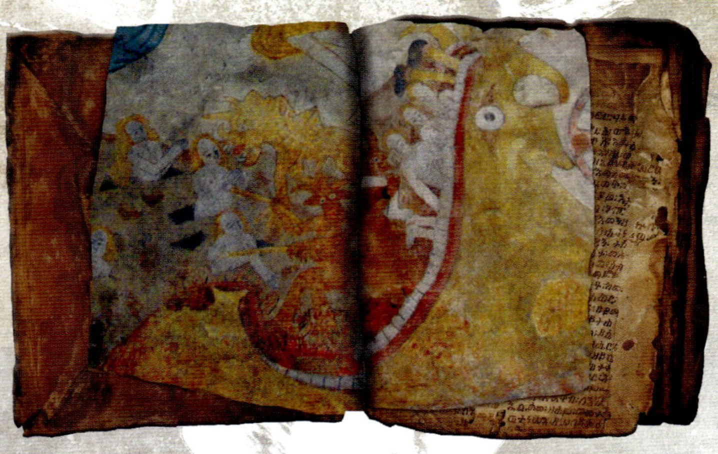

A Book of Flesh and Blood

***Necronomicon*. The book of the dead. Bound in human flesh and inked in blood, it holds the path to an unknown evil; an evil never meant for the world of the living. Created by iconic horror writer H.P. Lovecraft (1890–1937), this fictional grimoire is only ever hinted at throughout his works, its readers succumbing to a gruesome and horrific death should they ever utter its words.**

Making its first appearance in Lovecraft's short story 'The Hound', published in 1924, the book is said to be filled with bizarre burial rites, funeral incantations and demon resurrection spells. Whilst entirely fictional, avid Lovecraft fans have claimed ithat the book really does exist – seemingly convinced by the author's History of the Necronomicon published in 1938. Recounting the life of its author – the 'Mad Arab' Abdul Alhazred – the book quickly grew in popularity, with plenty of 'real editions' published to satisfy its devoted believers.

Books, video games and cult horror films have all referred to the ***Necronomicon*** in their works, with the likes of artist H.R. Giger (1940–2014) and filmmaker Sam Raimi (b. 1959) hugely influenced by its implied content. Suggesting demonic gods of outer-worldly existence, Lovecraft's ***Necronomicon*** remains a landmark in the creation of sci-fi horror, and its legacy continues.

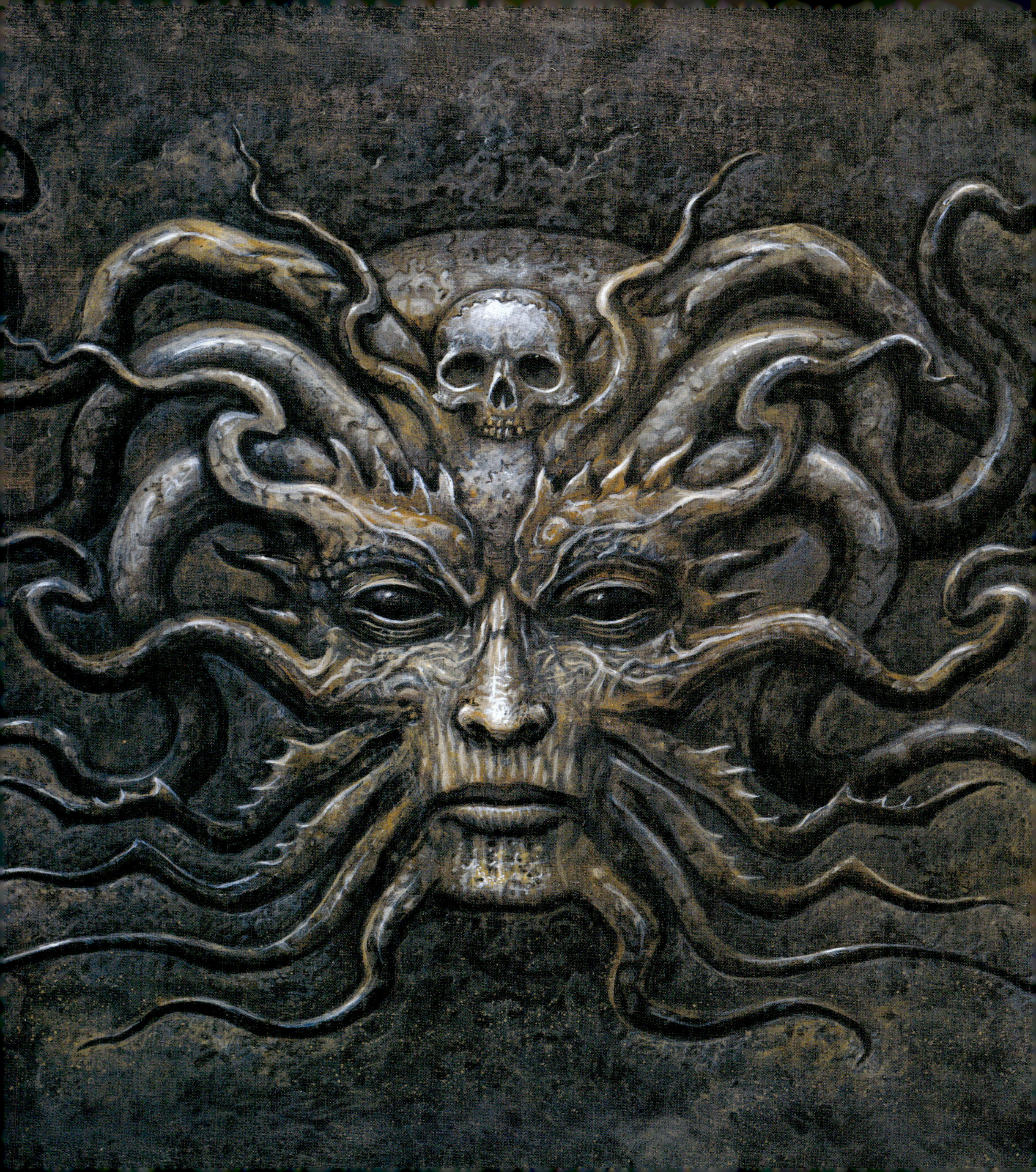

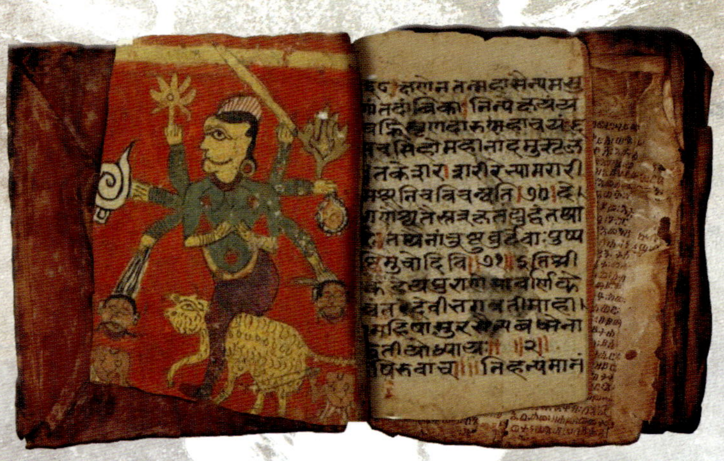

Occult Origins

H.P. Lovecraft

H.P. Lovecraft was weird; so weird in fact, that his work coined the term 'Weird Fiction'. This term harks back to the time in which his writing was published in an extensive range of pulp magazines including the likes of ***Amazing Stories***, ***Astounding Stories*** and the appropriately titled ***Weird Tales***.

Born in 1890 in Providence, Rhode Island, Lovecraft was the only child of Winfield Scott Lovecraft (1853–98) and Sarah Susan Phillips Lovecraft (1857–1921). When Lovecraft was three years old, his father suffered a nervous breakdown; he was hospitalized and died five years later. Lovecraft was subsequently raised by his mother, two aunts and maternal grandfather.

Cosmic Horror

Lovecraft suffered frequent illnesses – many said to be influenced by his mother's worry – that ensured he led a lonely, yet literature-filled life. Isolation is a prominent theme in Lovecraft's work, with many of his stories featuring lost cities and civilizations, including Atlantis and other lost continents. With a keen interest in chemistry, astronomy and Greek and Roman

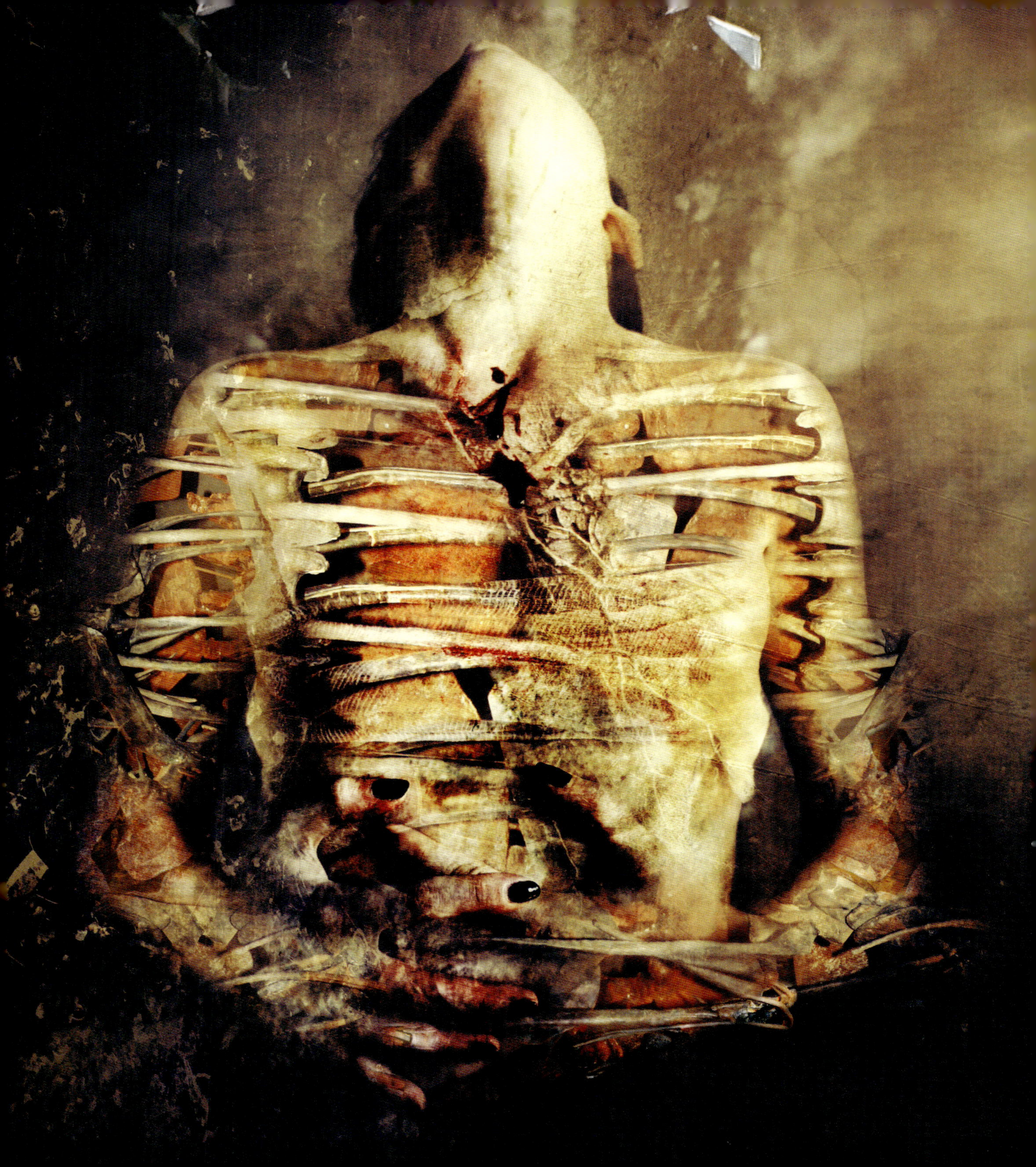

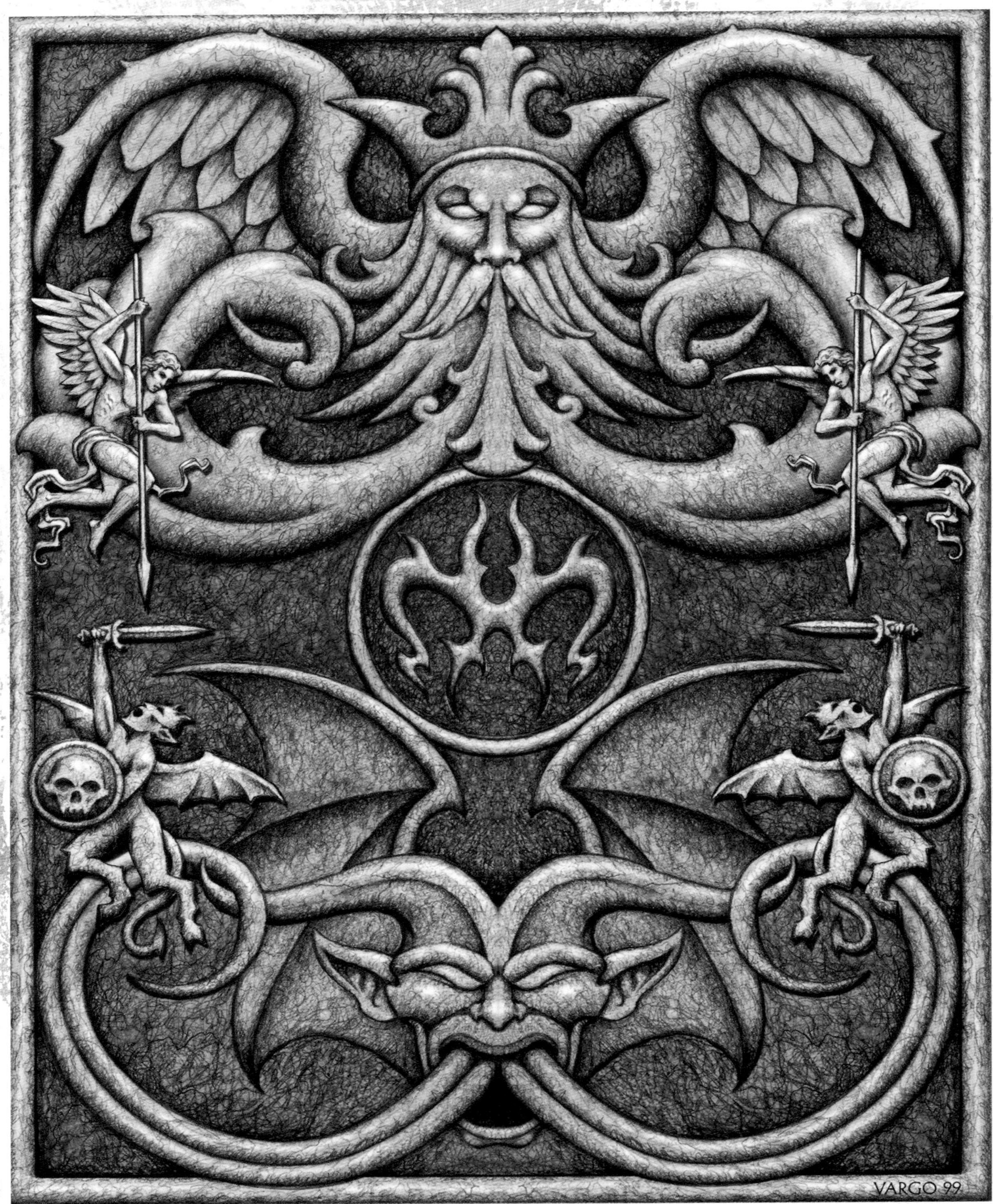
VARGO 99

cultures, his work developed a genre of its own – 'cosmic horror'. Featuring unknown, extraterrestrial and otherworldly creatures, gods and beings, Lovecraft's stories were some of the first to mix science fiction with horror. Often including mind-transfers, savagery and cannibalism, the psychological aspects of his stories have gripped just about anyone who comes across the works of this talented writer.

Cthulhu Mythos

In his famous Cthulhu mythos, Lovecraft created a universe in which the lines blurred between good and evil. Although Lovecraft's friend, August Derleth (1909–71) speculated that the Cthulhu mythos was 'basically similar to the Christian mythos', Lovecraft himself claimed that he was 'an indifferentist', and no-one knows exactly where he gained his inspiration. What we do know is that he created a world unlike any other, teaching us that there is more than one way to look at the universe and that we – as mankind – might not be as important as we think we are. 'One is a stranger in this century,' Lovecraft said, and in this fictional universe he created a world in which we can all immerse ourselves.

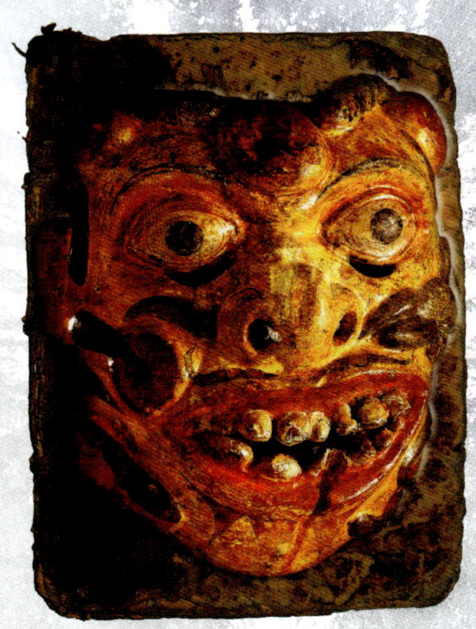

In the Pages

But how do we enter this terrifying Lovecraftian world? Thankfully, Lovecraft created a book in which all our nightmares could come true – the ***Necronomicon***. Filled with spells to raise the dead, summon demons and through which to glimpse a truly hideous world, this fictional work was only ever hinted at within the pages of 'The Hound', ***The Case of Charles Dexter Ward*** (published posthumously in 1941), ***At the Mountains of Madness*** (1936), and other works. Often causing the downfall of its solitary protagonists, the events surrounding the ***Necronomicon*** take place behind closed doors, in sporadic fragments, with only our imagination fuelling our fears. The names of otherworldly gods are whispered, and our planet and our way of life is proved to be just a mere dot on the spectrum of an entirely undiscovered and ghastly universe.

The Unknown

Lovecraft only ever hinted at the powers of the ***Necronomicon*** and never actually wrote a full edition of the book itself. He declared that 'if anyone were to try to write the ***Necronomicon***, it would disappoint all those who have shuddered at cryptic references to it'. Lovecraft based his works upon the unknown and through our fear of it the ***Necronomicon*** quickly became a reference point throughout his stories. He referred to it more than any other mystical book – real or fictional – and it is involved in 18 of his tales. And whilst it remains entirely fictional, the ***Necronomicon*** has been pinpointed as the grimoire of biblical stature concerning Lovecraft and all that follow the genre. It predicts the 'anti-future' of human beings, fueling our fear of the unknown and tapping into our natural, earthly fear of the outside.

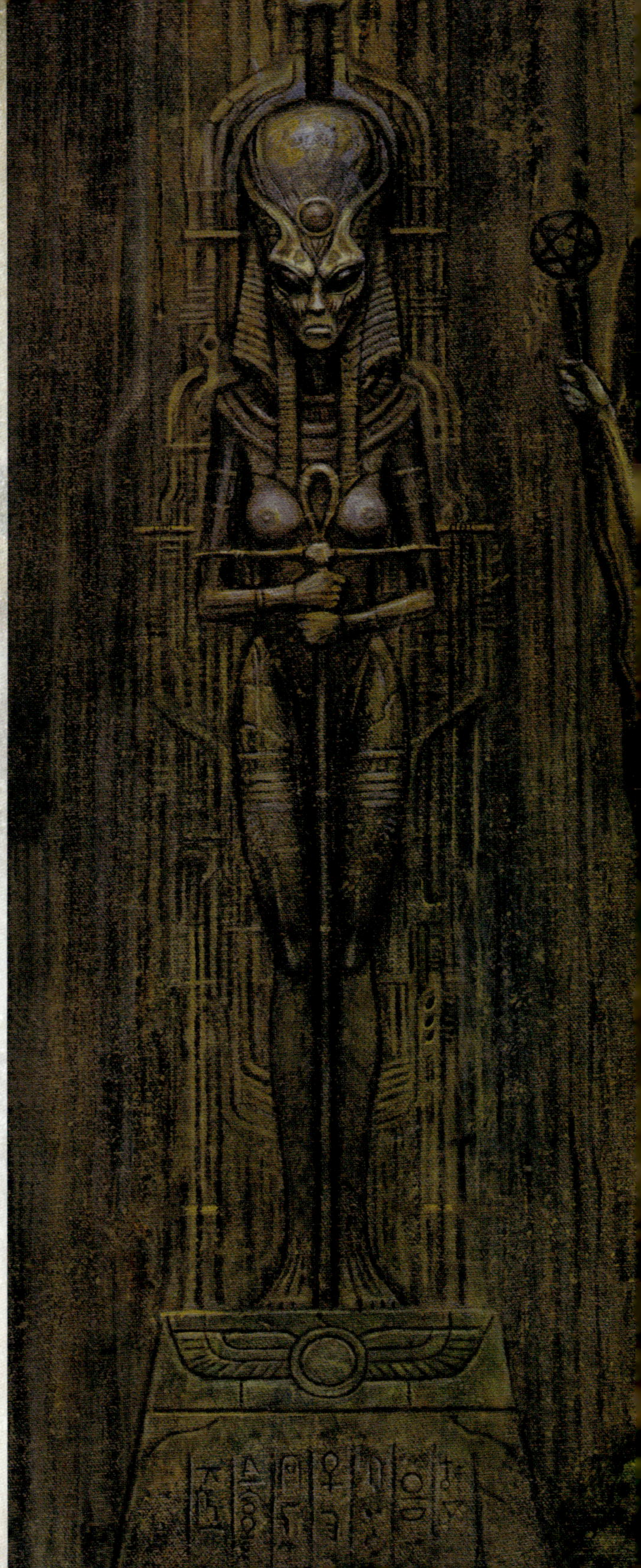

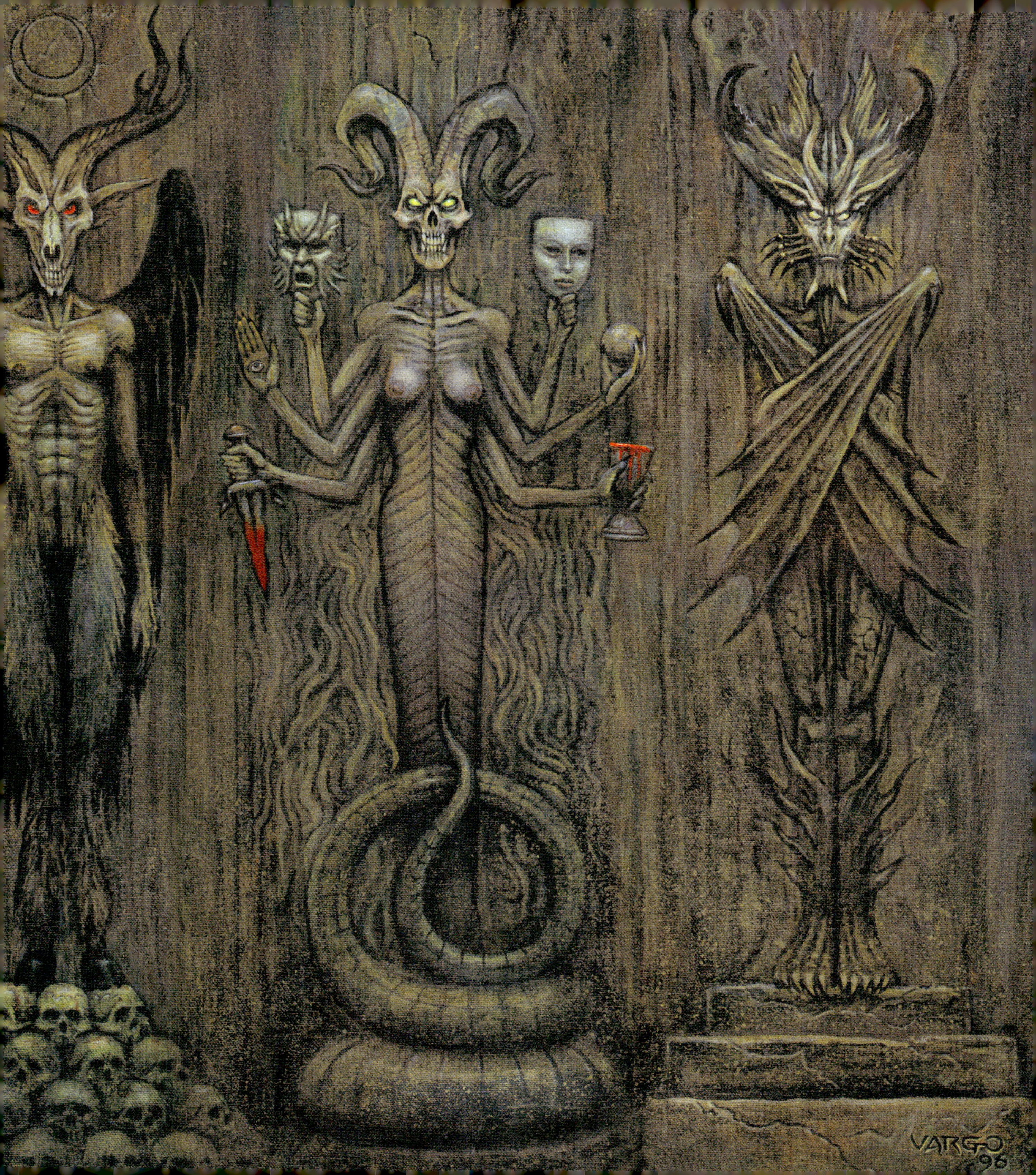
VARGO
96

The Fictional Author

So, what do we know of the ***Necronomicon's*** fictional author, Abdul Alhazred? Well, he was first mentioned by Lovecraft in 'The Nameless City' (1921), where he told of Alhazred singing an unexplainable couplet: 'That is not dead which can eternal lie / And with strange aeons even death may die.' Merely hinting at the character in true Lovecraft style meant that his readers would go on to discuss this couplet at great length. What does it mean? And who exactly is Abdul Alhazred? We were only to learn more about Alhazred in another short story, 'The Hound'. Lovecraft spoke of 'the forbidden ***Necronomicon*** of the Mad Arab Abdul Alhazred', and of the 'corpse-eating cult of inaccessible Leng, in Central Asia'. It was in this story that the unexplainable couplet was finally given its context; Abdul Alhazred wrote the dreaded ***Necronomicon*** before being mauled to death by an invisible demon in the middle of a busy market square in Yemen.

The Crimson Desert

As we delve in deeper, we learn of the ***Necronomicon's*** Arabic title. Penned by Alhazred in AD 730, he titled it 'Al-Azif', a word which is said to mimic the sound of insects summoning demons in the night. Alhazred spent 10 years alone in the southern desert of Arabia – the Roba el Khaliyeh – which was also nicknamed the 'crimson desert', due to the shelter it gave to evil spirits and monsters of death. Alhazred wrote the ***Necronomicon*** during his time in the desert before his inevitable and horrifically gruesome

'The unmentionable Necronomicon of the Mad Arab Abdul Alhazred … a book which I had never seen, but of which I had heard monstrous things whispered.'

'The Festival'

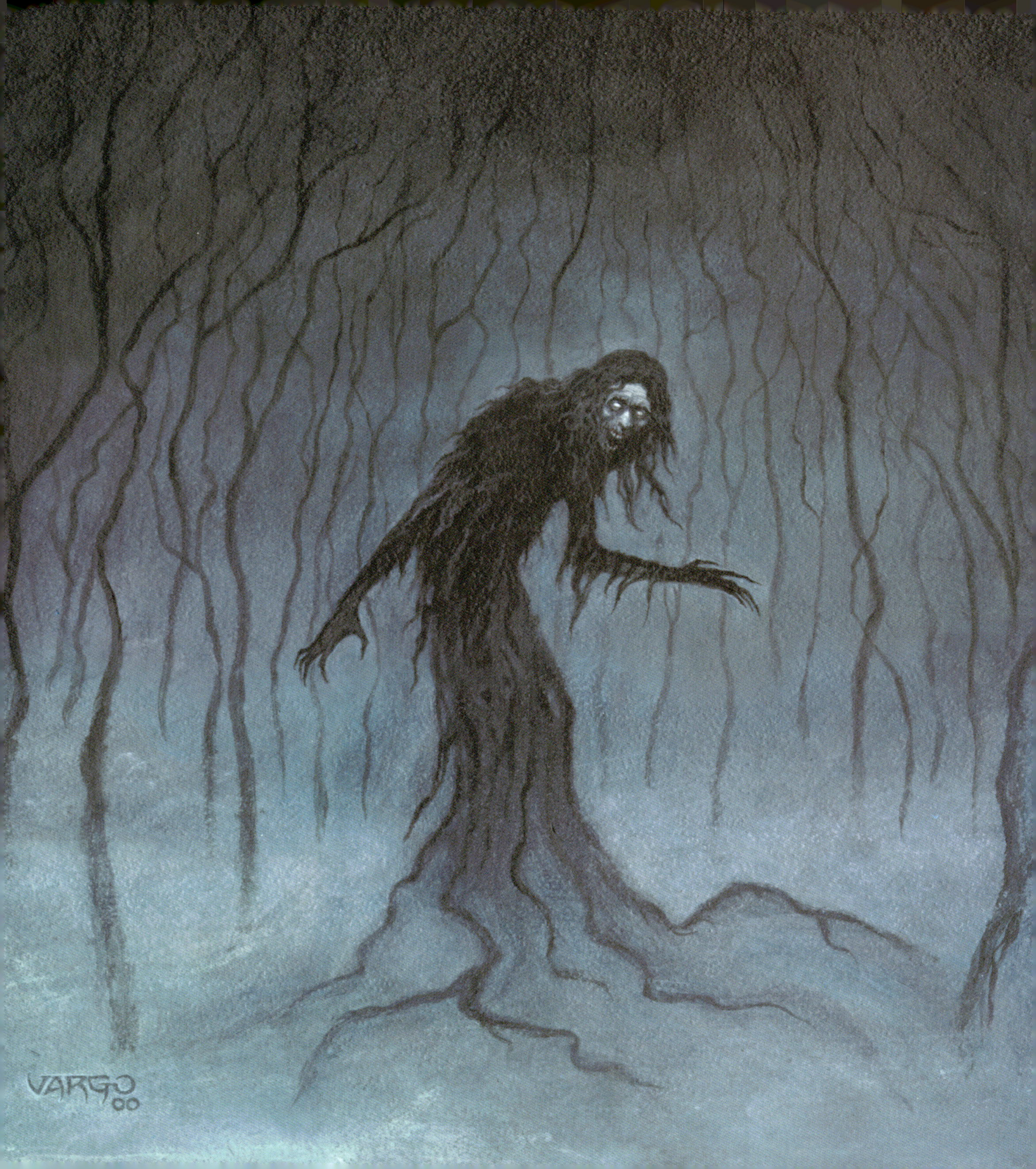
VARGO
00

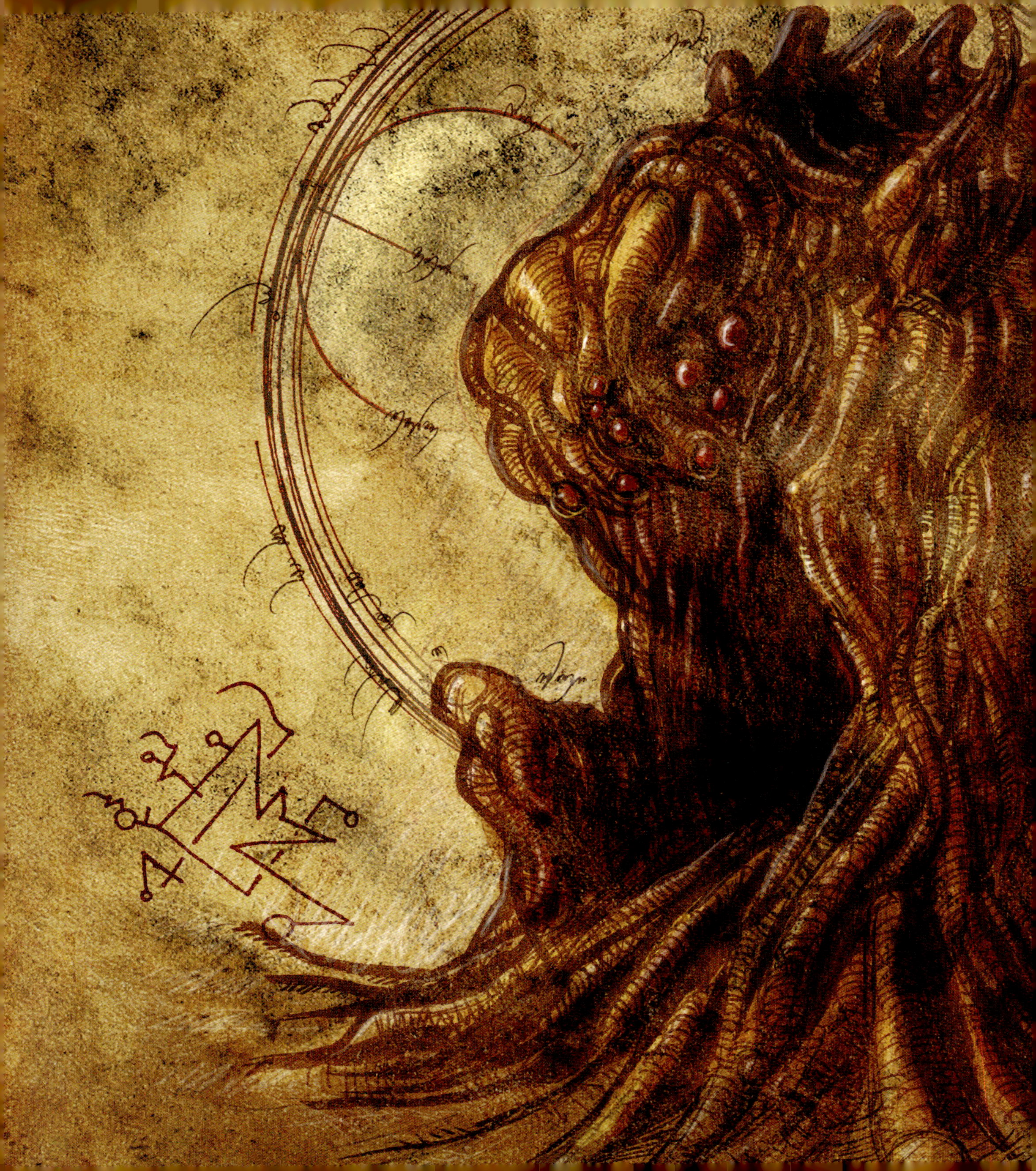

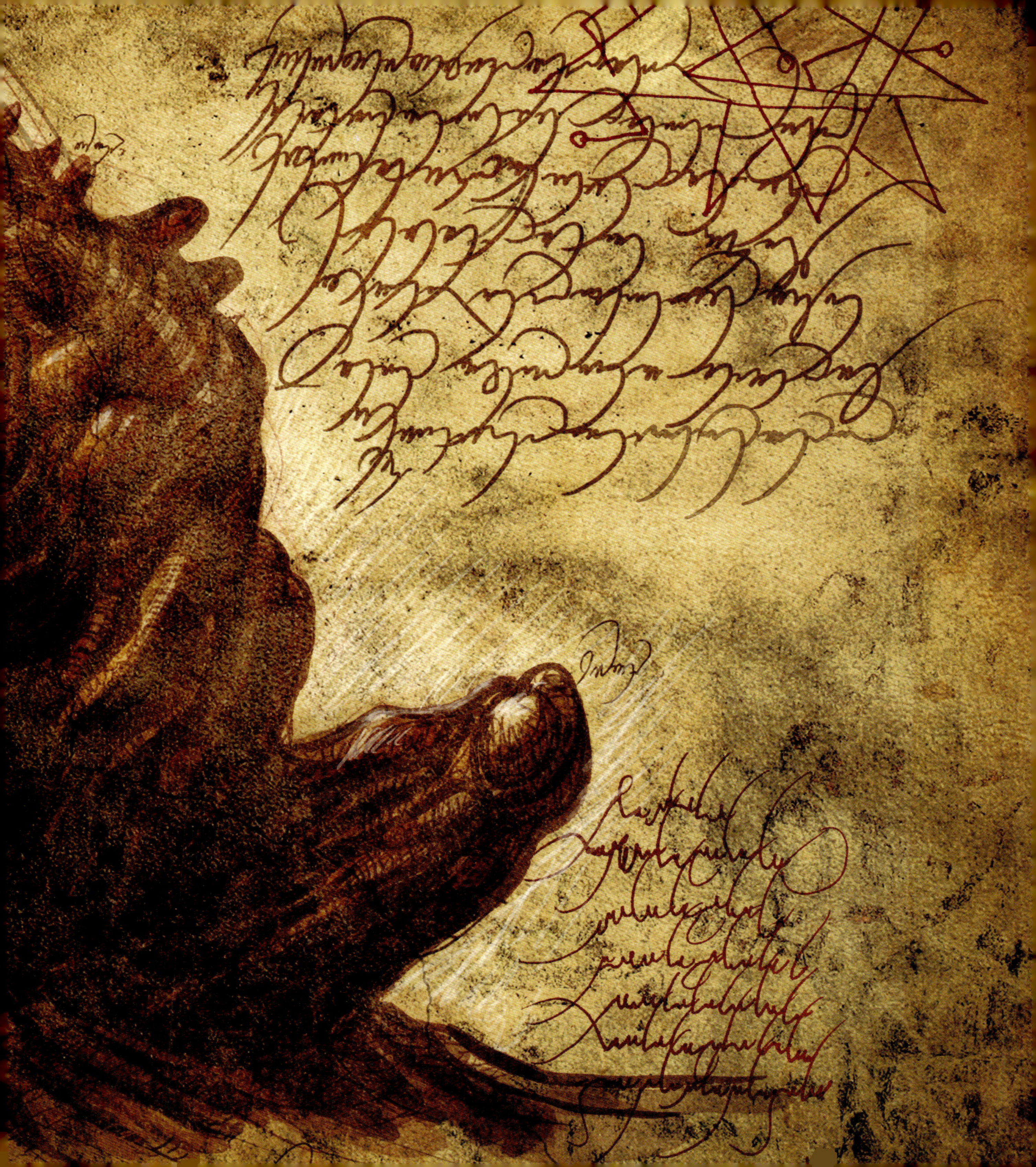

death in broad daylight. Though unable to travel huge distances during his lifetime, Lovecraft was able to pinpoint exotic locations as environments of evil, further tapping into both his personal and his readers' fear of the outside.

The 'Mad Arab'

The 'Mad Arab' and his given name is said to be an ode to Lovecraft's love of Andrew Lang (1844–1912) and his version of ***1001 Arabian Nights***, which Lovecraft read as a young boy. Whilst 'Abdul' is a typical Arabic name – though only usually used as an ending of another name – Lovecraft would be hard pressed to convince actual Arabic people of the names' authenticity. Nonetheless, it's a fun name to dissect, with 'Alhazred' transmuted into 'All has read' and the 'Hazred' aspect hinting at a 'hazard'. Leading authority on Lovecraft S.T. Joshi (b. 1958), suggested a more appropriate and traditional Arabic name in 'Abd-el-Hazred', but then that just wouldn't be Lovecraftian enough, would it?

The History of the Necronomicon

After all his clever referencing, Lovecraft finally gave his fans what they wanted – the short story, 'History of the Necronomicon'. Whilst still maintaining its fictional status, this simply encouraged those who believed the book to be real, with shops and libraries bombarded with enquiries. Lovecraft penned the 'History of the Necronomicon' in the autumn of 1927 before it was

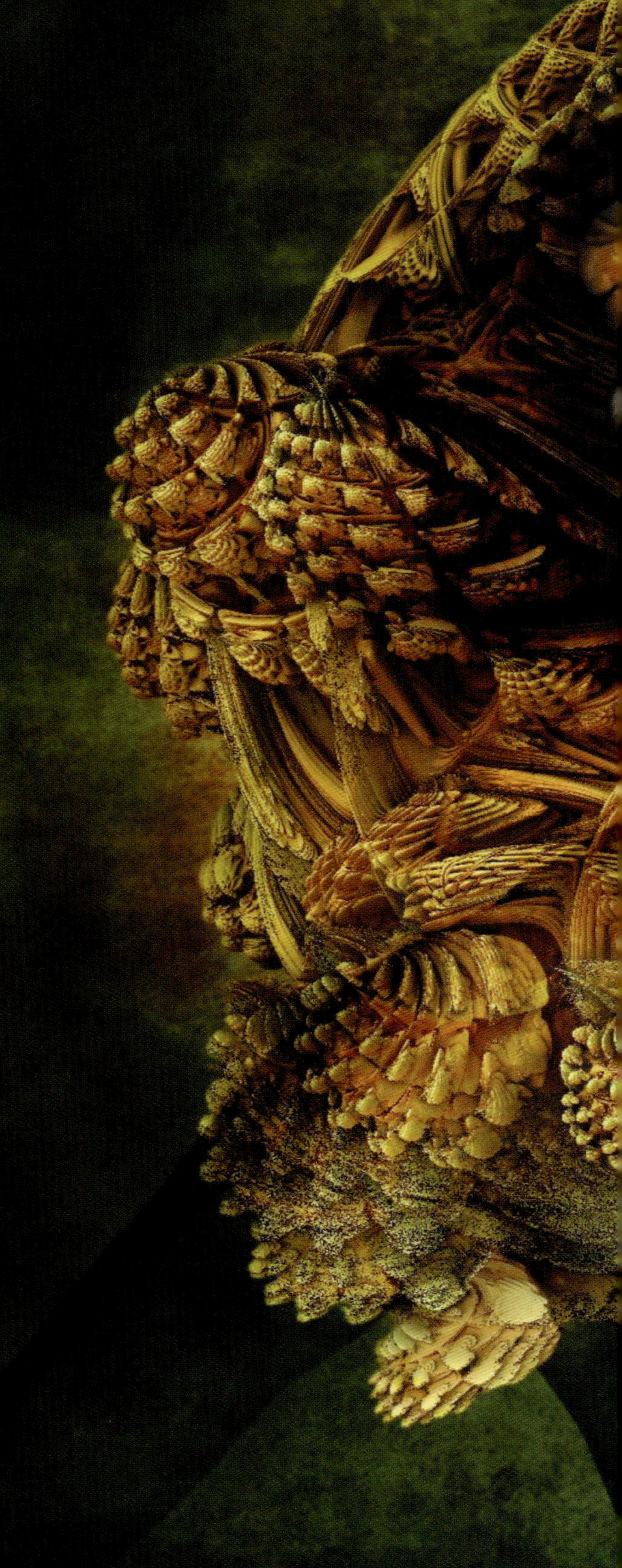

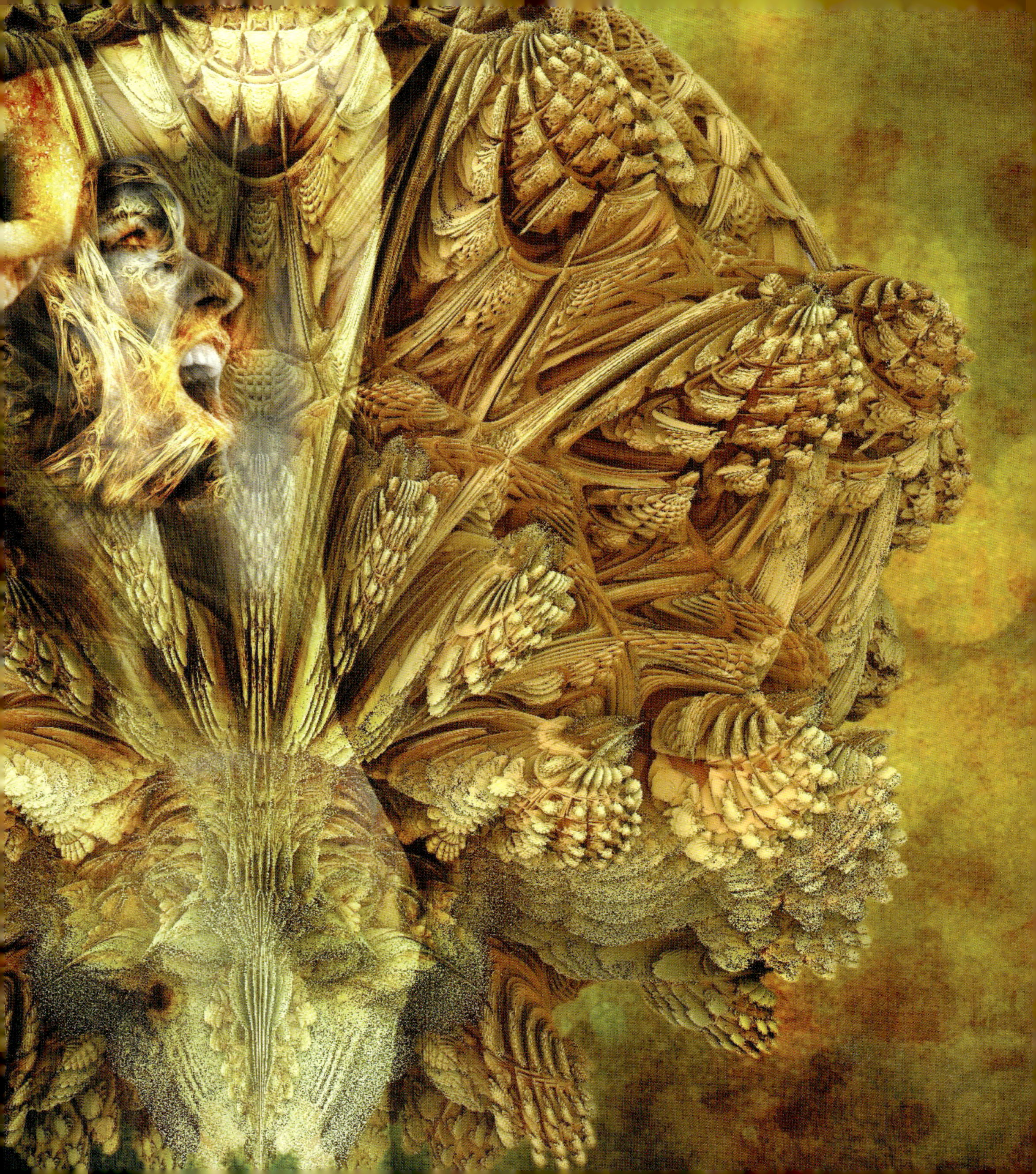

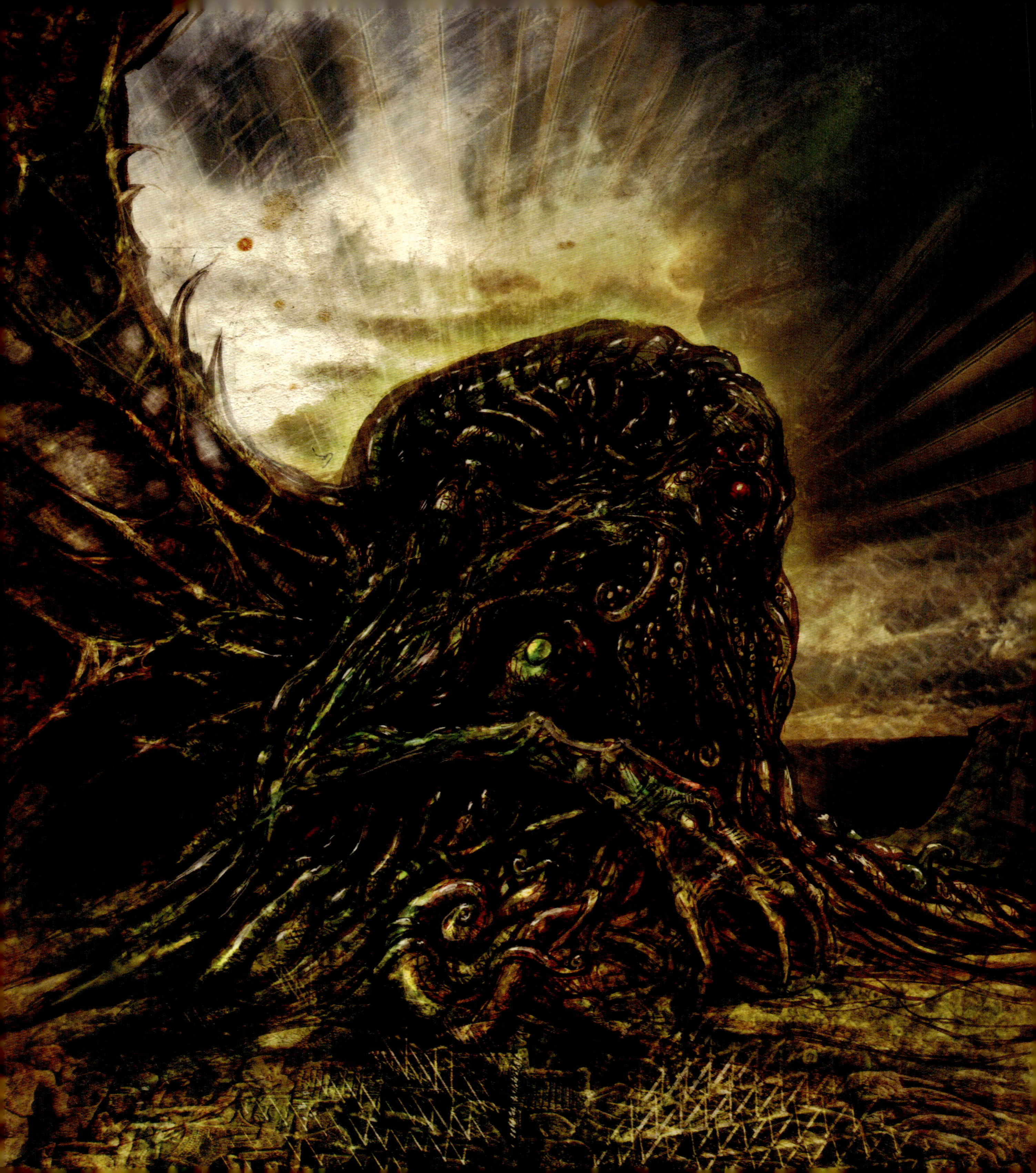

published in 1938 by Wilson H. Shepherd's Rebel Press. The story tells of Abdul Alhazred at great length; of the impenetrable and intensely hostile desert, his religion and his madness, explaining that in this madness, Alhazred 'claimed to have seen fabulous Irem, or City of Pillars', which cleverly harks back to the environment mentioned in ***At the Mountains of Madness***.

Playing with Religion

We learn that Alhazred was an indifferent Muslim, much like Lovecraft and his avoidance of Christianity, and that Alhazred worships the gods Yog-Sothoth and Cthulhu, adding to Lovecraft's infamous Cthulhu mythos. Mythology begins to take a much more prominenet role at this point, with the overall idea of the ***Necronomicon*** said to be inspired by Lovecraft's fascination with Greek and Roman tales. He continues to tell of its translation into Greek by Theodorus Philatas and of how it was suppressed and burnt by the Patriarch Michael. It was then translated into Latin by Olaus Wormius in the Middle Ages before both versions were banned by Pope Gregory IX in 1232. Though a man of religious indifference, Lovecraft certainly knew how to use religion to his advantage.

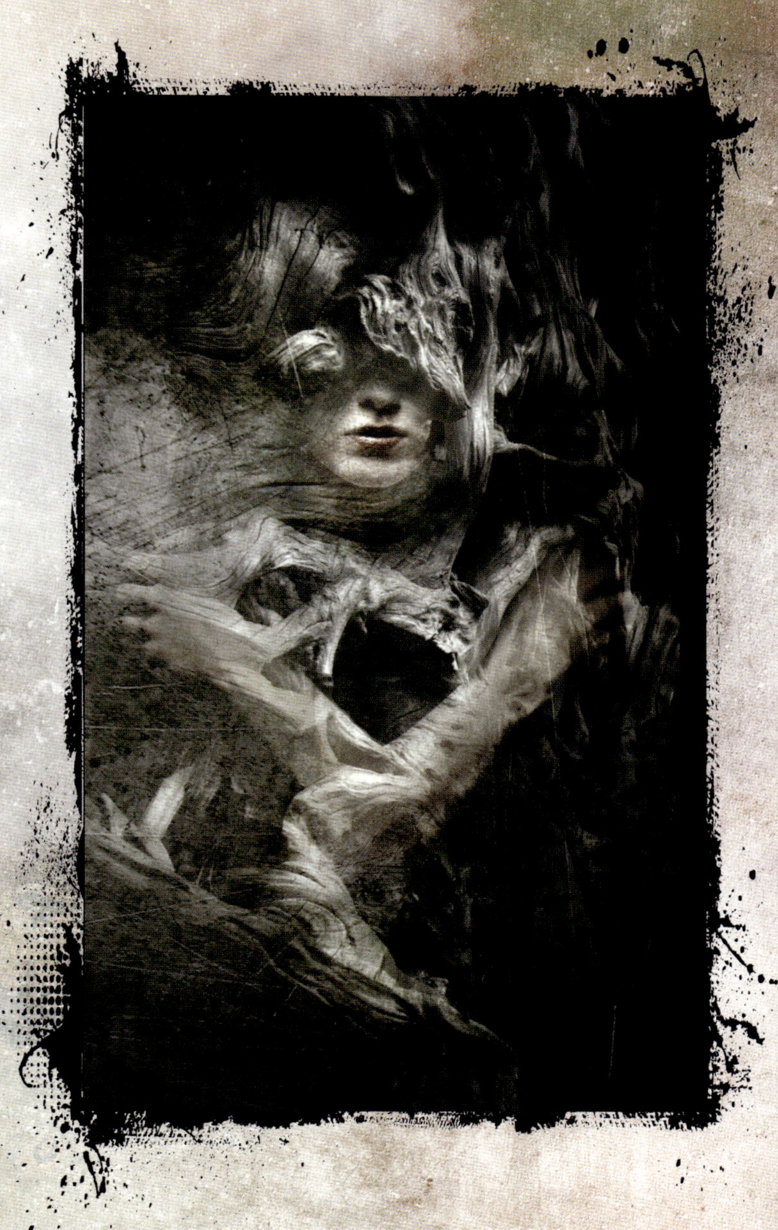

Roving between Italian publishers, Salem and English manuscripts, Lovecraft did what he did best – never giving too much away. Adding more fuel to the believers' fire, he spoke of the ***Necronomicon***'s existence at a number of famous museums (though of course, only the British Museum and the Bibliothèque nationale in Paris are real).

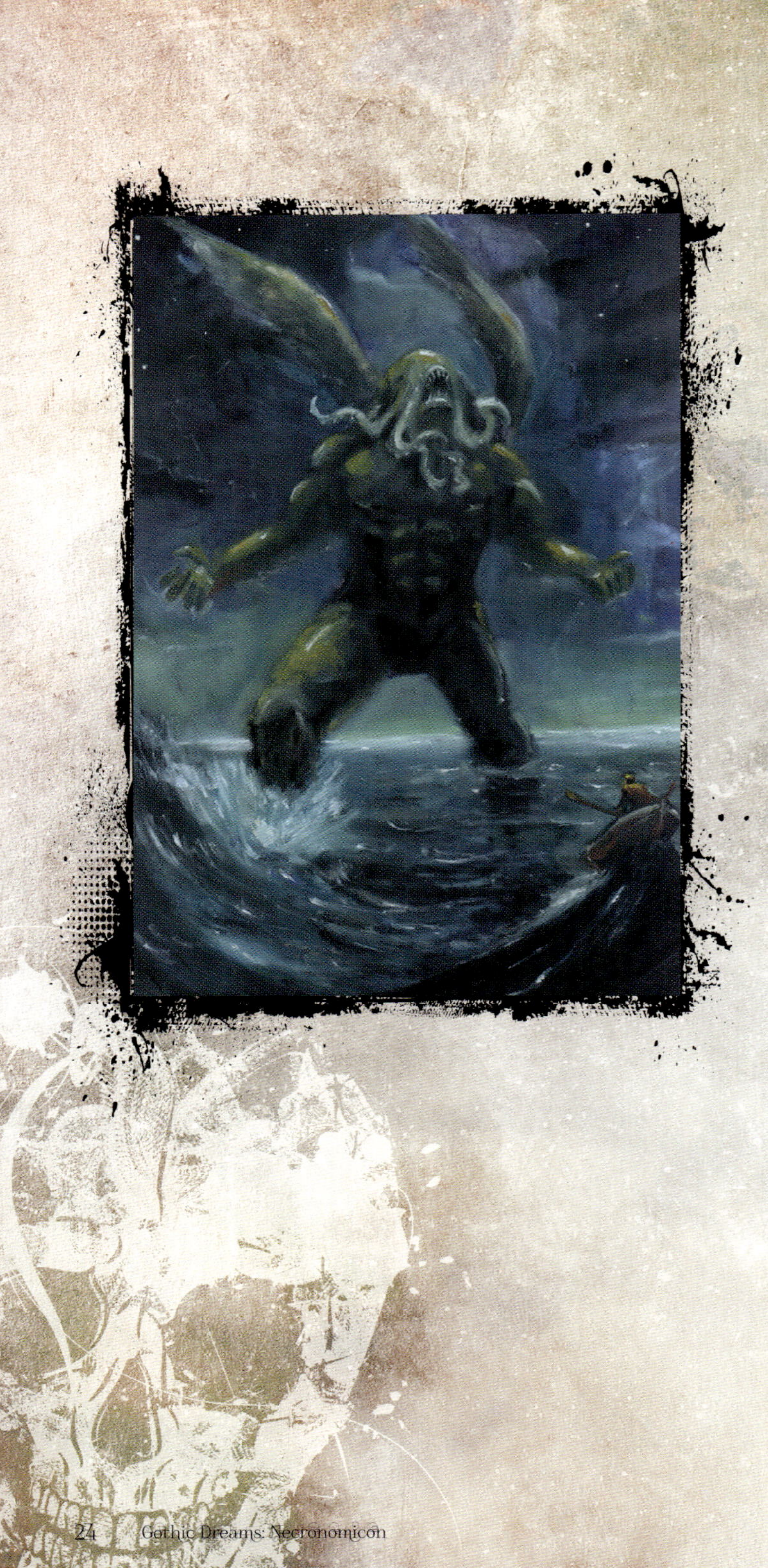

Personal Letters

Lovecraft loved to write letters, especially to his close personal friends who also happened to be authors themselves. Corresponding with the likes of Robert E. Howard (1906–36), Robert Bloch (1917–94) and Willis Conover (1920–96), Lovecraft would often relate his bewilderment at the endless inquiries into the authenticity of the ***Necronomicon***. 'As for writing the ***Necronomicon*** – I wish I had the energy and ingenuity to do it!' he says in a letter to Howard in 1932.

Despite telling his readers that the ***Necronomicon*** was 100 per cent fiction, Lovecraft continued to write to his friends, telling them of the endless enquiries he received. There's a hint of guilt in these letters for leading on his readers so regularly, as he says in a letter to Margaret Sylvester (1918–unknown) in 1934: 'Of course none of us has the least wish actually to mislead readers.' Sylvester originally began correspondence with Lovecraft in 1934 after writing to ask him to explain the origin and meaning of the term 'Walpurgisnacht' – she later became Margaret Ronan and wrote the preface to a school edition of Lovecraft's tales, ***The Shadow Over Innsmouth and Other Stories of Horror*** (1971). Maybe Lovecraft would have finally given in to the urge to write his very own version of the ***Necronomicon*** – we can but dream!

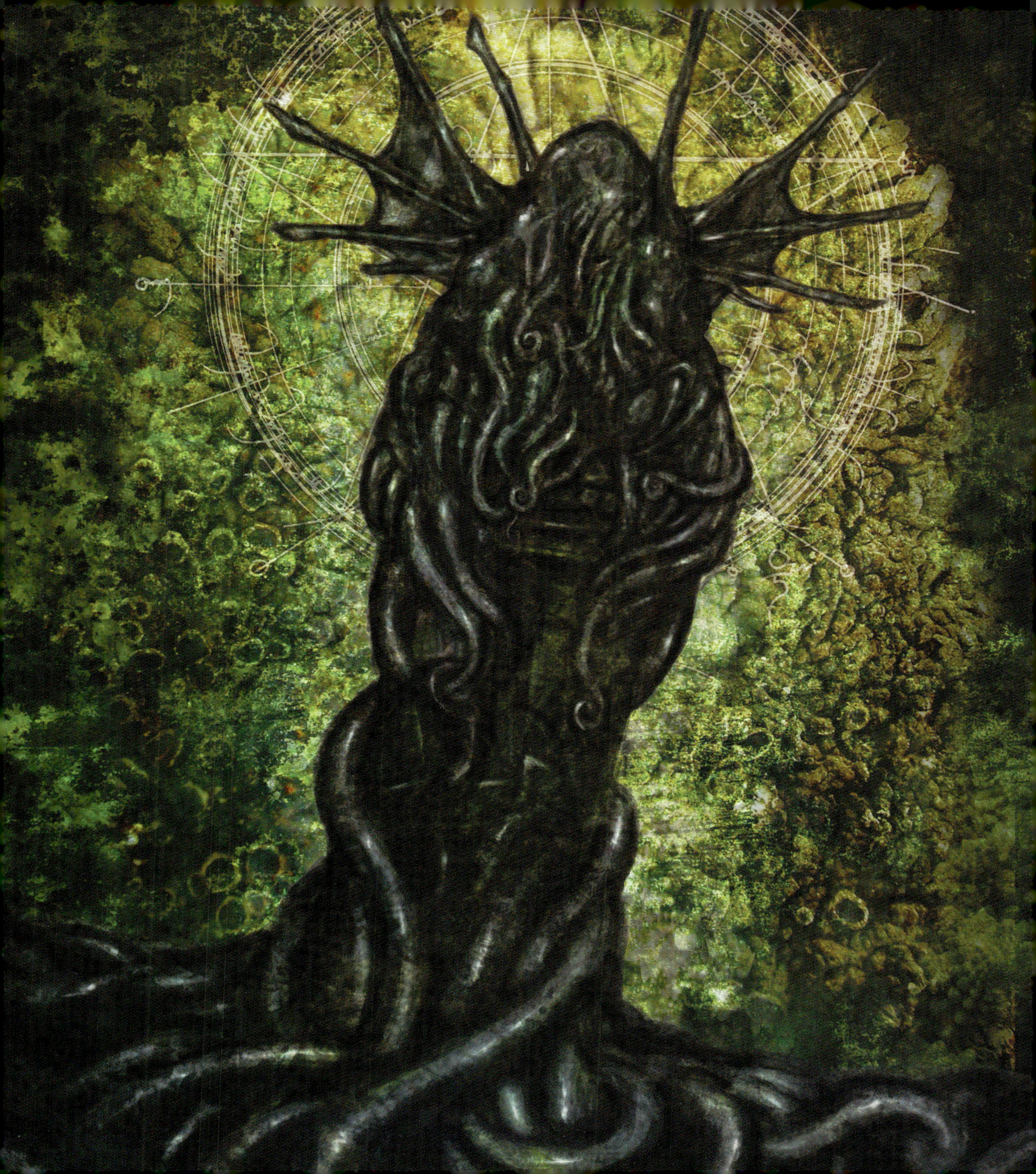

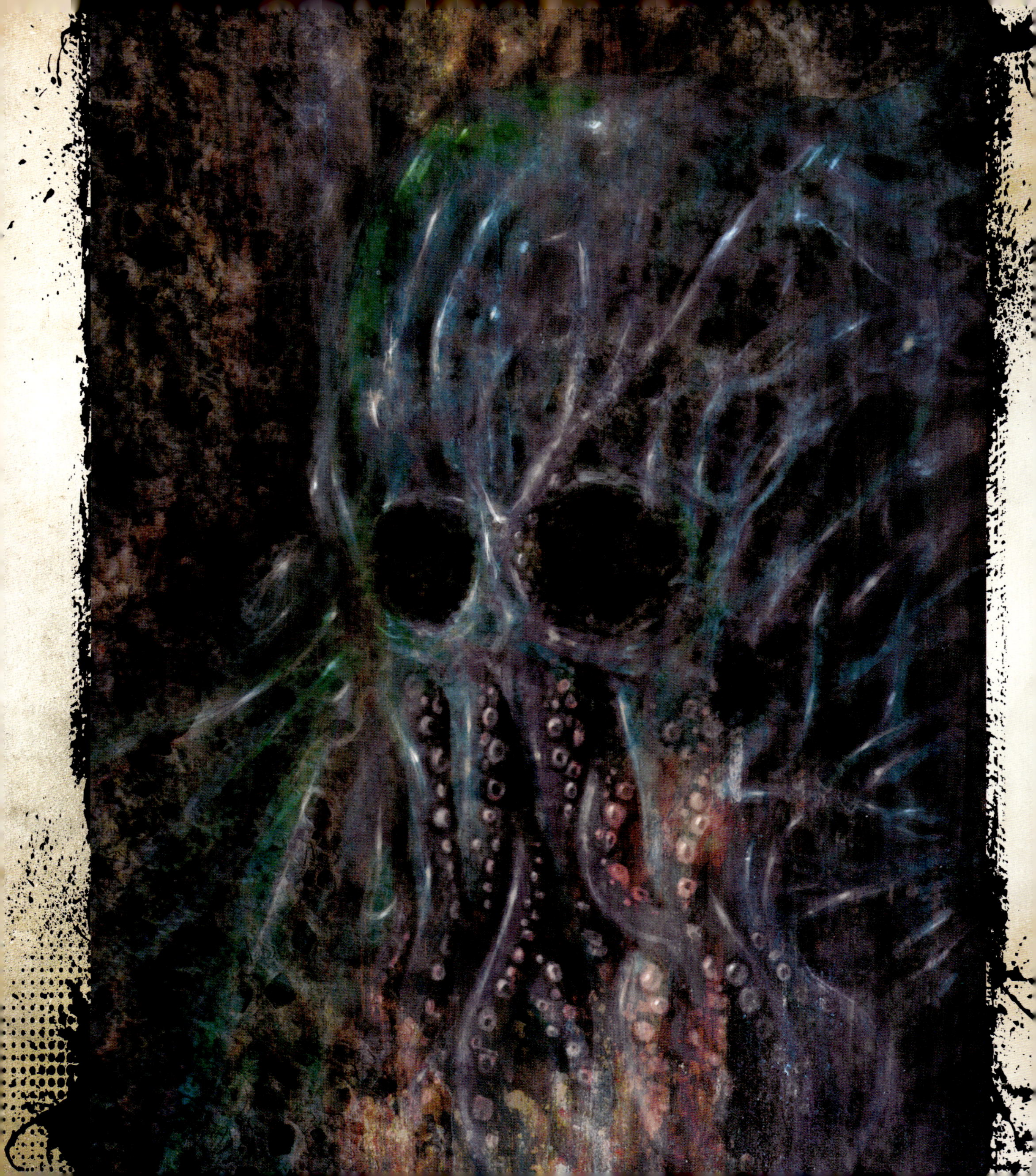

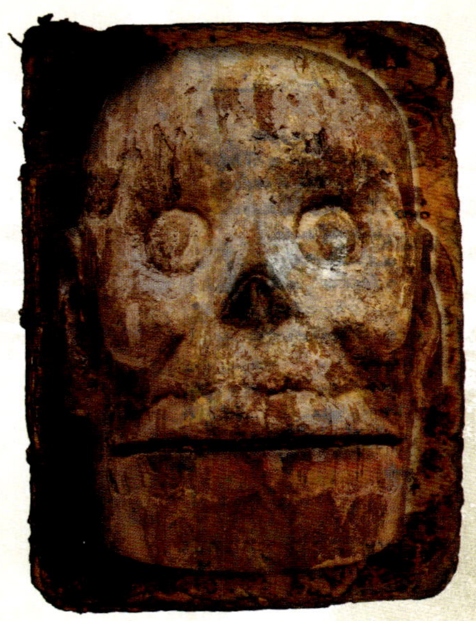

The Inspiration

Where Lovecraft initially came up with the idea for the ***Necronomicon*** can never truly be known but we do know a few things; as a huge fan of Nathaniel Hawthorne (1804–64), especially his ***Tanglewood Tales*** (1853) and ***A Wonder Book*** (1851), Lovecraft set out to read Hawthorne's entire body of work. He immersed himself in letters, novels, stories and even notebooks – one of which is said to be of huge inspiration for the ***Necronomicon***. Hawthorne often scribbled down ideas for stories and one is particularly relevant: 'An old volume in a large library – everyone to be afraid to unclasp and open it, because it was said to be a book of magic.' Again, it's all speculation but immersing yourself so profusely into another's work is bound to have an impact.

The King in Yellow

Another source of inspiration is sometimes conjectured to be a collection of short horror stories, ***The King in Yellow*** (1895), by Robert W. Chambers (1865–1933). The fictional play linking the stories is of the purest evil, with its words engendering a terrible fascination among its readers, eventually rendering them mad. Condemned by church and state, there are obvious similarities between this play and the ***Necronomicon***.

In one story, an artist finds the yellow sign mentioned in the fictional play 'The King in Yellow'. This sign carries a guardian, and when the sign is found, this evil guardian emerges.

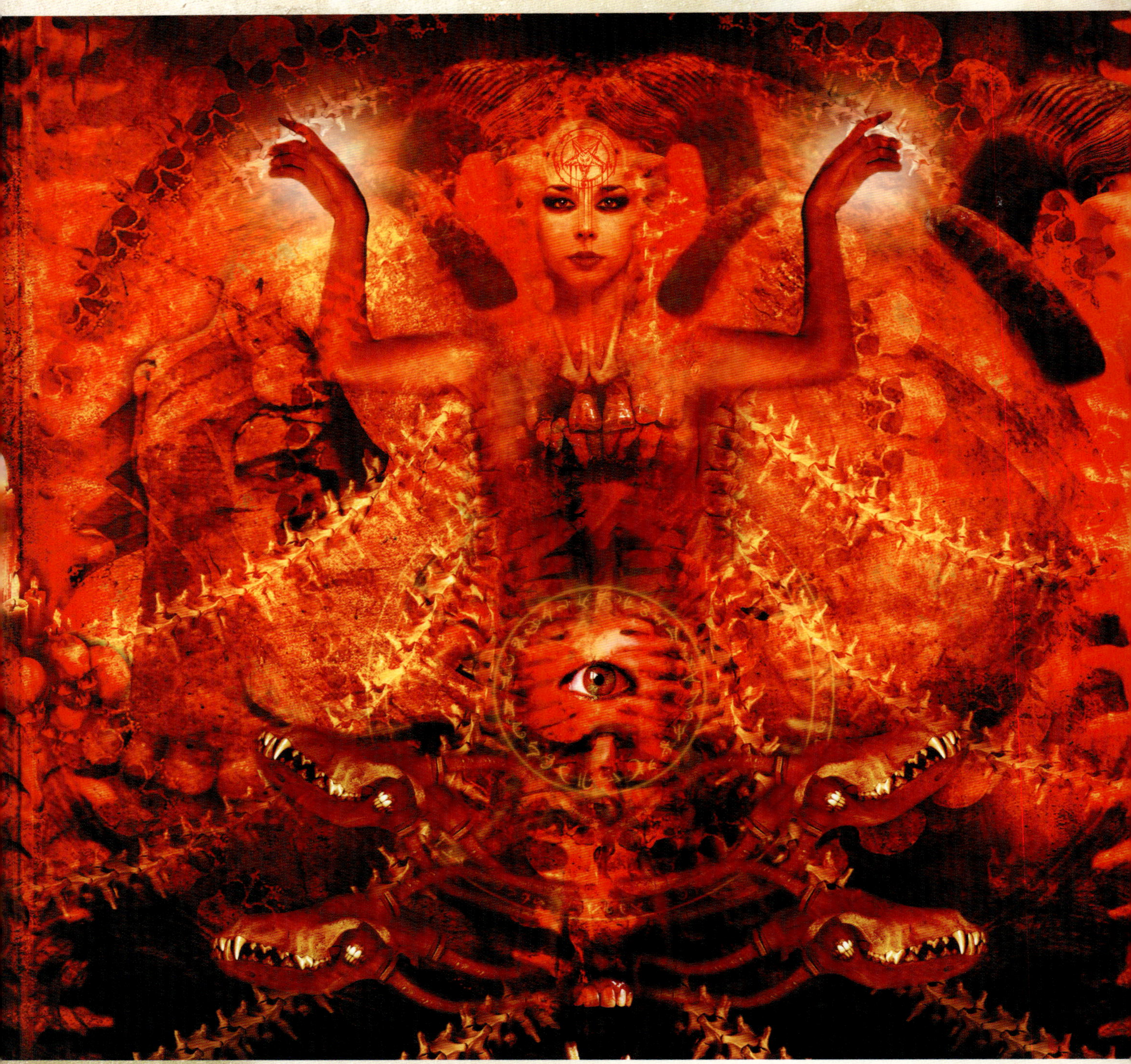

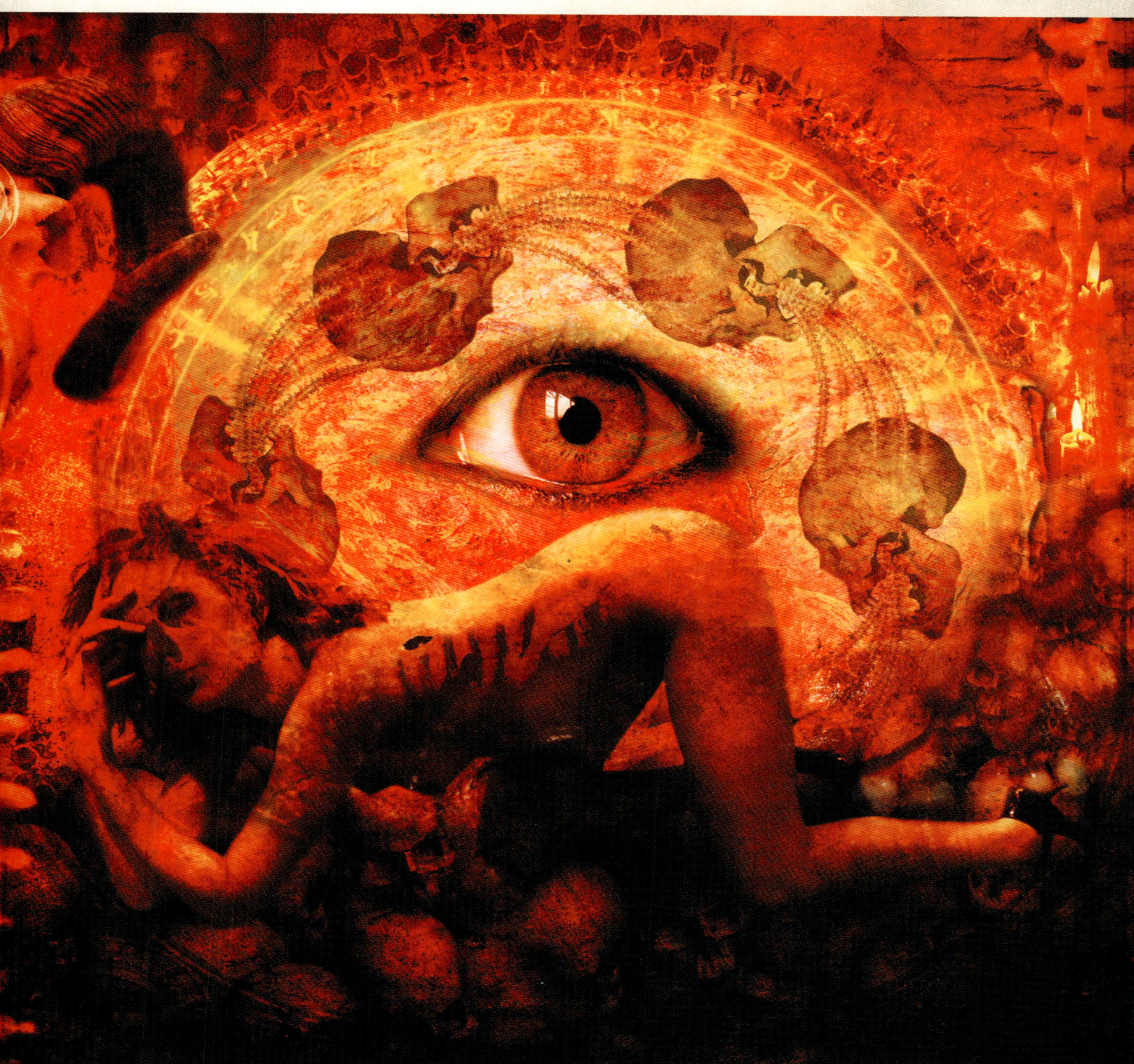

Whilst these tales nicely complement the ***Necronomicon***, there is a huge difference: Chambers' play drives its readers mad, whilst the ***Necronomicon*** simply places its readers' surroundings and situations within a terrifying, yet real, structure. And although there are similarities, S.T. Joshi claims that Lovecraft first read ***The King in Yellow*** five years after he had already referenced the ***Necronomicon*** in 'The Hound', meaning it could not be the inspiration for it.

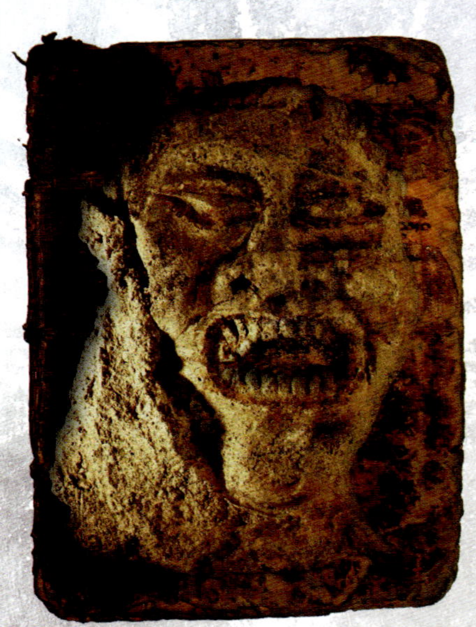

Pretty much everyone will have their own opinion of where the idea of the ***Necronomicon*** originated, but one thing's for sure – it's one of the most influential fictional books to have entered the pop culture spectrum.

'The Old Ones were, the Old Ones are, and the Old Ones shall be. Not in the spaces we know, but between them, They walk serene and primal, undimensioned and to us unseen.'

'The Dunwich Horror'

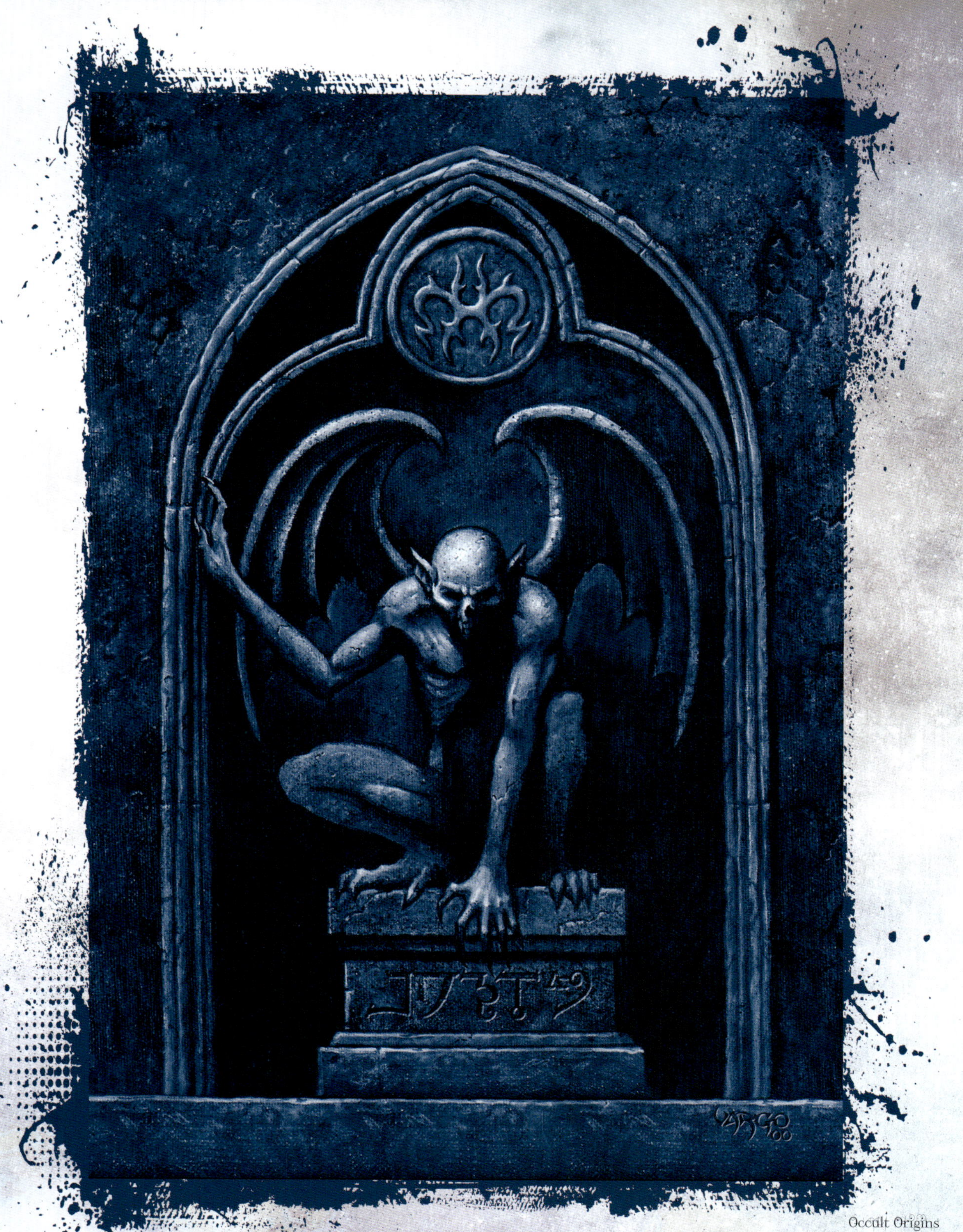

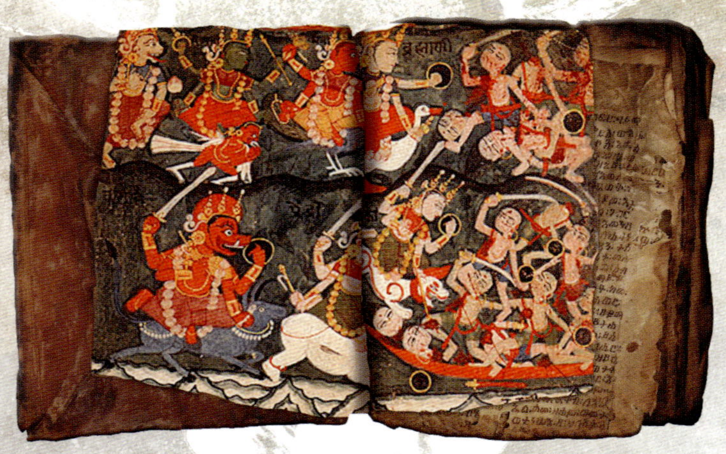

Its Power Grows: The Lovecraftian Legacy

Lovecraft sadly died relatively young in 1937. Did that mean the end of his works? Did it, heck! His dear friend and collaborator August Derleth decided to keep his spirit alive by incorporating fragments of Lovecraft's stories into his own short stories. Mainly published by Lovecraft's ever-supportive Arkham House, the books include ***The Lurker at the Threshold*** (1945), ***The Survivor and Others*** (1957) and ***The Watchers Out of Time and Others*** (1974).

Collaboration

However, some have argued that these stories are not collaborations at all, and that only a sentence or two from Lovecraft inspired Derleth's stories. 'In most cases, the stories were based on one or more ideas noted in Lovecraft's ***Commonplace Book***,' explains S.T. Joshi in his ***H.P. Lovecraft: A Comprehensive Bibliography*** (2009).

'The Fisherman of Falcon Point' (1959) was based on this entry: 'Fisherman casts his net into the sea by moonlight – what he finds.' Plotting, description, dialogue, characterization and other elements were entirely by Derleth. As much as we might have wanted an actual collaboration between the two writers, sadly these seem slightly too good to be true.

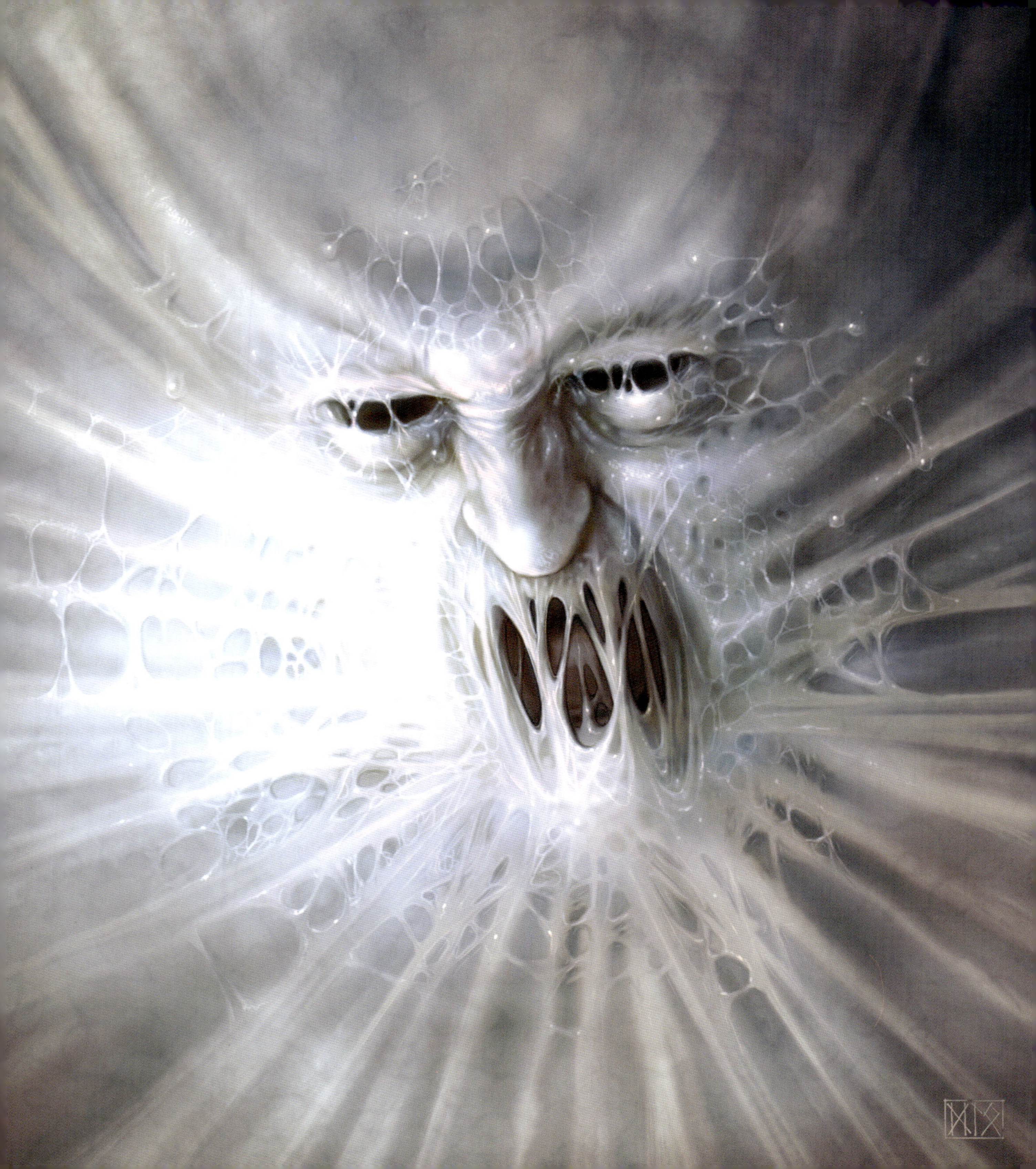

Posthumous Prose

However, Derleth did at times manage to incorporate actual prose passages from Lovecraft into his works, ensuring the collaboration dream was kept alive. In ***The Lurker at the Threshold***, Derleth included roughly 1,200 words from Lovecraft – though seeing as the book was around 50,000 words, it still wasn't that much of a collaborative effort. Lovecraft was known to keep in touch with his friends through regular letters, so it's no surprise that Derleth was inspired by his personal collection of letters, as in ***The Lamp of Alhazred*** (1957), the title of which is quite obviously Lovecraftian in essence.

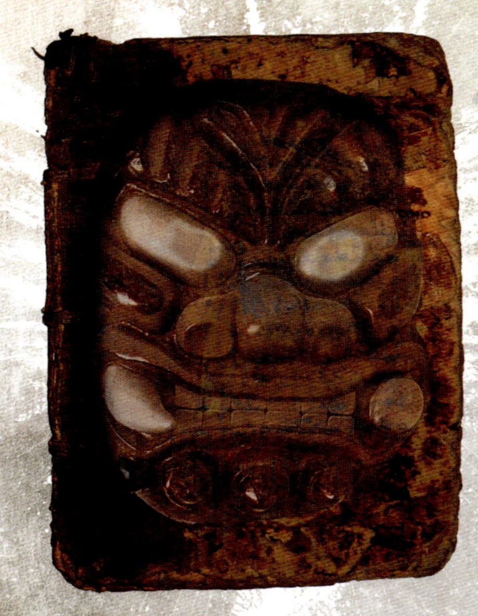

Necronomicon Press

The invention of the ***Necronomicon*** also led to the creation of the Necronomicon Press. A small publishing house based in Rhode Island, it was initially set up to showcase short stories, poetry, novels and criticism of the horror, fantasy and sci-fi genres. Although it wasn't established until 1976 – almost 40 years after Lovecraft's death – the press went on to gain a roster of endless Lovecraftian and ***Necronomicon***-inspired authors and writers.

Clark Ashton Smith (1893–1961) is a notable example, as his work garners influence from Lovecraft and his brand of Weird Fiction. Death, yearning and loss are always key factors in his work, especially in 'The Hunters from Beyond' (1932), which speaks of a book by Goya entitled ***Proverbes***. The protagonist, Mr Hastane, picks up this

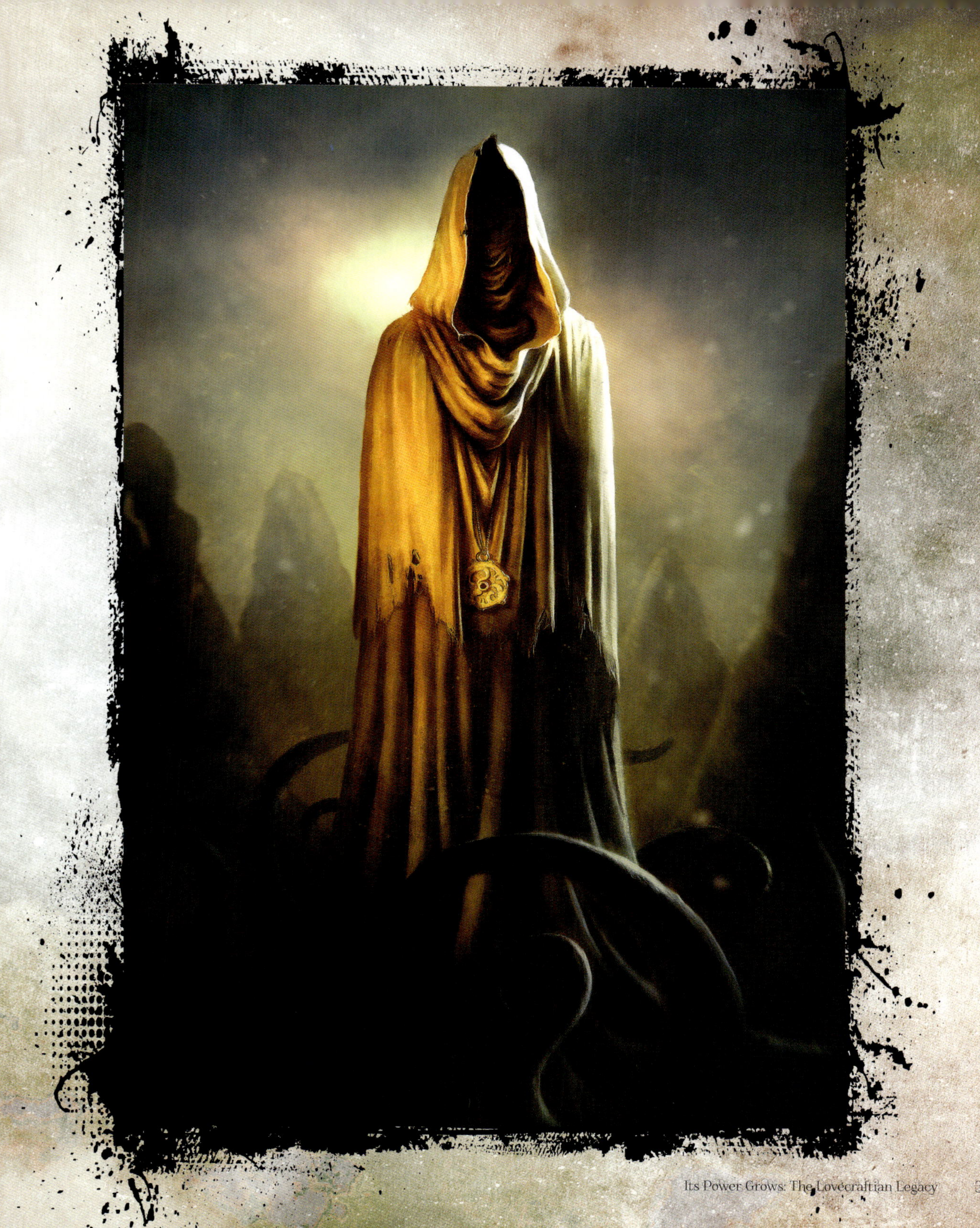

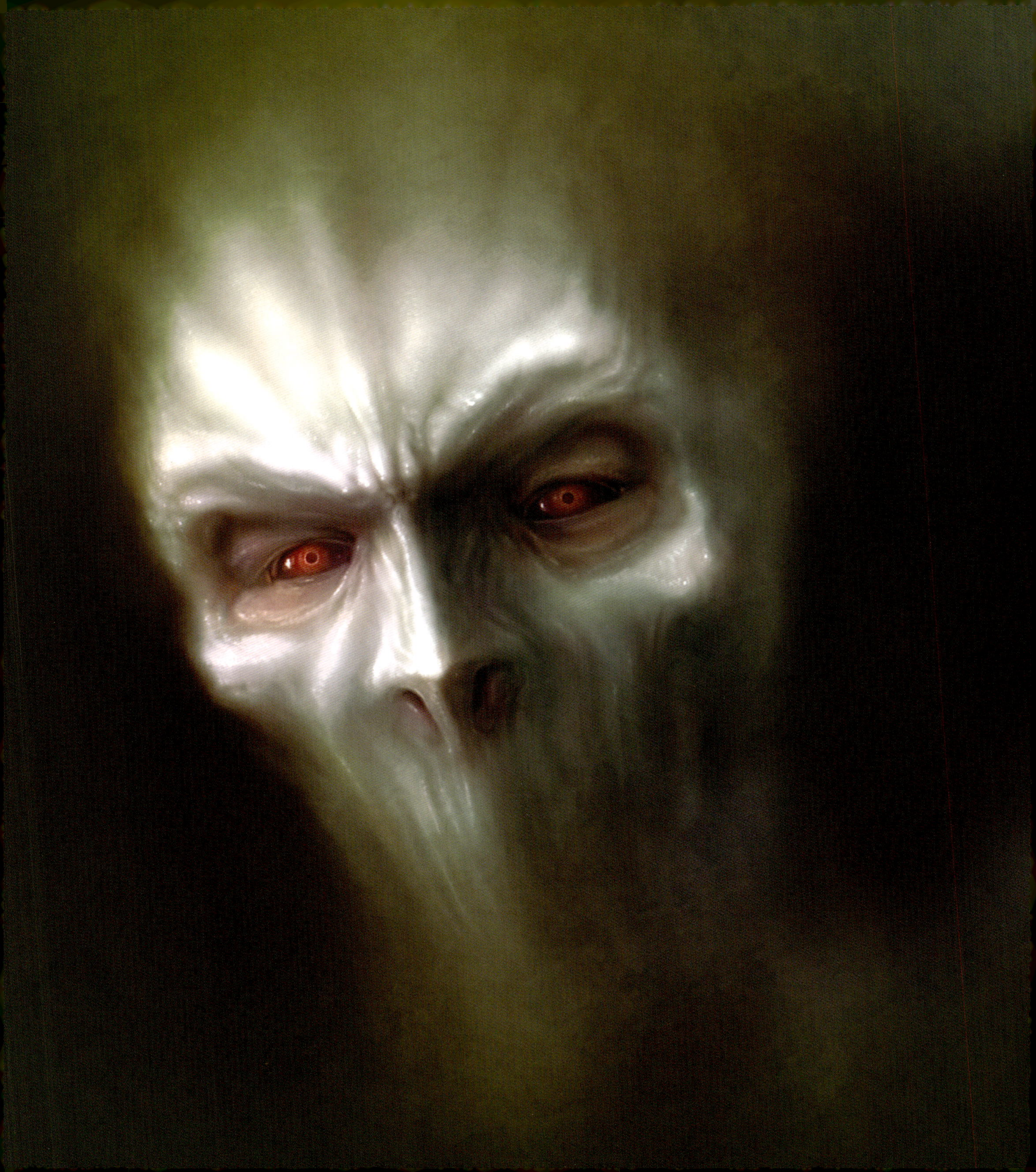

book in a strange, devoid-of-customers shop and begins seeing the creatures portrayed in the pages of the Goya – the 'diabolic art of these nightmare-nurtured drawings'. Already, we're noticing similarities to the ***Necronomicon***, as both books tell of nightmarish, outer-worldly creatures, reminding the characters within the stories that we may not be as alone on Earth as we like to think.

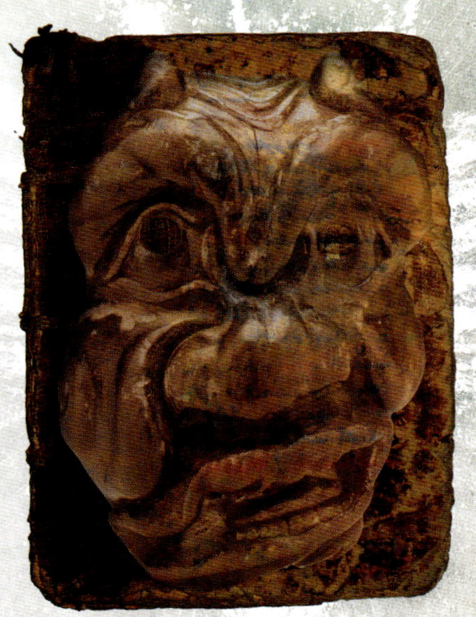

The Cyprian

The story then introduces us to the 'Cyprian' – an artist who creates drawings and statues of these inherently terrifying creatures. As Mr Hastane tells of his apparition, the Cyprian reveals statues of an almost identical aesthetic. 'Anything may exist, in a boundless universe with multiple dimensions,' he explains. 'Anything may be real – or unreal. Who knows? It is not for me to say. Figure it out for yourself, if you can – there's a vast field for speculation – and perhaps for more than speculation.'

Here we can see the influence of Lovecraft's famous Weird Fiction, where horror meets sci-fi. Like Lovecraft, Smith questions the universe and its realm, hinting at something further, something unknown – this unknown quickly creates the fear factor within the story and, again, corresponds with Lovecraft's fear of 'others'.

'Their hand is at your throats yet ye see Them not'

'The Dunwich Horror'

Other Worlds

The ***Necronomicon*** was a device through which Lovecraft linked the terrifying surroundings and situations that his

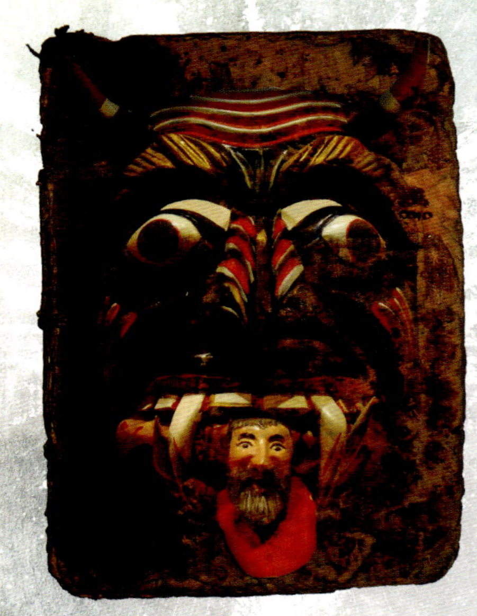

characters faced to the scriptures in the book. Mr Hastane does this with the Goya – linking the hellish characters to the artwork within the book, it causes him to question his sanity and yet, having this solid, almost evidential book to refer to enables him to place these existential happenings in his 'known' world. 'It seemed to me that I had gone astray from the normal, familiar world into a land of detestable mystery, of prodigious and unnatural menace,' he says.

Science Fiction

The gargoyle-like creatures described within 'The Hunters from Beyond' are 'summoned' by the Cyprian, which again relates to the spells and scriptures within the ***Necronomicon*** to summon demons and otherworldly gods. They walk the fine line in horror literature between what's real and what's not, with authors such as Lovecraft and Smith forever hinting about a world immersed in sci-fi elements. 'The world in which we live isn't the only world; and some of the others lie closer at hand than you think,' says the Cyprian. 'The boundaries of the seen and the unseen are sometimes interchangeable.'

Obsession

Much like the characters in Lovecraft's ***The Case of Charles Dexter Ward***, Smith's characters become transfixed – obsessed even – with otherworldly books. In 'The Hunters from Beyond', Mr Hastane buys the Goya book almost subconsciously, only noticing it in his hands

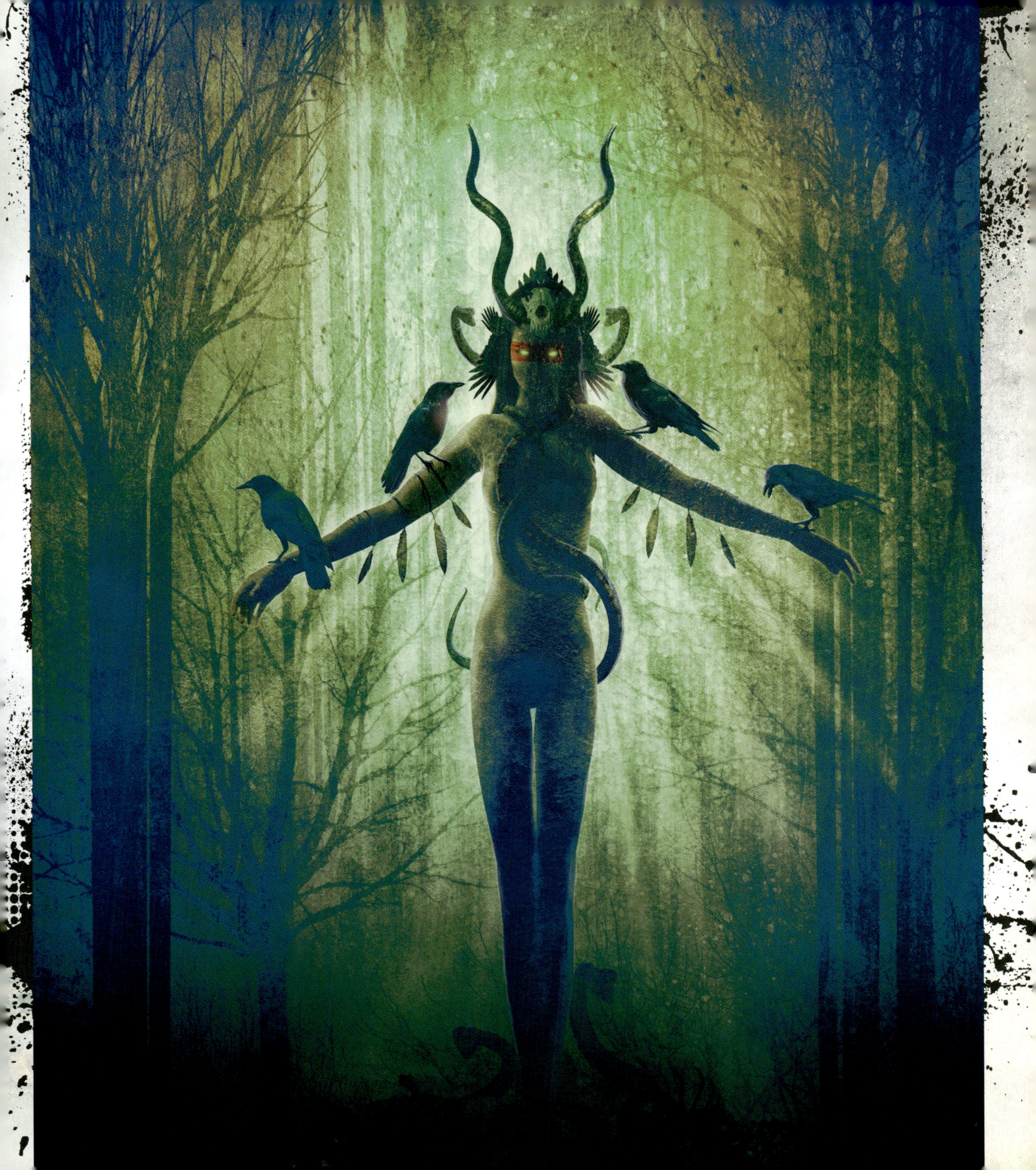

once he's left the shop. With an 'automatic impulse', it's clear that – just like the ***Necronomicon*** – the book has a certain power over its readers, one that will cause them to become obsessed with its content. The Cyprian, too, becomes obsessed with the idea of capturing these horrific creatures, to 'do in sculpture what Poe and Lovecraft and Baudelaire have done in literature, what Rops and Goya did in pictorial art'. Perhaps Smith was speaking of his own personal goals, but nonetheless it's a wonderful tribute to the authors before him.

Insanity

The Cyprian becomes so obsessed that, according to his model Marta, his mental health starts to deteriorate. Mental health was a huge theme in Lovecraft's writing, no doubt influenced by the problems concerning his parents, and Smith brilliantly ties this in with his story. In the tales of both authors, their characters often become obsessed with the supernatural and creatures of nightmares that cause their loved ones to label them mentally ill. Whilst Lovecraft never out-rightly states that the ***Necronomicon*** causes madness, it's often implied throughout his works – much as it is in those of Smith.

Ramsey Campbell

Another notable author on the Necronomicon Press roster is Ramsey Campbell (b. 1946). A self-confessed Lovecraft super fan, the Liverpudlian became engrossed in the author as a child, falling in love with one of Lovecraft's stories,

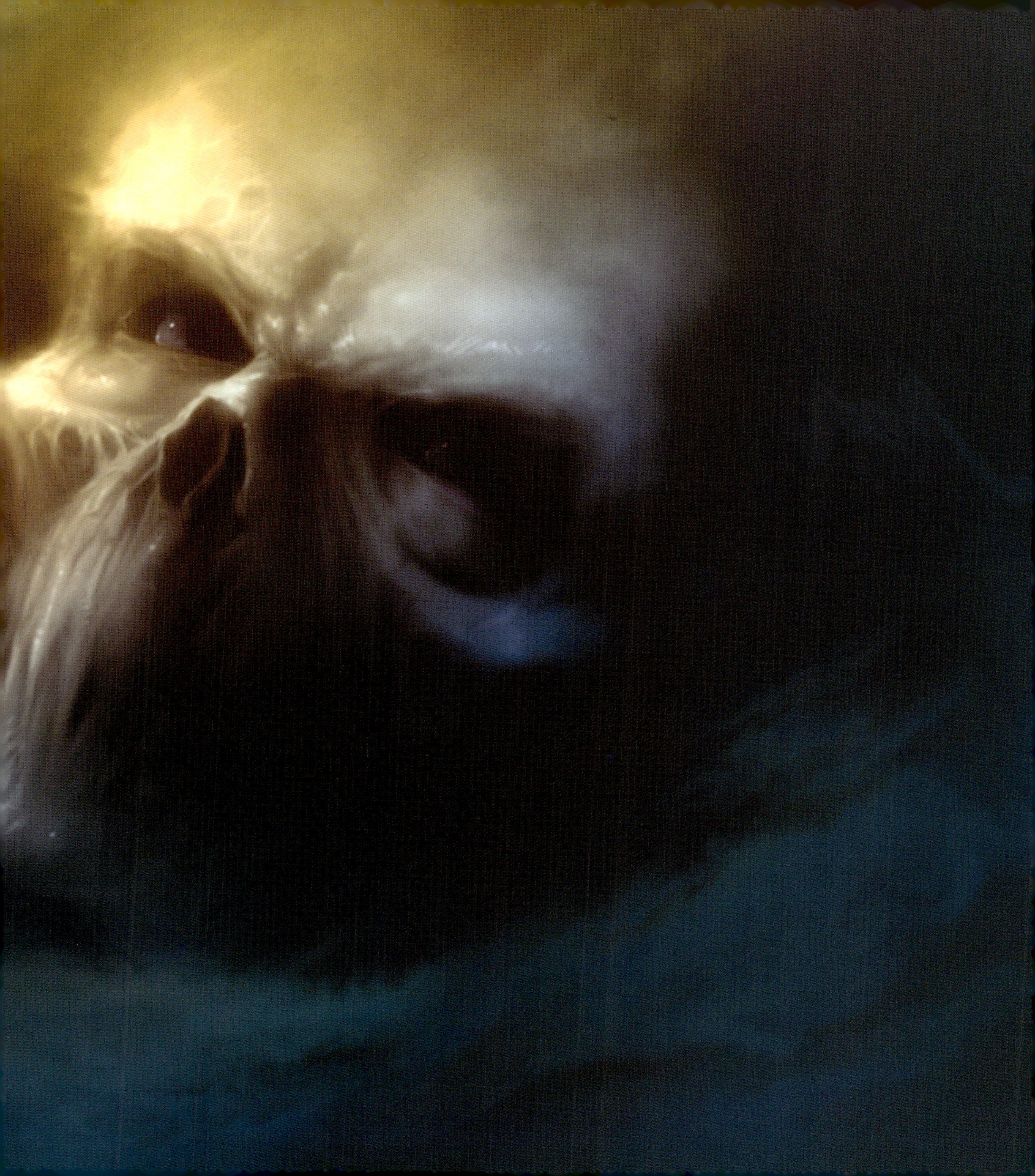

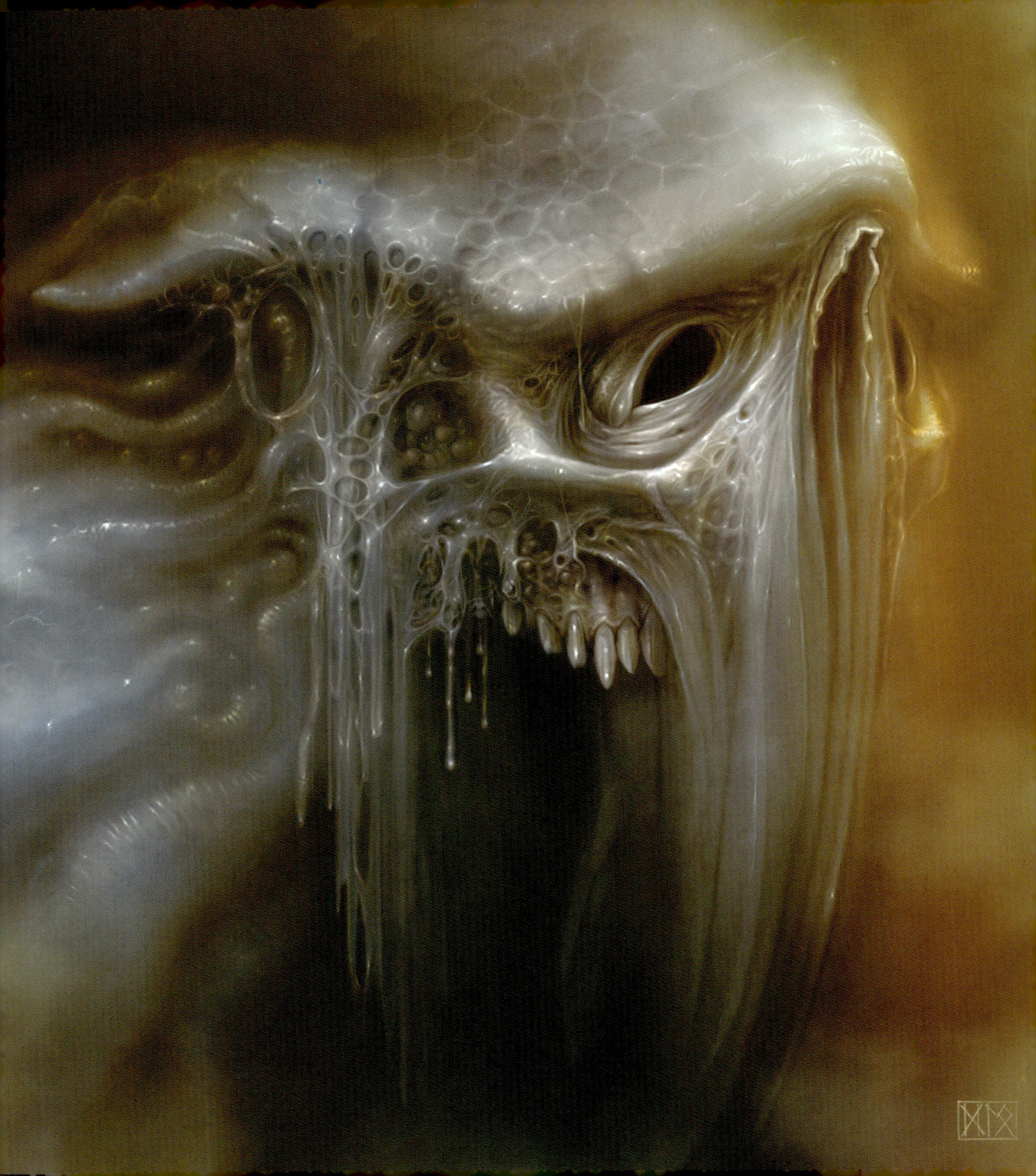

'The Color Out of Space' (1927). His first collection of short stores, ***The Inhabitant of the Lake and Less Welcome Tenants*** (1964), was published when he was just 18 years old and showcased his Lovecraftian influences to a tee. The first story, 'The Revelations of Gla'aki', told of Gla'aki, a 'Great Old One' who dwells in a lake in the Severn Valley. Said to have arrived on Earth through being trapped inside a meteor, Campbell cleverly incorporates science fiction into horror, à la Lovecraft.

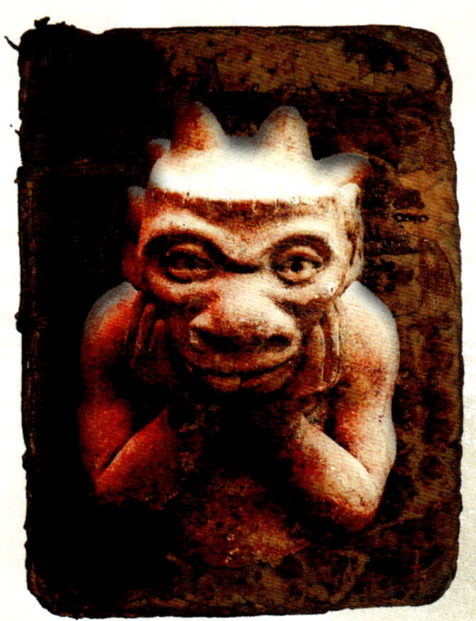

Extruding tentacles, with a slug-like exterior, Gla'aki certainly resembles creatures often described in the ***Necronomicon***. Many of these creatures came from the sea, said to be inspired by Lovecraft's fear of the water – again, touching on the 'fear of the unknown' … after all, we mere humans have only found roughly 10 per cent of the species lurking beneath the depths!

The Revelations of Gla'aki

As part of the Cthulhu mythos, Gla'aki had his very own undead cult who worshipped him every hour of every day. They produced a book, ***The Revelations of Gla'aki***, that included everything they could remember of their master's thoughts. The manuscripts made up the entire book and it was quickly included in the library of the Cthulhu mythos, where the ***Necronomicon*** kicked off everything. Here, we're starting to see the circle of Lovecraft devotees forming, with Smith and Campbell just the tip of the iceberg.

'Men know him as the Dweller in Darkness, that brother of the Old Ones called Nyogtha, the Thing that should not be.'

The Burrowers Beneath

The Cthulhu Mythos Collection

The ***Necronomicon*** sparked a wide range of tomes from many authors inspired by Lovecraft and his Weird Fiction. Whilst the ***Necronomicon*** remains the most influential of them all, the others allowed each author to pay homage to one another. Adding their own grimoire to the spectrum, the likes of Lin Carter (1930–88), Brian Lumley (b. 1937) and Jonathan L. Howard joined Ramsey Campbell and August Derleth in their post-***Necronomicon*** productions. There are about 1,000 stories to date within the Cthulhu mythos, so it would probably take you a fair few months to get through the entire back catalogue.

Lin Carter

Carter is arguably one of the most notable creators of Lovecraft pastiche. A difficult style to emulate, some adore his work whilst others prefer to stick to the original Lovecraft masterpieces. In 1971, Carter created ***The Doom of Yakthoob***, which purported to produce translations from the ***Necronomicon***. In it, we learn of the death of Abdul Alhazred's mentor, the 'Saracen' wizard Yakthoob. By summoning one of the 'Great Old Ones' for the curious Alhazred, Yakthoob meets a grisly fate, before Alhazred flees the scene – curiosity once again seals the fate of these characters. It was a brilliant way to touch upon what might have happened before the ***Necronomicon*** was created, giving die-hard Lovecraft fans a glimpse into the past of Alhazred.

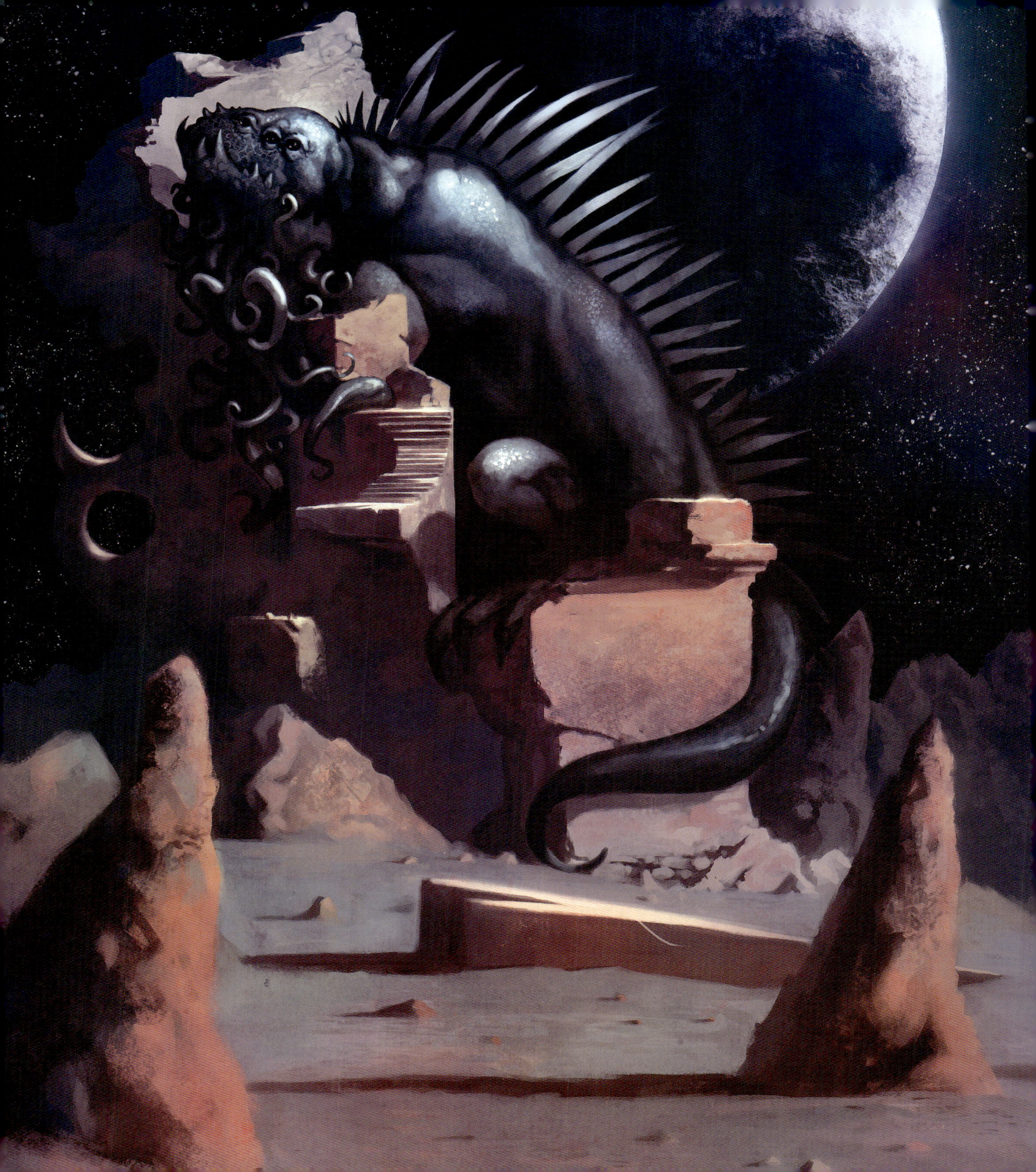

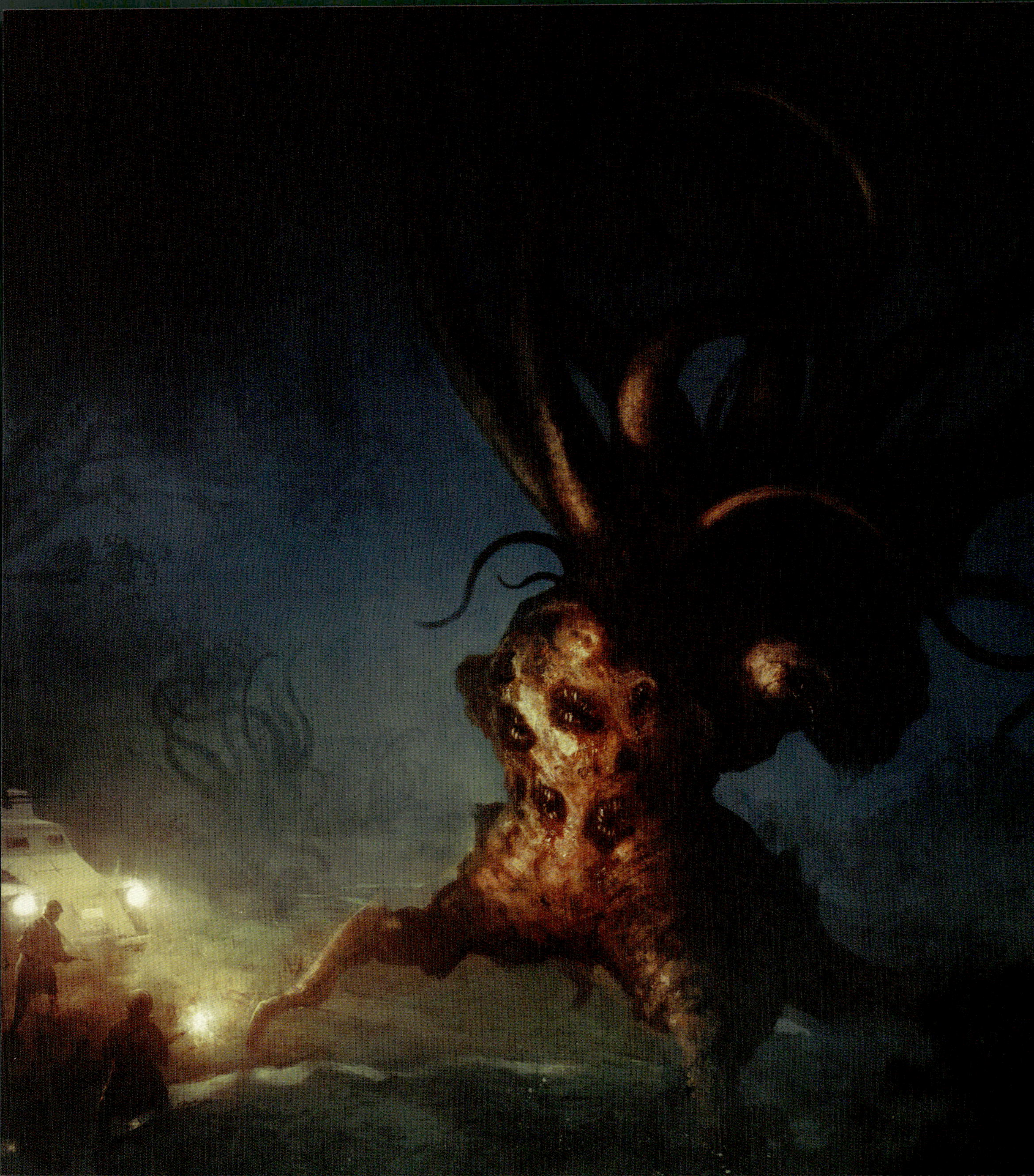

The Book of Eibon

There are significant similarities between Carter's ***The Doom of Yakthoob*** and ***The Book of Eibon***. Created by Clark Ashton Smith, the latter features in a number of Lovecraft stories, including 'The Dreams in the Witch House' (1933) and 'The Shadow Out of Time' (1936). Smith describes it as 'the rarest of occult forgotten volumes … from a prehistoric original written in the lost language of Hyperborea', in his tale 'Ubbo-Sathla'. It centres on the wizard Eibon, who supposedly wrote the book whilst dwelling in the land of Hyperborea. Much like Alhazred, Eibon is a curious child with no family, who is taken in by the sorcerous necromancer Zylac, who much like Yakthoob disappears after a magical accident at the hands of another 'Great Old One'.

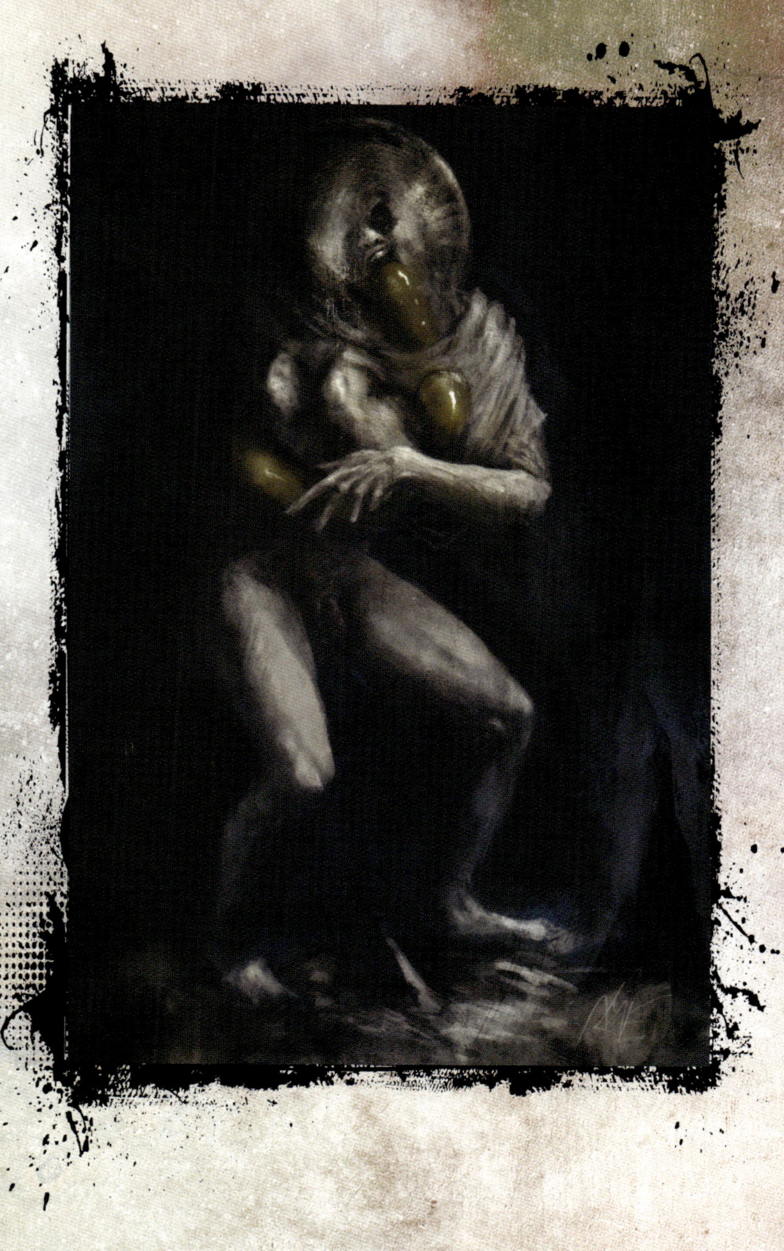

De Vermis Mysteriis

Plenty more odes to the ***Necronomicon*** were published, with great sci-fi, horror and Weird Fiction authors trying to replicate the terrifying magic and mystery Lovecraft had evoked so brilliantly. Robert Bloch created ***De Vermis Mysteriis*** and its fictional author Ludvig Prinn – although its original Latin title was actually invented by Lovecraft himself. A contributor to pulp magazine ***Weird Tales***, Bloch and Lovecraft are seamlessly joined in both style and substance, with Bloch even writing to Lovecraft as a young writer seeking advice, and Lovecraft dedicating 'The Haunter of the Dark' (1936) to Bloch through the character of Robert Blake.

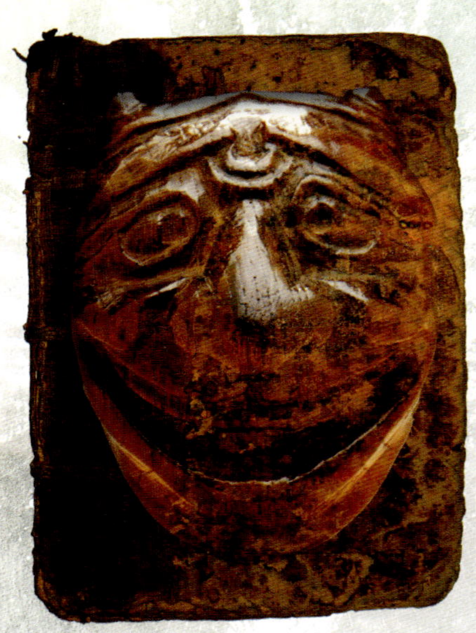

De Vermis Mysteriis first appeared in Bloch's short story 'The Shambler from the Stars' (1935), with the story created in close contact with Lovecraft himself – after all, Bloch was about to kill off a Lovecraft-inspired figure in the tale, so it's understandable he would want some kind of permission from his mentor. Like so many that have sealed their fate with the ***Necronomicon***, the ***De Vermis Mysteriis*** book contains spells and enchantments that eventually lead to a character's death after summoning horror of otherworldly stature.

The Circle Continues

The Lovecraft circle allowed these authors, as well as others including Brian Lumley, Henry Kuttner (1915–58) and Richard F. Searight (1902–75), to pay homage to the ***Necronomicon***. The book allowed them to create worlds in which the line between horror and science fiction blurred, adding more fuel to the fire for the believers in the 'Great Old Ones'. 'For the fun of building up a convincing cycle of synthetic folklore, all of our gang frequently allude to the pet daemons of others,' Lovecraft lovingly stated in a letter to William Frederick Anger (***c.*** 1920–97) in 1934. Whilst each creation of the circle and the Cthulhu mythos has certainly made an impact in the literary world, none have come close to the ***Necronomicon*** and its timeless influence on authors past, present and future.

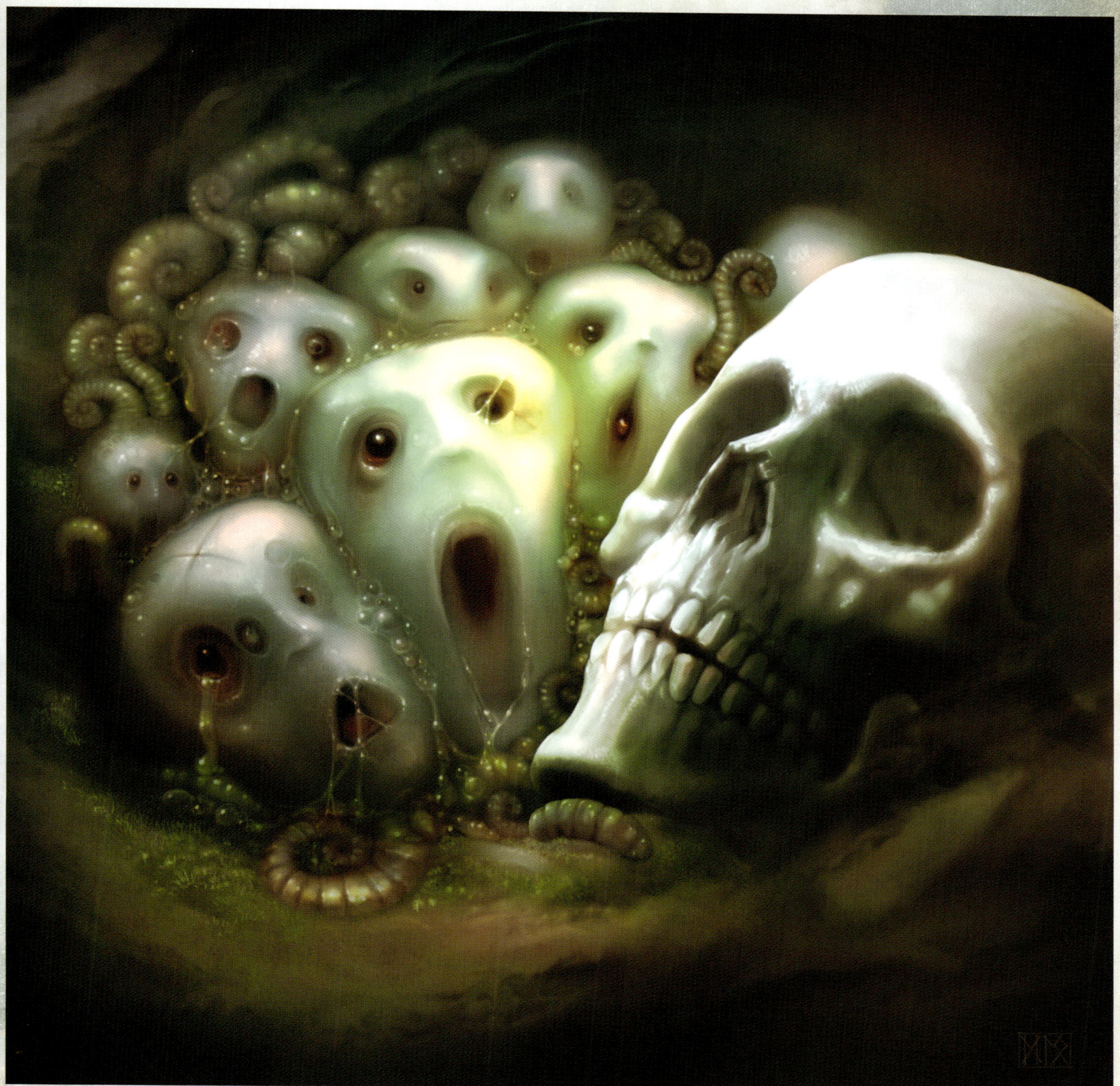

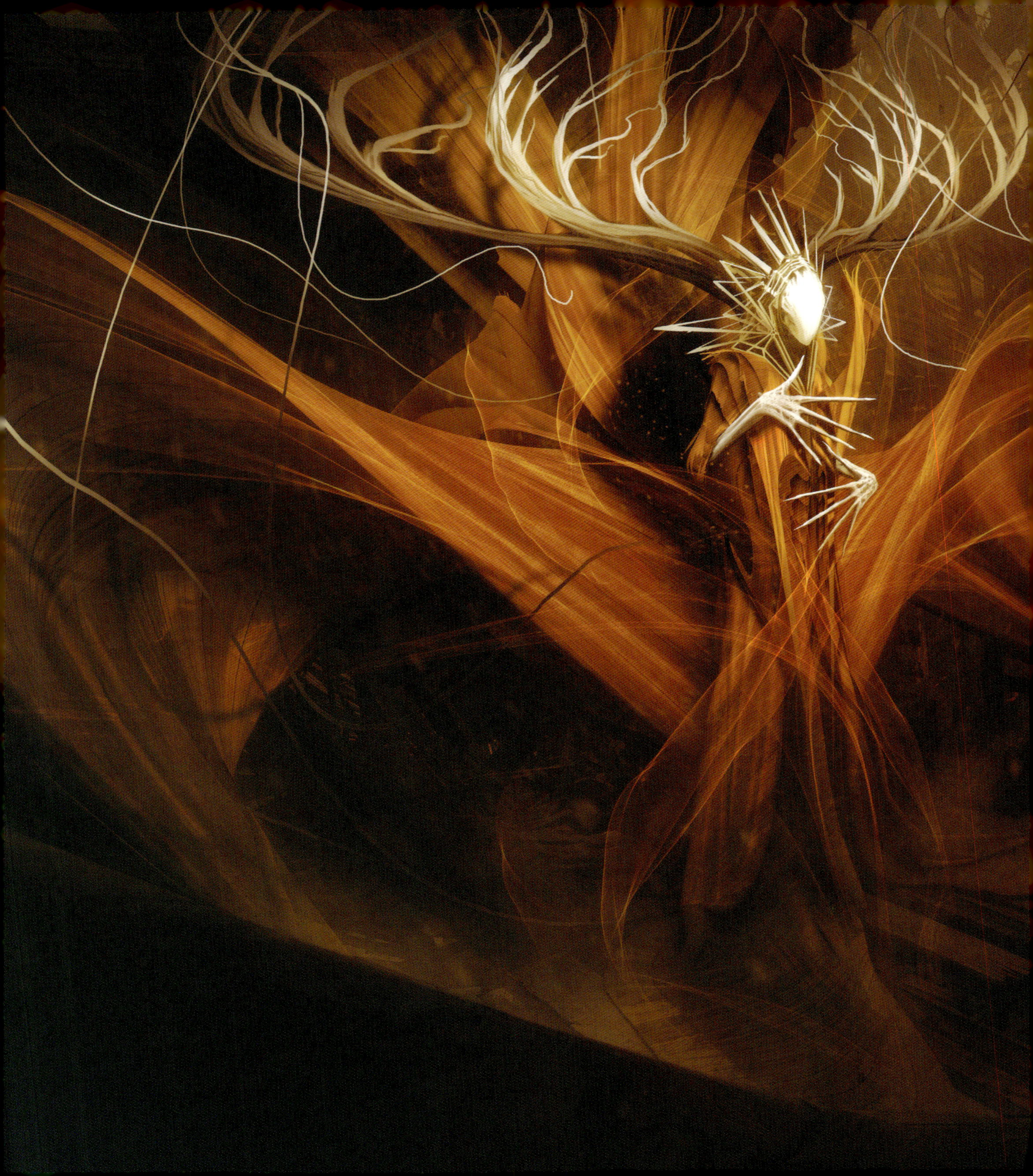

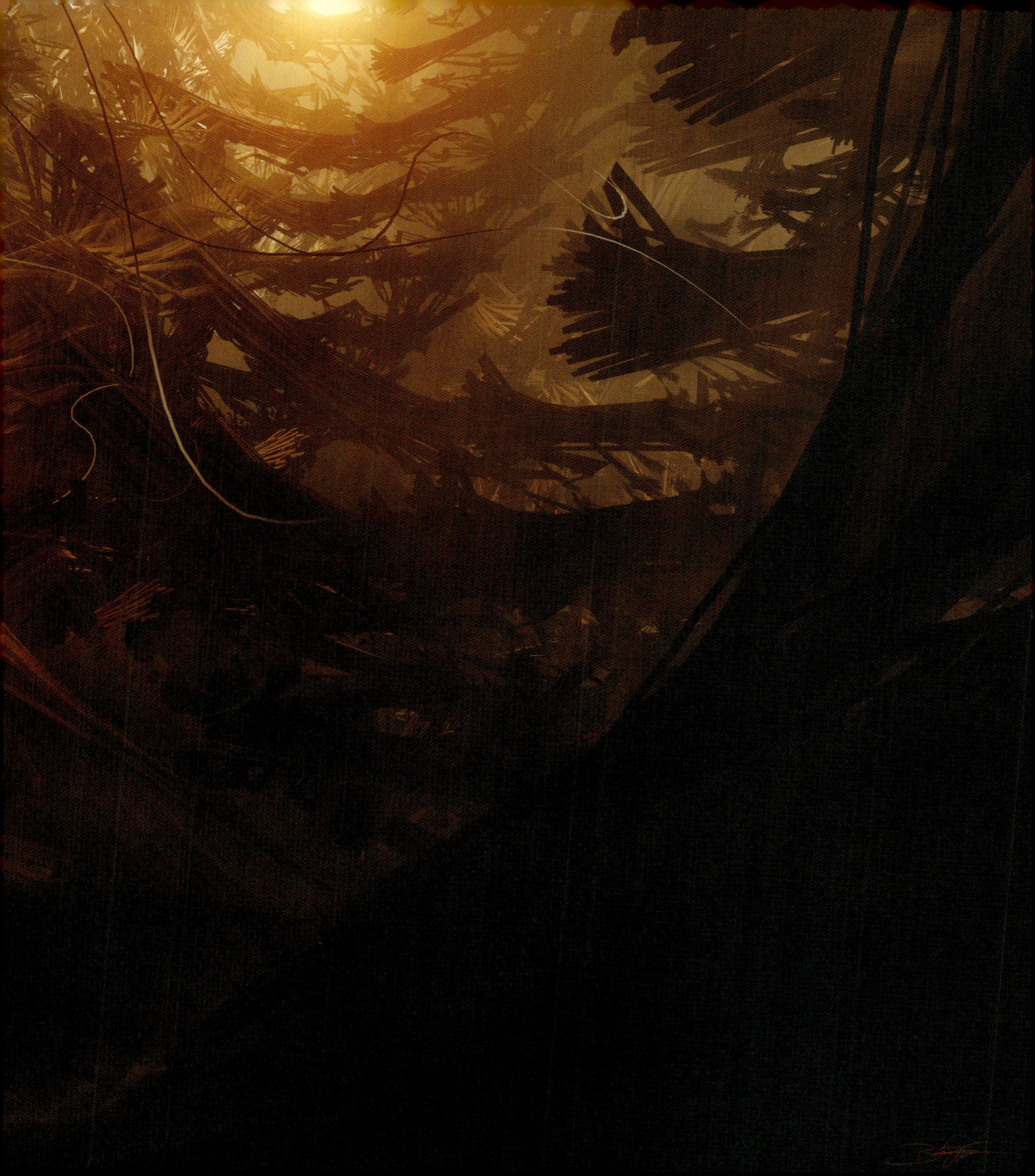

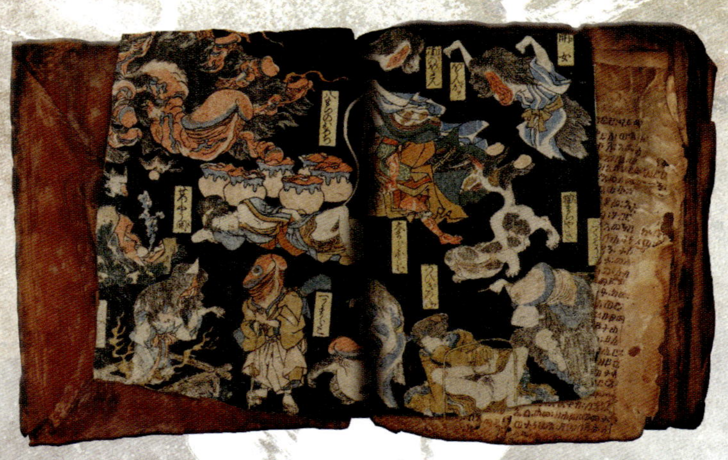

The Pages Unfold: More Modern Fiction

The continuation of the *Necronomicon* and its influence in the horror genre didn't stop with the Cthulhu mythos circle. For decades it was perpetuated in the tales of iconic writers such as Stephen King (b. 1947) and Neil Gaiman (b. 1960), as well as inspiring the production of 'real' *Necronomicons* – namely, the *Simon Necronomicon* in 1977. Further proving the timelessness of Lovecraft's invention, the book of the dead allows authors and its readers to enter a world of extraterrestrial gods, terrifying demons and horrific creatures. It's clearer than ever that the ***Necronomicon*** is yet to have a best-before date, with fans of the Weird Fiction genre lapping up tales of its torture.

The Simon Necronomicon

After his death, Lovecraft became something of a cult figure. Convinced of its authenticity, fans desperately wanted to get their hands on a copy of the dreaded ***Necronomicon***, bombarding shops and libraries with daily requests.

Some saw this as an opportunity, resulting in a range of volumes claiming to be the real ***Necronomicon***. In 1977, the ***Simon Necronomicon*** was published – released as a paperback version in 1980 – reaching thousands of avid ***Necronomicon*** believers.

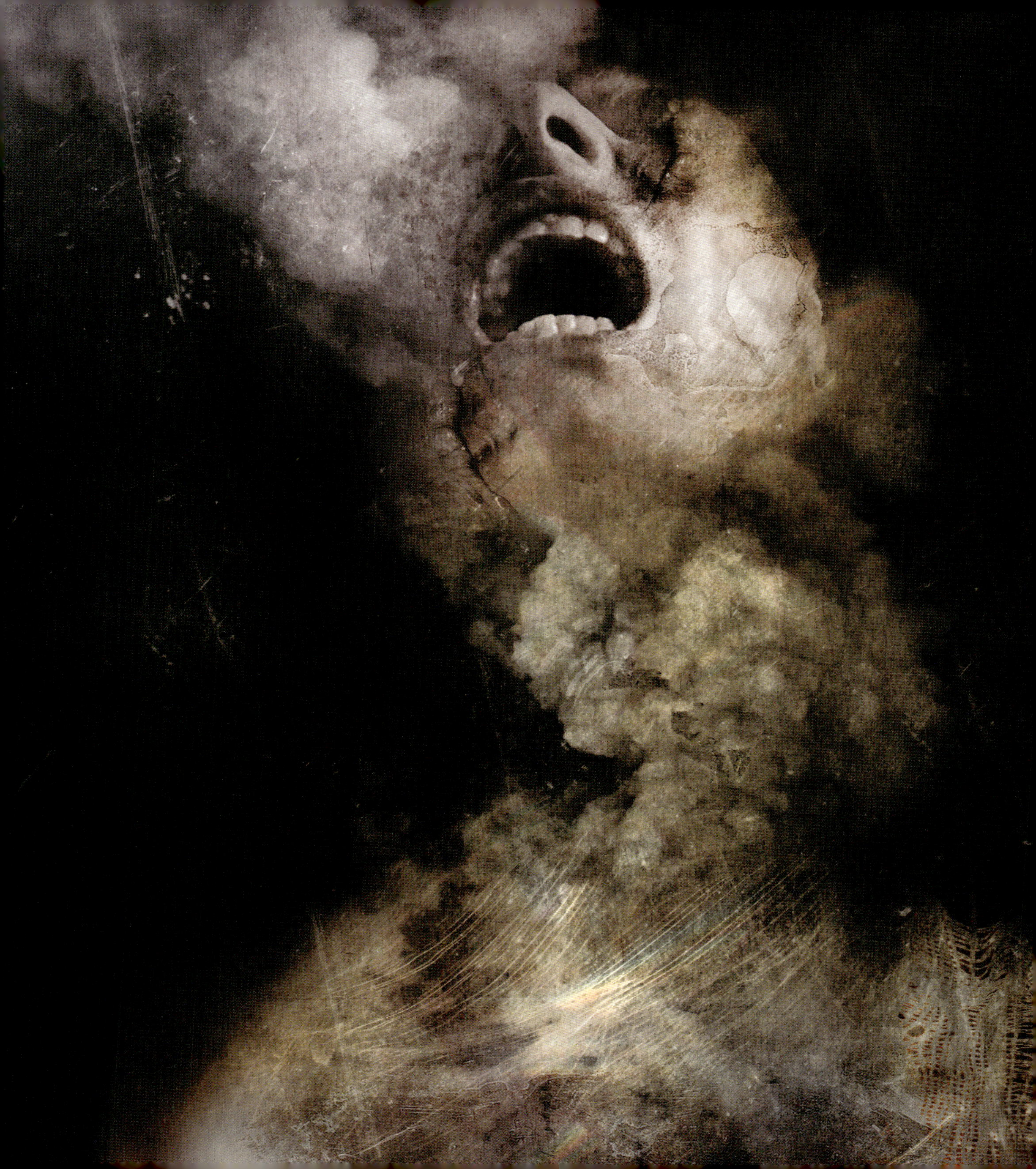

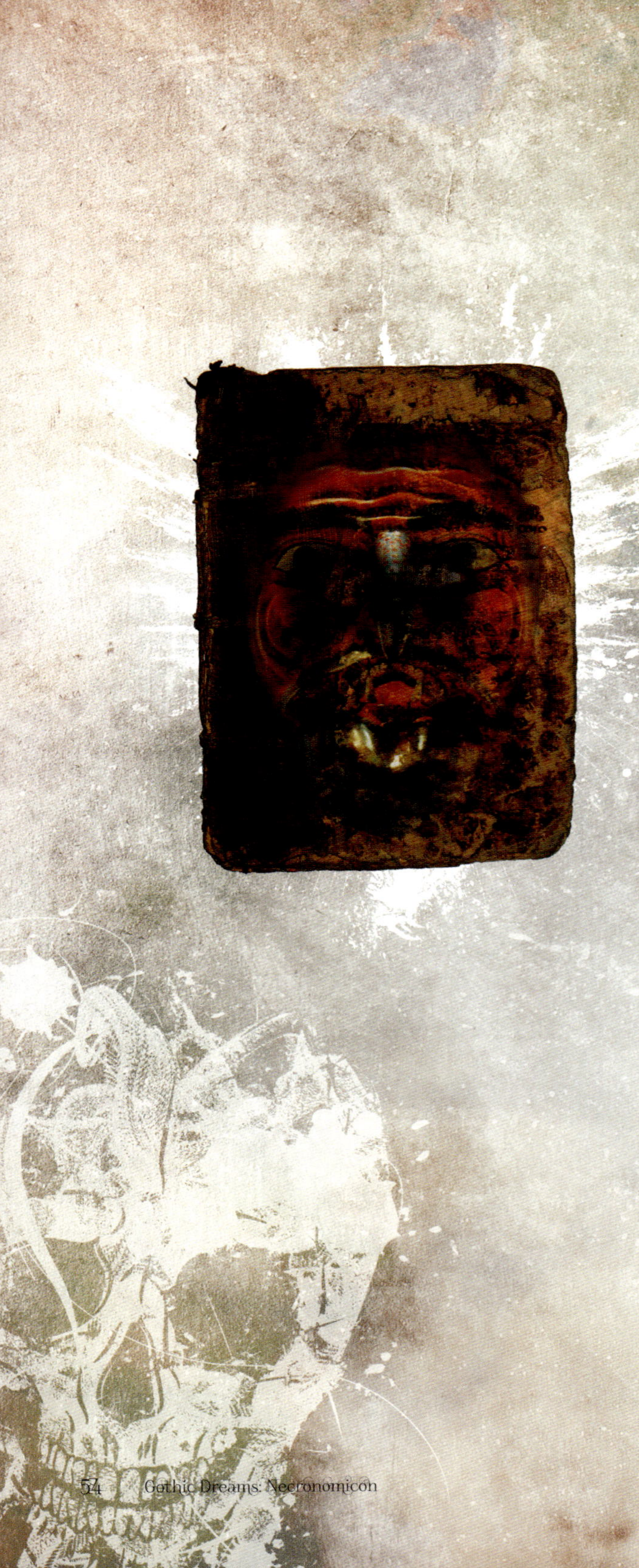

Authored by a man who simply called himself 'Simon', the book blended Gothic ritual with the names of creatures crafted to resemble Lovecraft's infamous monster gods. As the market demanded it at the time, 'Simon' was clever to publish the volume, with the gullible succumbing to a brilliant marketing tactic.

George Hay

Another man to contribute arcane text to the ongoing ***Necronomicon*** mythos was George Hay (1922–97), whose ***Necronomicon: The Book of Dead Names*** (1978) was published just after the Simon version. Supposedly a transcription of an encoded manuscript found in a library, this ***Necronomicon*** hoax was led by Colin Wilson, whose back-story more than satisfied the consumer.

Mentioning that the manuscript is in fact a set of charts of letters created by John Dee nicely ties in with Lovecraft's 'History of the Necronomicon' – Dr John Dee transcribed Abdul Alhazred's original ***Necronomicon*** into the English language. This version of the ***Necronomicon*** is certainly among one of the book's most famous incarnations, but opinions of its success as a post-Lovecraftian tribute differ widely among die-hard fans.

The Night Watch

In 1998, Ukrainian author Sergei Lukyanenko (b. 1968) integrated the ***Necronomicon*** into his novel ***The Night Watch***. Lukyanenko created a team of magicians,

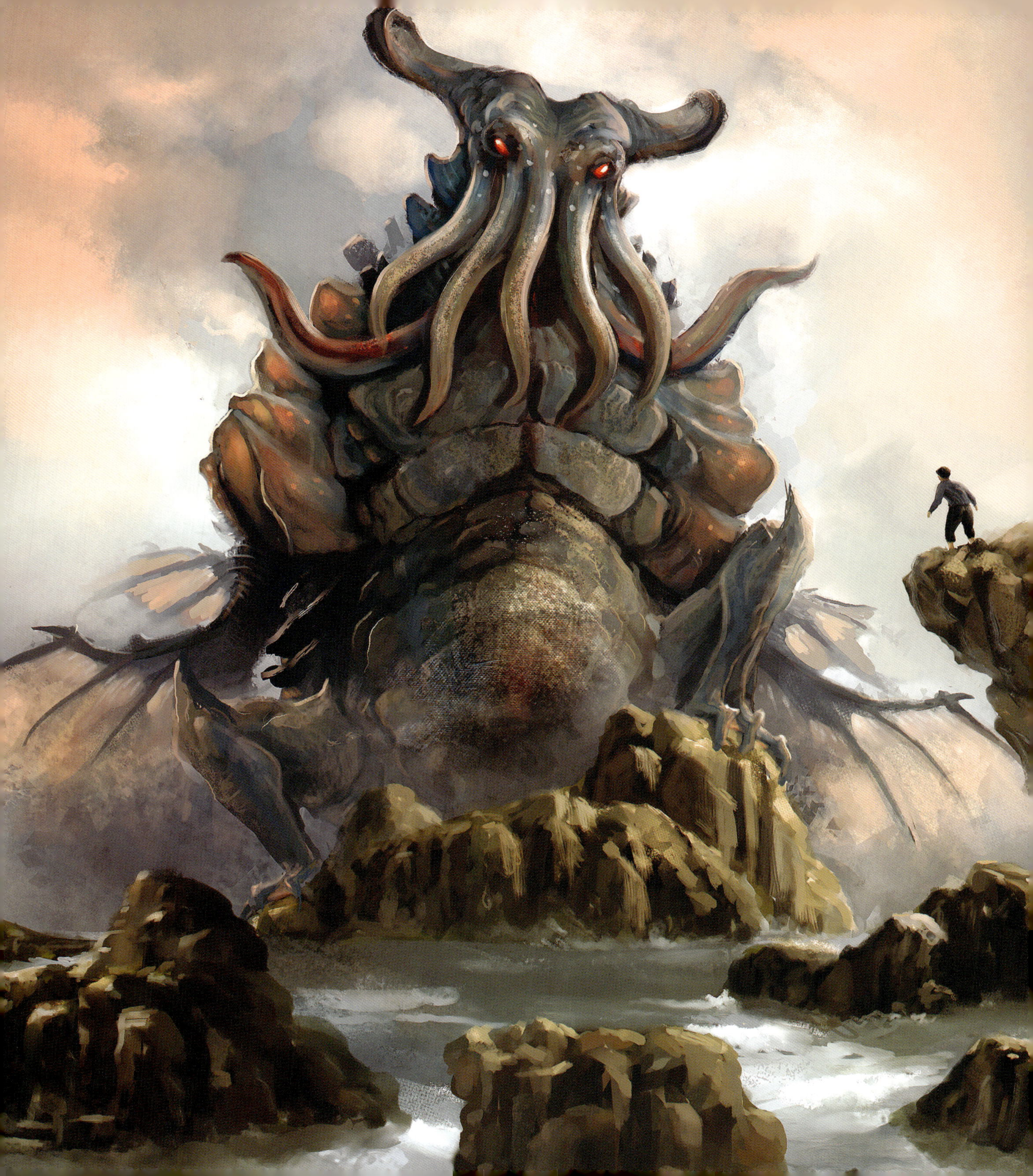

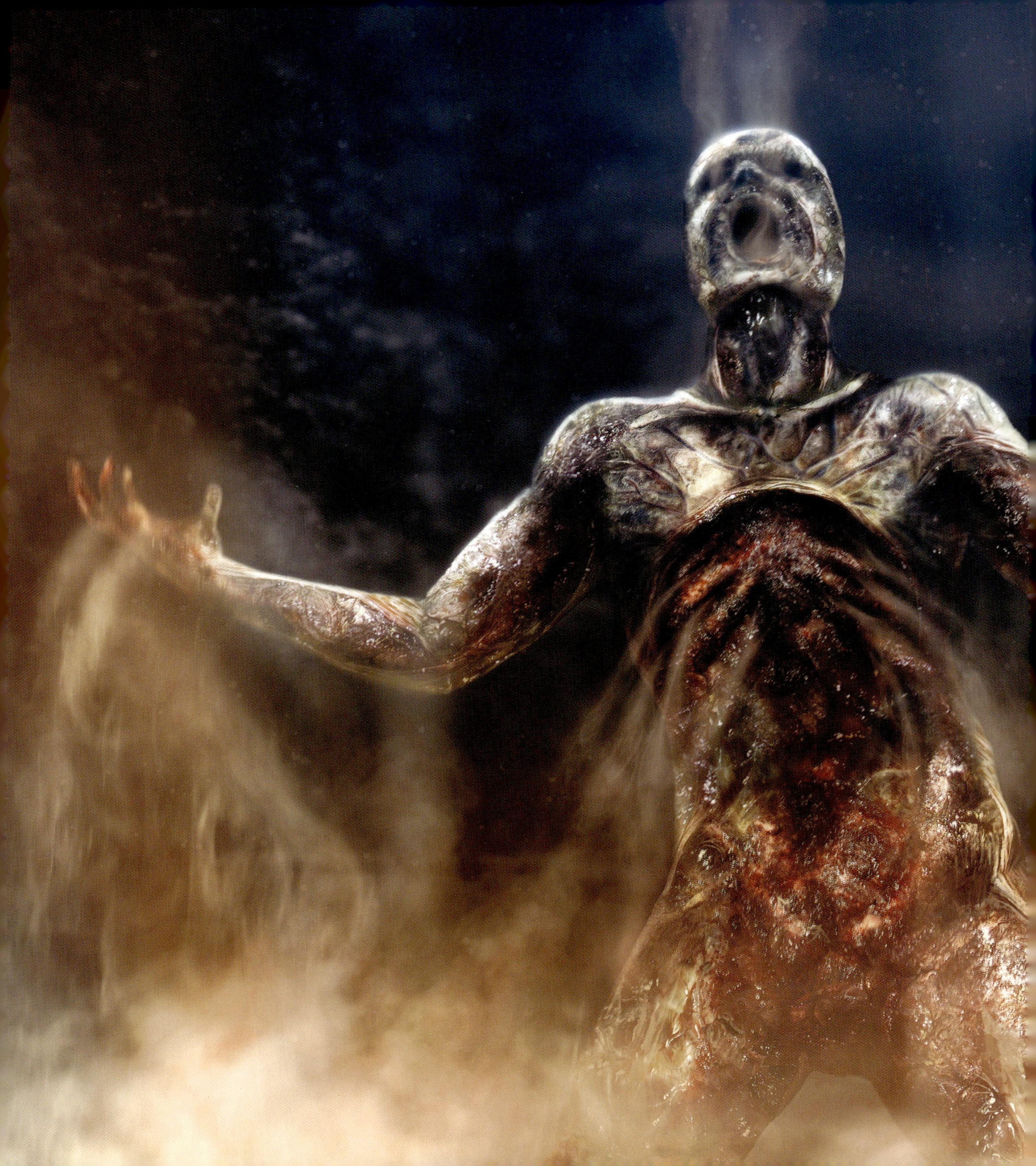

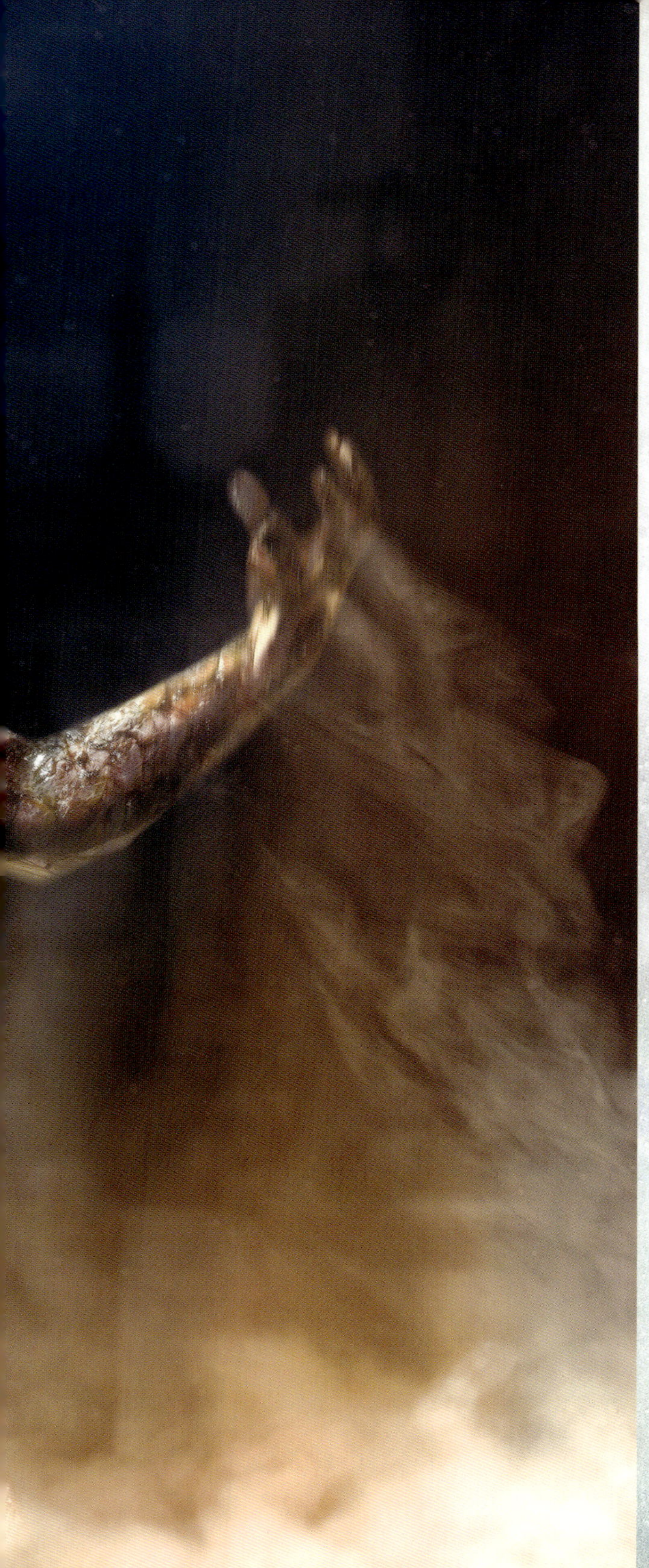

shape-shifters, vampires and healers who live among the humans of Earth; upon coming of age, they must choose between the Light and the Dark, with a prophecy stating that one supreme 'Other' will arise to spark a cataclysmic war. Lovecraft, too, built an idea into his stories that the future would involve a war with aliens, creating his 'cosmicism'.

The 'Others'

Touching upon these ideas, Lukyanenko uses the ***Necronomicon*** to build his world of the 'Others', brilliantly blending science fiction into fantasy and horror. He tells of 'The Twilight' – a magical realm that exists beneath our Earthly surface and of how 'Others' came to be by tapping into this twilight. There's the 'Book of Destiny' and the 'Book of Fate' mentioned within the story, as well as the magical book 'Fuaran'. This magic book is capable of transforming humans into 'Others', so that when used by an 'Other' every human in their sight is transformed into an 'Other' themselves. Mixing the otherworldly realm, as well as the Fuaran, ***The Night Watch*** is inherently influenced by the ***Necronomicon***; books that possess truly terrifying powers, transforming innocent into evil and exuding a kind of magical presence that only Lovecraft's brand of horror could inspire.

Neil Gaiman

Lovecraft's ***Necronomicon*** also went on to inspire some of the best fantasy and horror writers of this generation. No doubt having a book of the dead to play with would spark many an idea in the heads of some of the world's most creative storytellers. One such storyteller is Neil Gaiman, who is recognized as one of the most influential comic and fiction writers in recent decades. From ***Stardust*** (1999) to ***American Gods*** (2001), his works feature a range of mythical creatures that only the likes of Lovecraft and his ***Necronomicon*** could conjure.

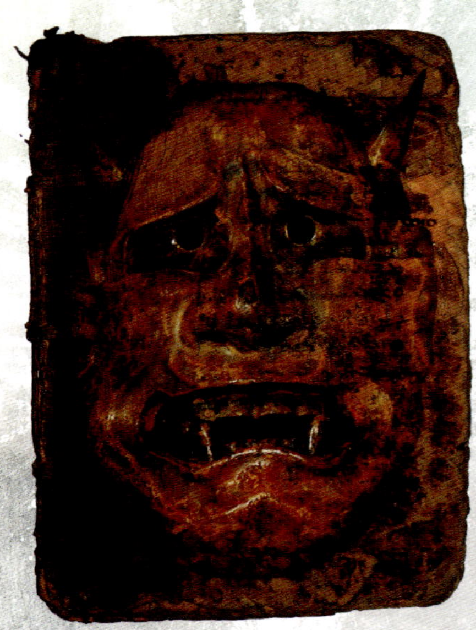

Whilst Gaiman has certainly created his own unique brand of Weird Fiction and science fiction horror, he hasn't shied away from the impact that the ***Necronomicon*** has had on his work; once stating that everyone should read Lovecraft as 'that's where the darkness started', the author has used this darkness throughout his extensive work.

'I Cthulhu'

In 1986 Gaiman wrote a short story called 'I Cthulhu', which is no doubt an ode to the Rhode Island writer. 'Cthulhu, they call me. Great Cthulhu,' it begins. Followed by 'Nobody can pronounce it right,' it's an early indication of Gaiman's satirical approach to the mythos as well as to the book of the dead. Anyone who's a fan of his work will know that Gaiman loves a sarcastic quip within his words, and it's this approach that ensures his odes to the ***Necronomicon*** are some of the most entertaining. 'I was spawned uncounted aeons ago, in the dark mists of Khhaa'ynhnaiih (no, of course I don't know how to spell it. Write it as it sounds), of nameless nightmare parents, under a gibbous moon,' continues the story, as Gaiman brilliantly pokes fun at those ***Necronomicon*** and Cthulhu fans that take it so very seriously – or rather, believe that it's real.

'It was never meant for the world of the living.'
Army of Darkness

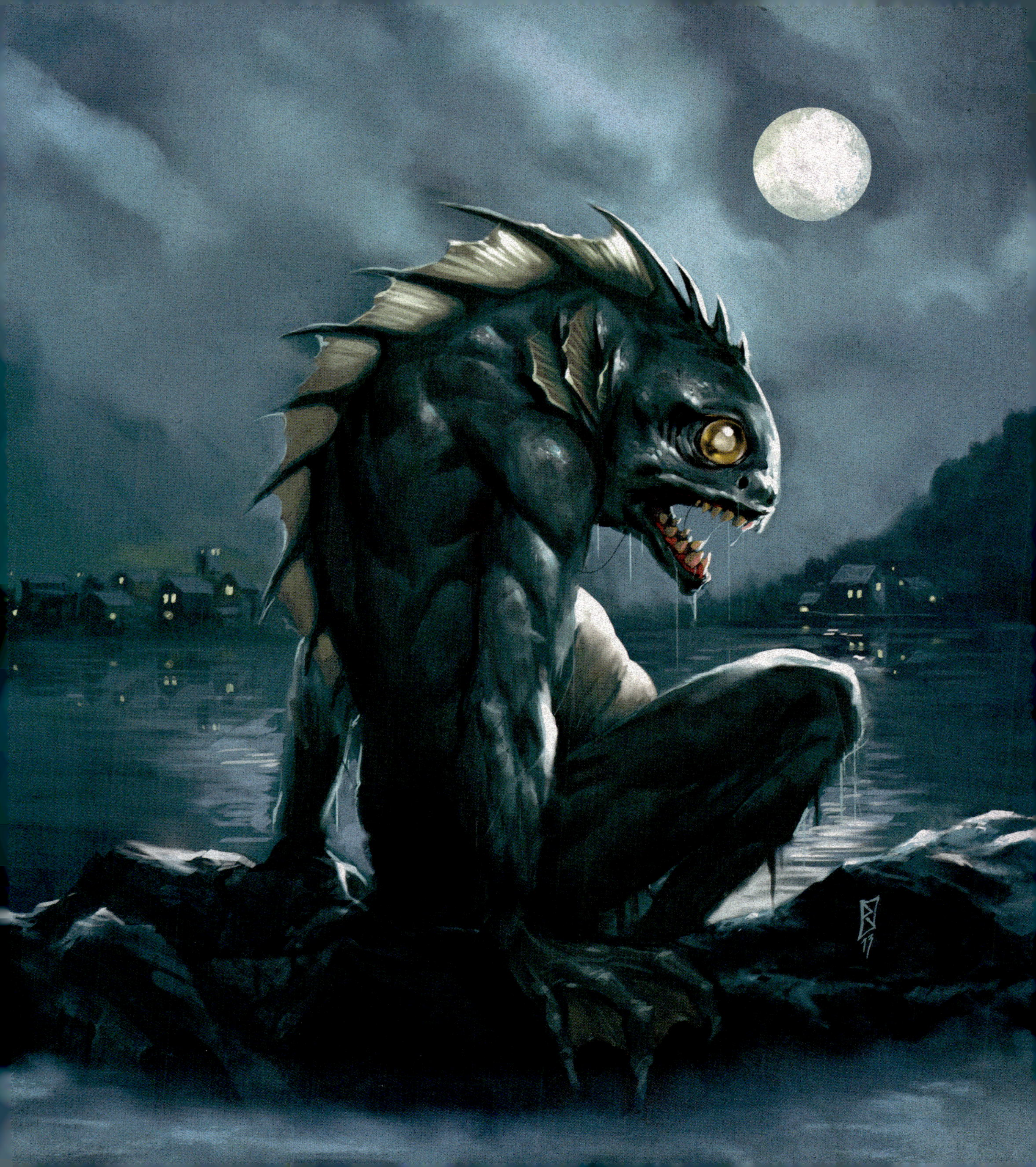

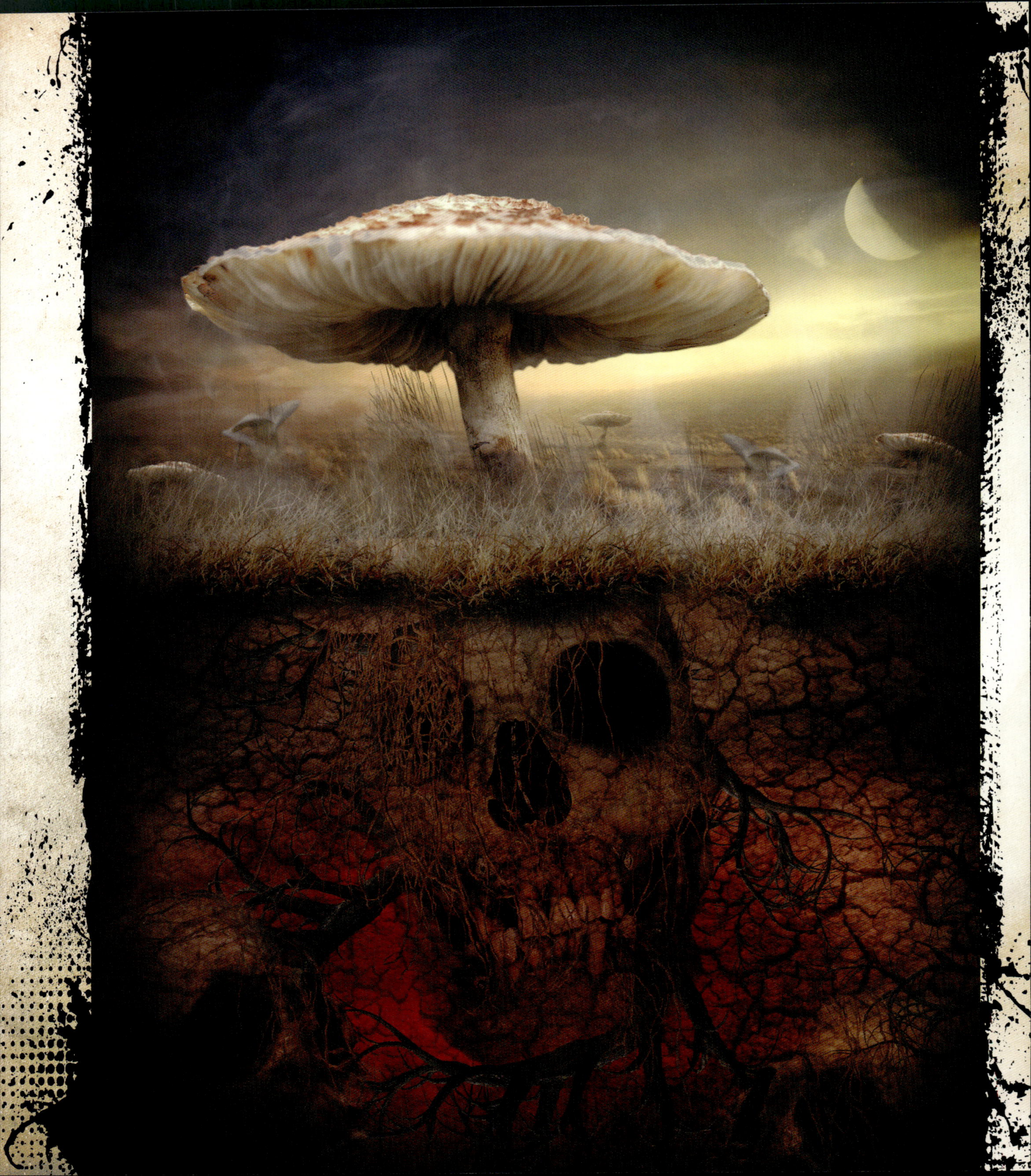

No Explanation Needed

It's clear now that the ***Necronomicon*** had reached such a point in pop culture that it could be satirized without too much background knowledge needed. Of course, Gaiman fans were more than likely familiar with the work of Lovecraft, but in the late 1970s and early 1980s the ***Necronomicon*** was beginning to be referenced without any prior explanation – people were already aware of its origins, connotations and, basically, that something pretty terrible was about to happen once it was mentioned.

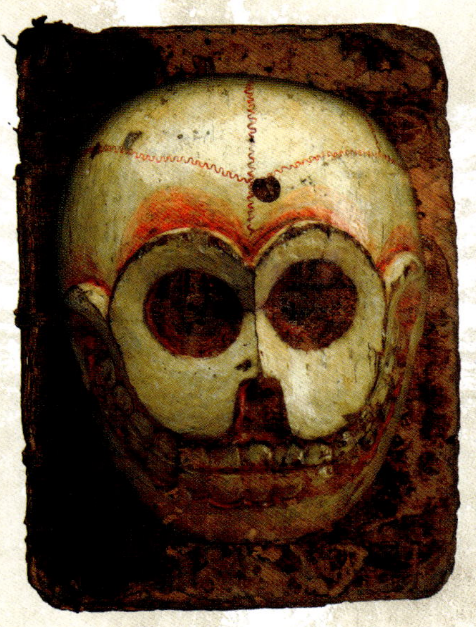

The Necrotelicomnicon

Gaiman wasn't the only author to poke fun at the ***Necronomicon***. Sharing a mutual love for the book was English author Terry Pratchett (b. 1948), who together with Gaiman, created the ***Necrotelicomnicon***. Much like its name suggests, it's sort of a phone book for contacting the dead, with its Latin name 'Liber Paginarum Fulvarum' translating as 'The Book of Yellow Pages'. It was used to summon all manner of horrifying demons and other otherworldly denizens of darkness, with both Gaiman and Pratchett featuring it in a range of their works – almost like creating their own Lovecraftian circle with this clever and hilarious homage to the originator.

Al Aksandir Garambel

The authors state that the ***Necrotelicomnicon*** was created by the 'Mad Arab' Al Aksandir Garambel after summoning the terrifying Wa'tz'ynn, whose names not only reference Lovecraft's 'Mad Arab' Abdul Alhazred but also cleverly reference the inventors of the telephone, Alexander Graham Bell and Thomas A. Watson. Moreover, Bell was the first to speak an intelligible sentence over the phone and, of course, this also ties in nicely with the ***Necrotelicomnicon*** – why? It was a summoning – not of a demon, unfortunately, but a command nonetheless: 'Mr Watson – come here – I want to see you.'

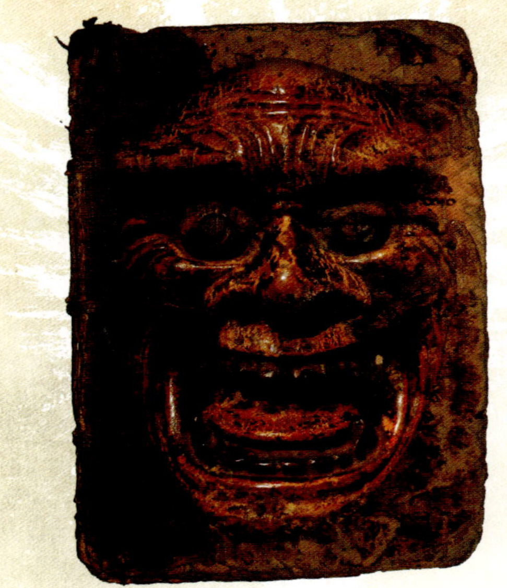

Terry Pratchett

'It is said that the book [the ***Necrotelicomnicon***] was written in one day after Klatchian necromancer Achmed – and fictional author of the ***Necrotelicomnicon*** – drank too much of the strange thick Klatchian coffee which doesn't just sober you up, but takes you through sobriety and ***out the other side***,' claims Pratchett in the tenth volume of his 'Discworld' series, ***Moving Pictures*** (1990). He continues: 'You glimpse the real universe beyond the clouds of warm self-delusion that sapient life usually generates around itself to stop it turning into a nutcake.'

The Necrotelicomnicon Continues

It's clear that both authors were having a lot of fun with their creation, as it continued to feature in a wide range of their works. As mentioned above, it was a welcome inclusion in Pratchett's 'Discworld' series collection – especially in ***Equal Rites*** (1987), which spoke of the unfortunate fate of

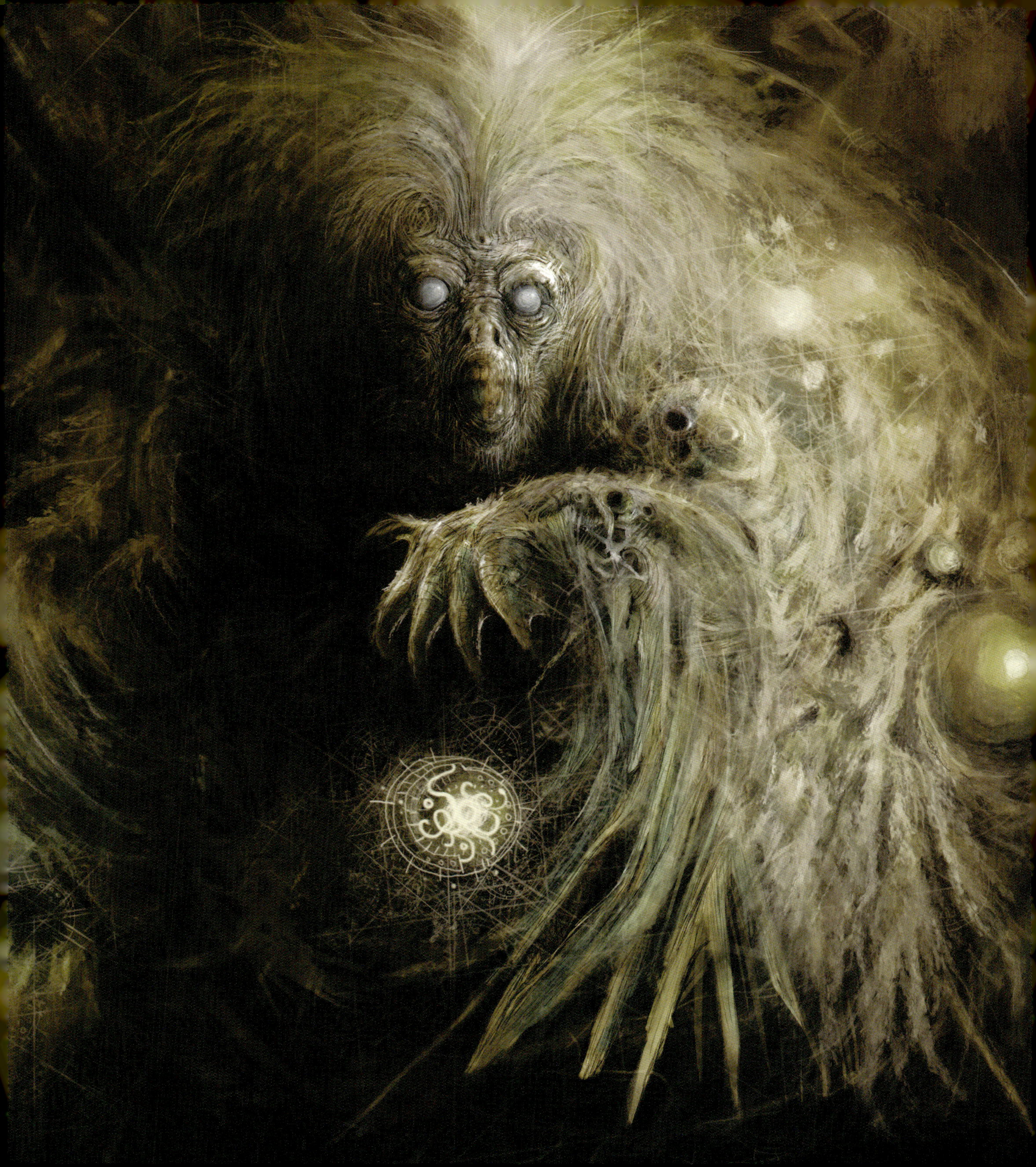

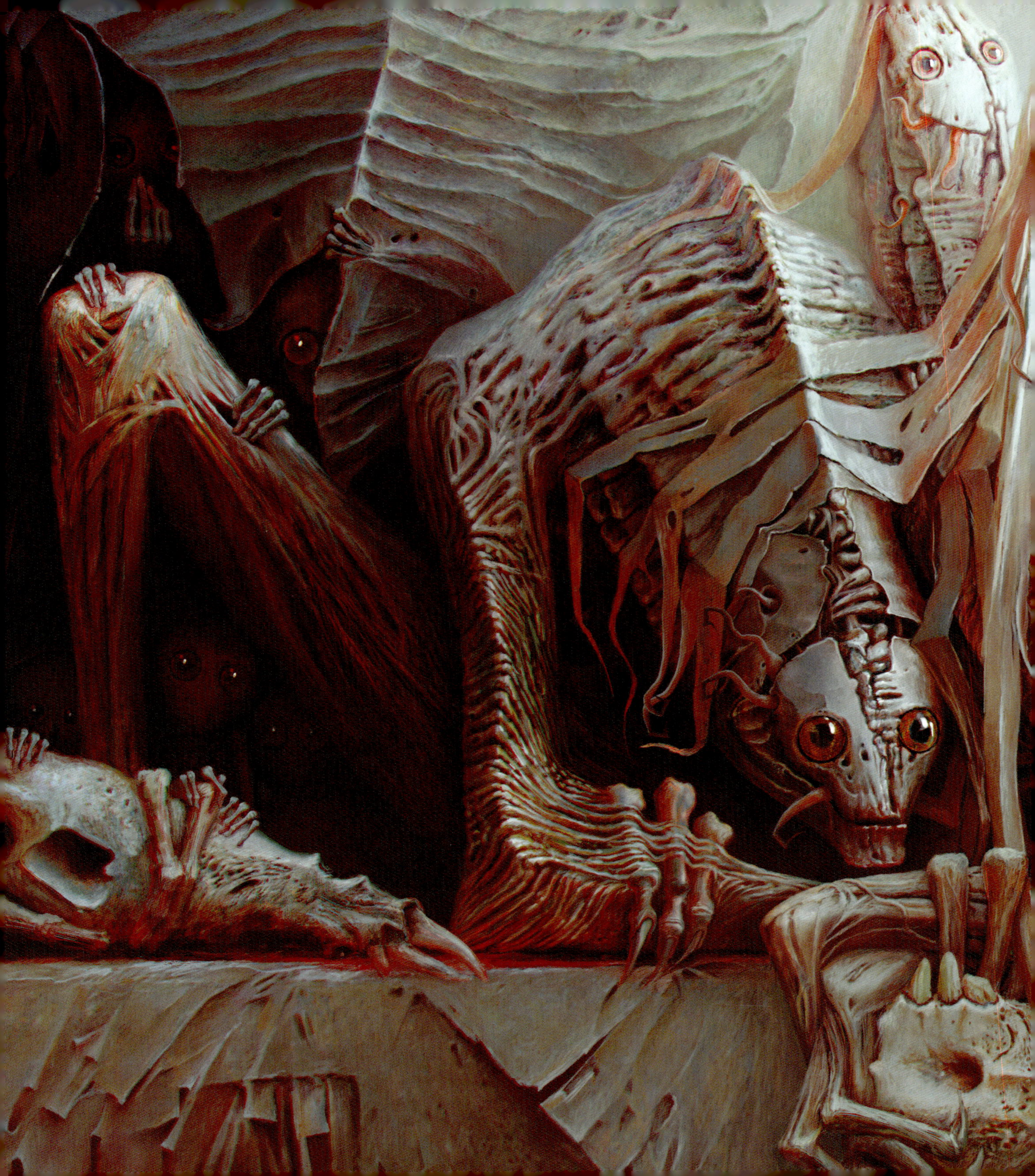

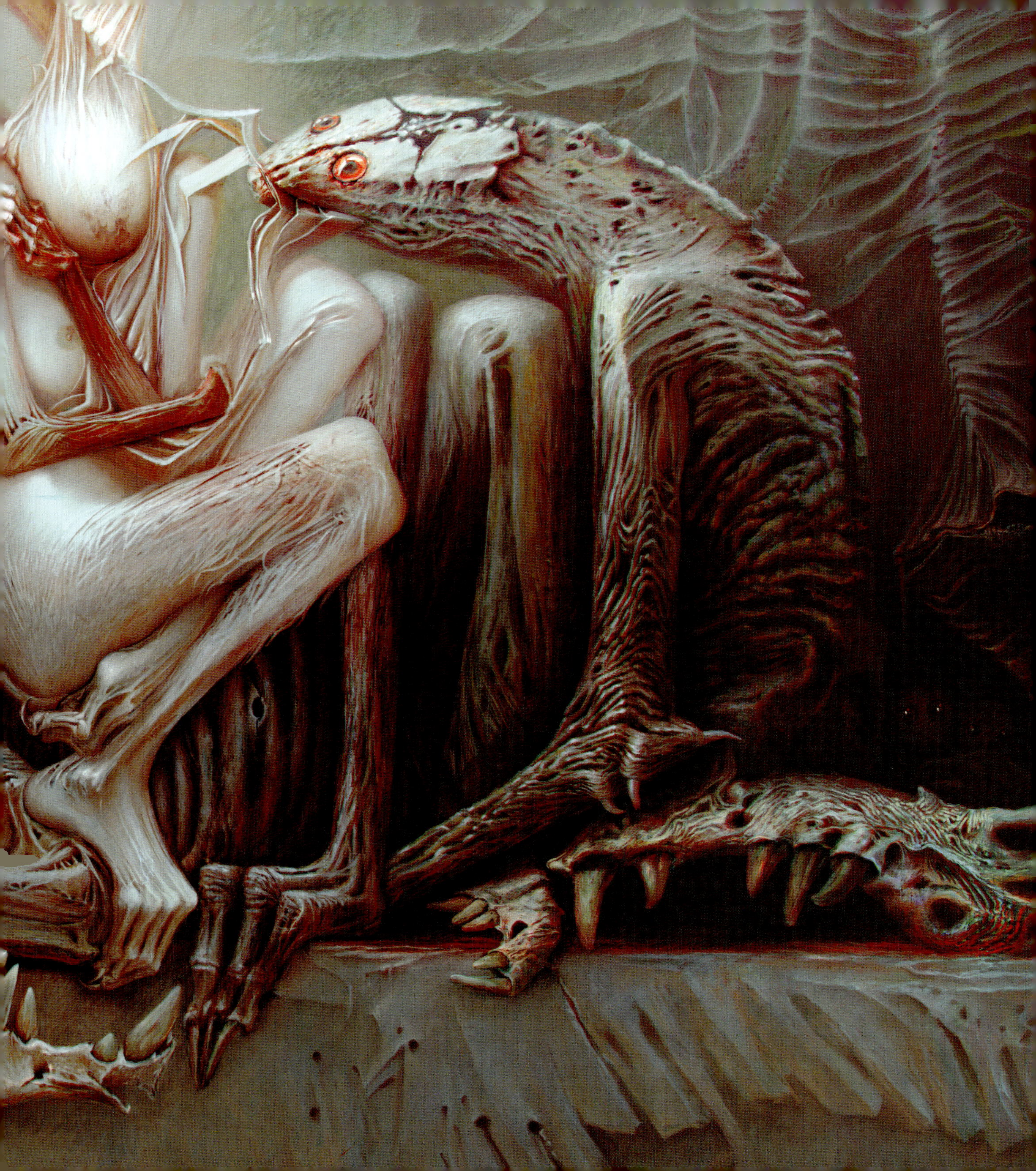

those who read the ***Necrotelicomnicon*** (**spoiler:** they were never seen again and the book became mysteriously thicker). The book also features in Neil Gaiman's ***The Sandman*** (1991), using its Latin title of 'Liber Pagnarum Fulvarum' in the Library of Dream. Pratchett and Gaiman also collaborated on ***Good Omens*** (1990), in which the ***Necrotelicomnicon*** makes another appearance.

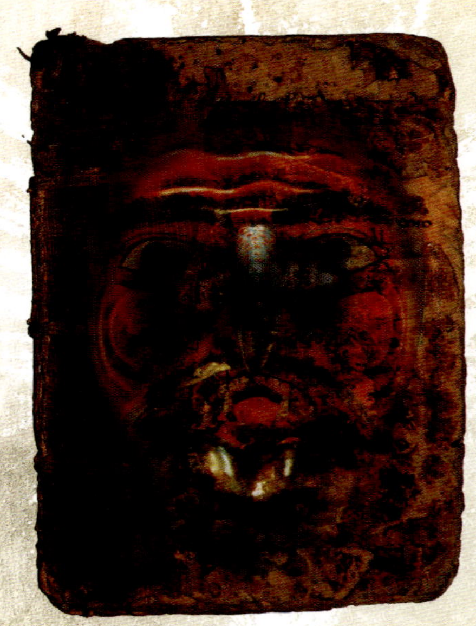

The Unseen University Library

It seems that the shelves of this fictional library were full of Pratchett-made grimoires, fuelling the plots of his cult-classic novels. Much like Lovecraft and his ***Necronomicon***, most of these inventions were crafted by priests or people of religious descent, their content alluding to an unpleasant mind of its own as Pratchett hints at the grisly fate of those who may come into contact with such books.

The Octavo

Pratchett alluded to a number of grimoires in his 'Discworld' series and with the ***Necronomicon*** being the first grimoire of its kind, the production of similarly attributed volumes is a clear indication of the book's impact on popular literature. First mentioned in ***The Colour of Magic*** (1983), one of his most famous creations is 'The Octavo' which contained the eight most powerful spells left behind on the Disc by its creator. Kept locked in the basement of the Unseen University's Library – much like the ***Necronomicon*** and its placement in both fictional and real libraries – the dark magic undertones nicely complement the content of Lovecraft's original grimoire.

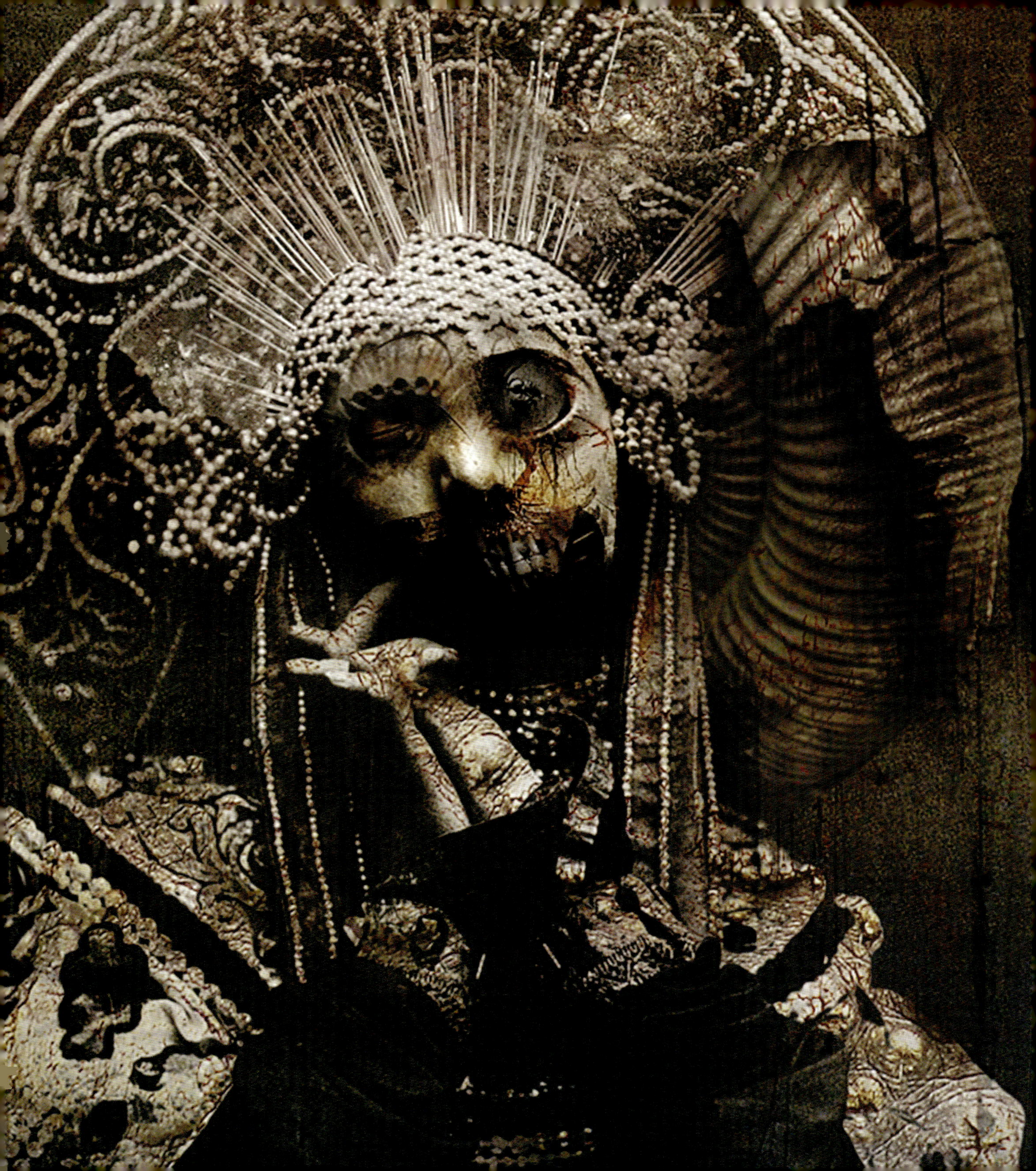

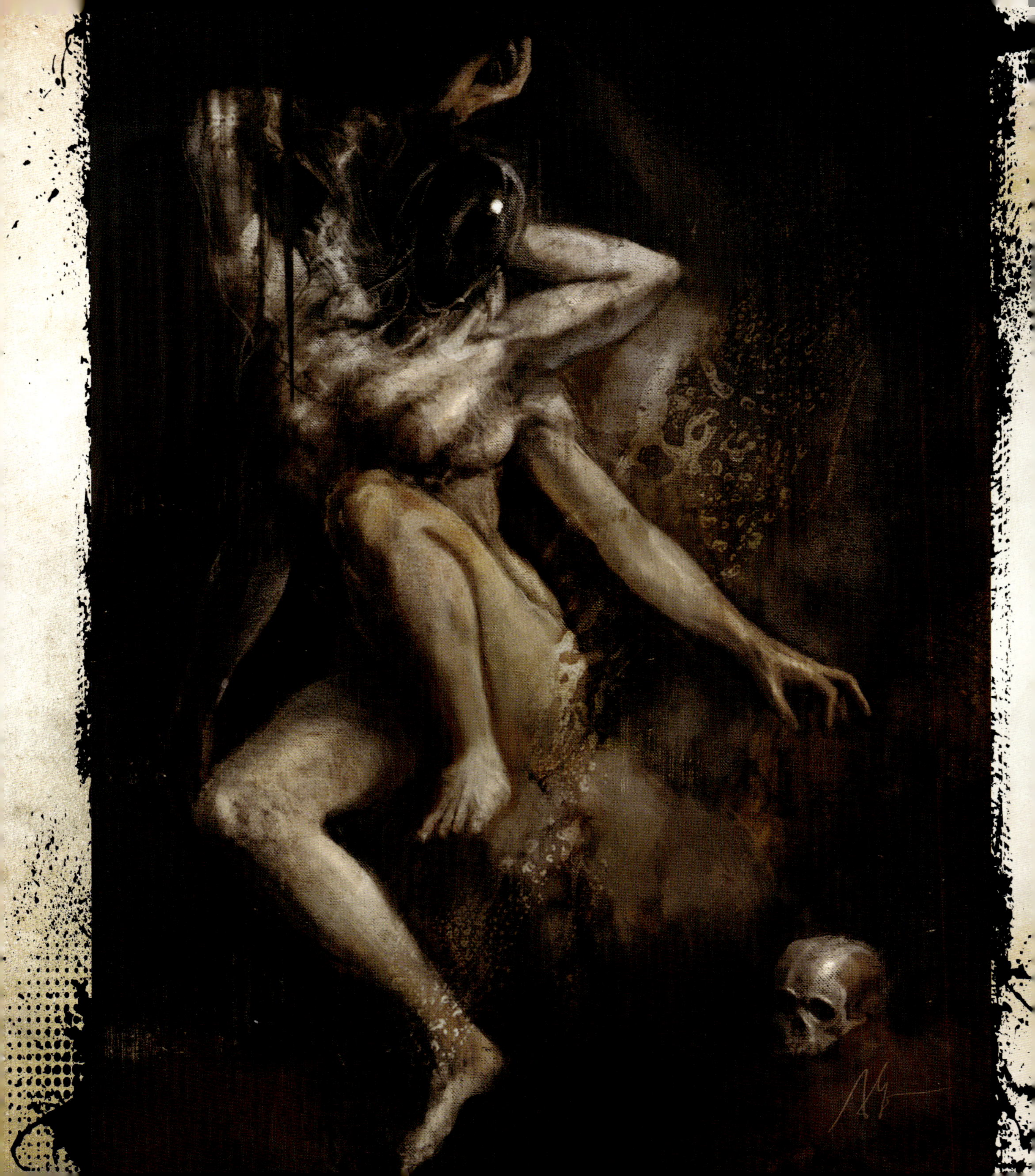

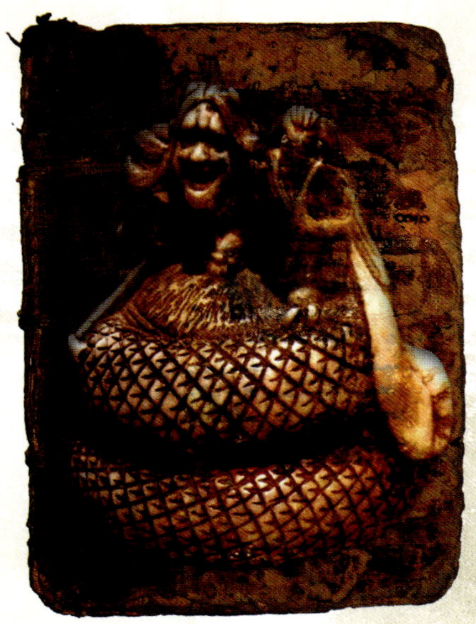

Protection

Contained in a room full of precautions for the protection of its visitors, the room's walls are covered in symbols and octagrams. No one person may stay in the room for more than a very specific 4 minutes and 32 seconds – a figure that was arrived at after almost two centuries of cautious experimentation with the book. Despite its importance in Pratchett's novels, the Octavo's appearance as a book bound in leather with a simple illustration of Bel-Shamharoth on the cover makes it fairly underwhelming.

Stephen King

Today, it could be said that Stephen King is arguably one of the most successful and well-known horror and fantasy writers. Movie adaptations of his novels have gone on to become hugely popular in their own right, whilst his original novels have gone down as some of the best cult classic offerings of the past few decades. Widely known as an expert in fantasy horror, King has been incredibly vocal about his love and inspiration from Lovecraft and the ***Necronomicon***.

The ***Necronomicon*** is most notably used in King's novel ***The Eyes of the Dragon*** (1987), in which one of its main characters, Flagg, uses a spell book to disappear and escape death; this 'spell book' is merely described as being written on the plains of Leng by a man named Alhazred – ring any bells? And as Flagg is described as a 'demonic being', the ***Necronomicon*** ties in nicely with the attributes of the character.

Night Shift

Mentioned in King's first collection of short stories, ***Night Shift*** (1978), the author has created some of the best homages to Lovecraft and his ***Necronomicon***. 'Jerusalem's Lot' is one particular story that has stuck out for Lovecraft fans, as King manages to effortlessly capture the archaic language without being a complete copycat, solidifying his own style of Weird Fiction in the process.

King often associates the ***Necronomicon*** with characters that emit a mysterious and creepy air – adding to their sinister personalities and unpredictable actions. In 'I Know What You Need', a social outcast called Ed Hamner Jr owns a copy of the ***Necronomicon***; it cleverly mimics Hamner Jr's paranormal abilities and the other characters' uneasiness around him.

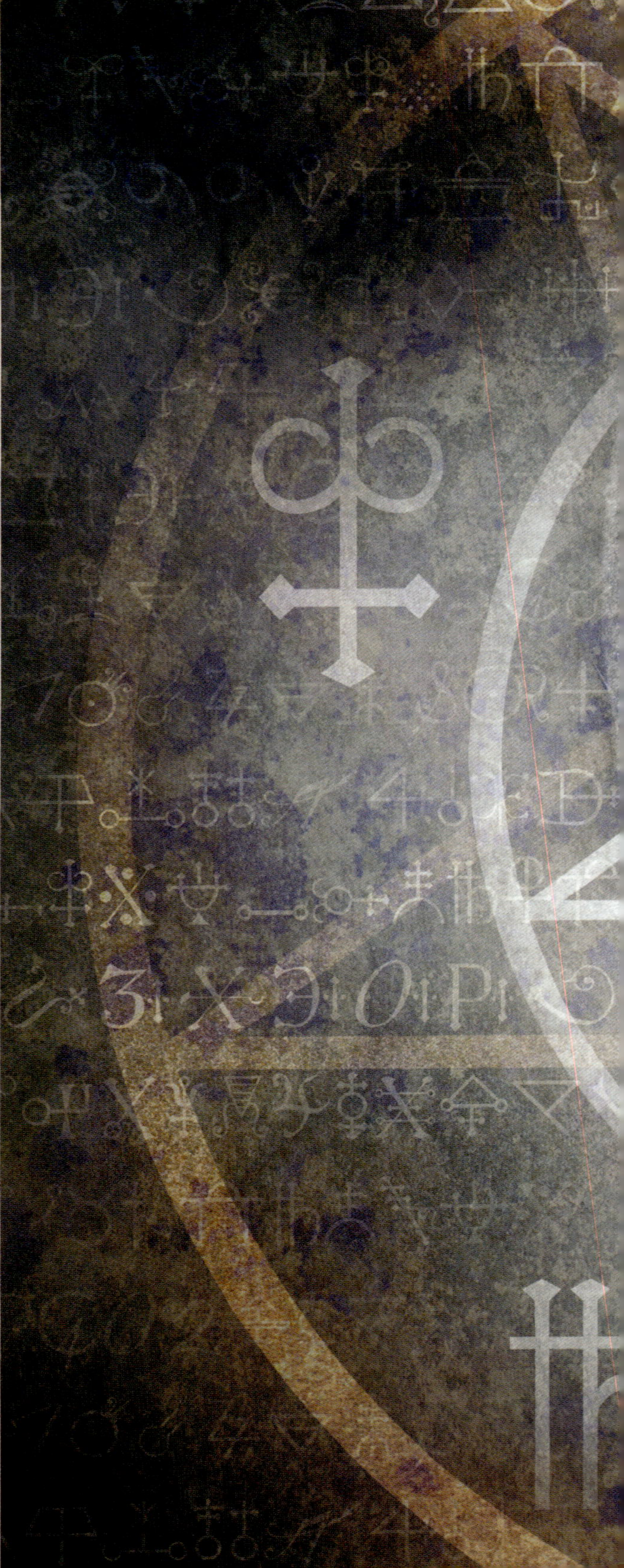

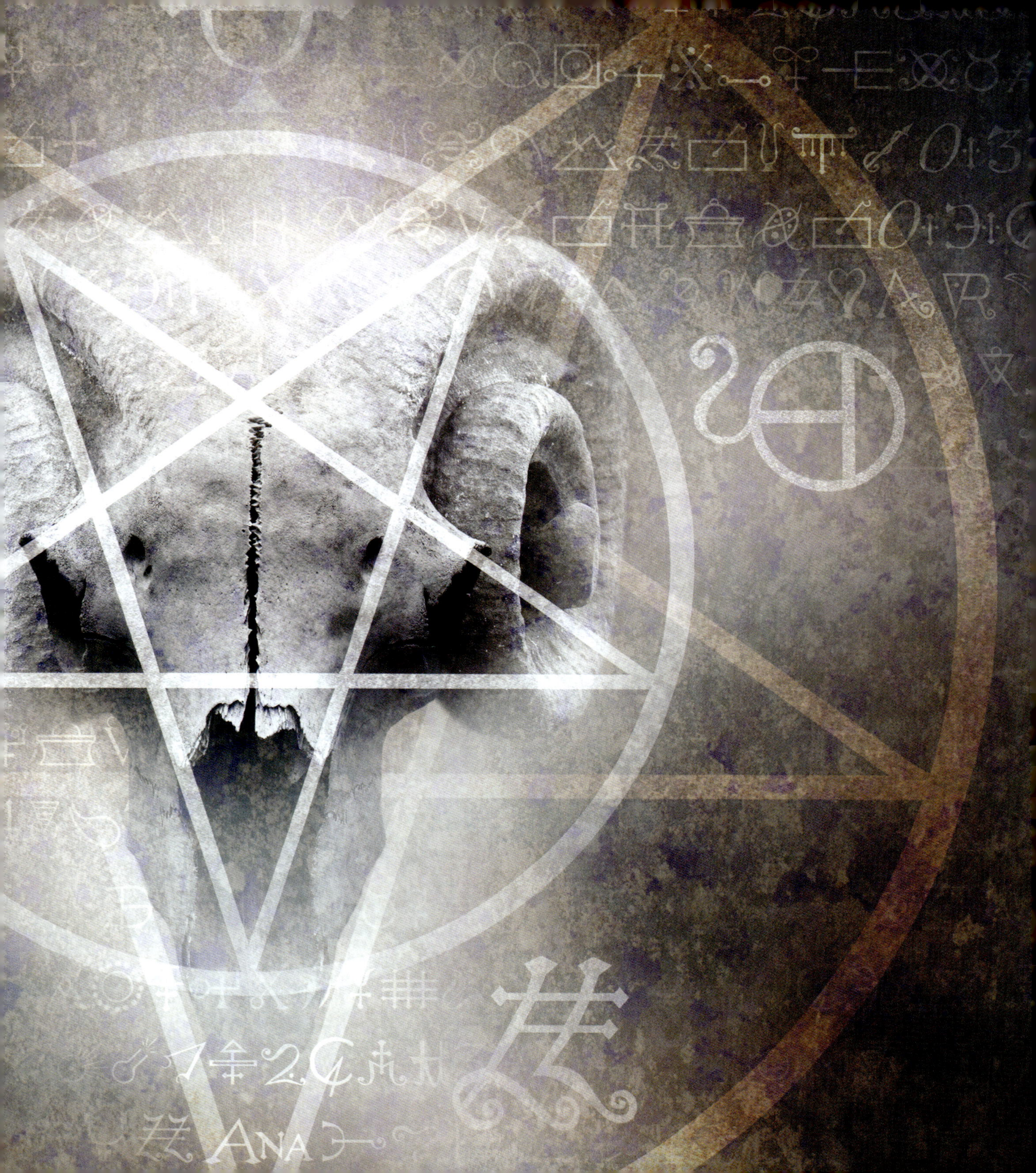

Trouble in the Pages

King also goes on to mention the ***Necronomicon*** in a range of his stories, including ***Salem's Lot*** (1975) and ***The Stand*** (1978). In the latter, King speaks of the book showcasing 'details that made him [Isaac] feel a little bit sick deep down' and compares it to 'the way papop's arms used to look when he would carry Glen and put him in the car'. Again, King takes Lovecraft's lead by only hinting at the atrocities within the pages, as the character of Isaac says: 'Some books you should only judge by the cover. Some books you shouldn't read at all.'

The Go-To Horror Device

Proving its sustainability throughout modern literature, the ***Necronomicon*** has been and will continue to be the go-to device in creating otherworldly undertones and summoning horrifying creatures only the minds of Lovecraft, King, Pratchett, Gaiman and more could come up with. King once stated that the ***Necronomicon*** is 'The twentieth century horror story's dark and baroque prince'; pretty much summing it up for writers and fans the world over.

'All life is only a set of pictures in the brain, among which there is no difference betwixt those born of real things and those born of inward dreamings ...'

'The Silver Key'

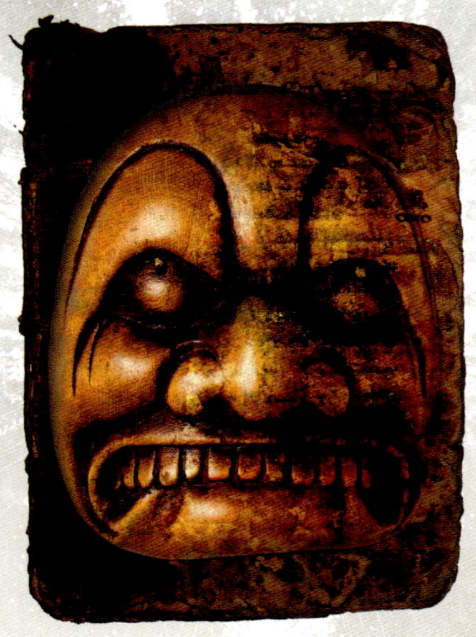

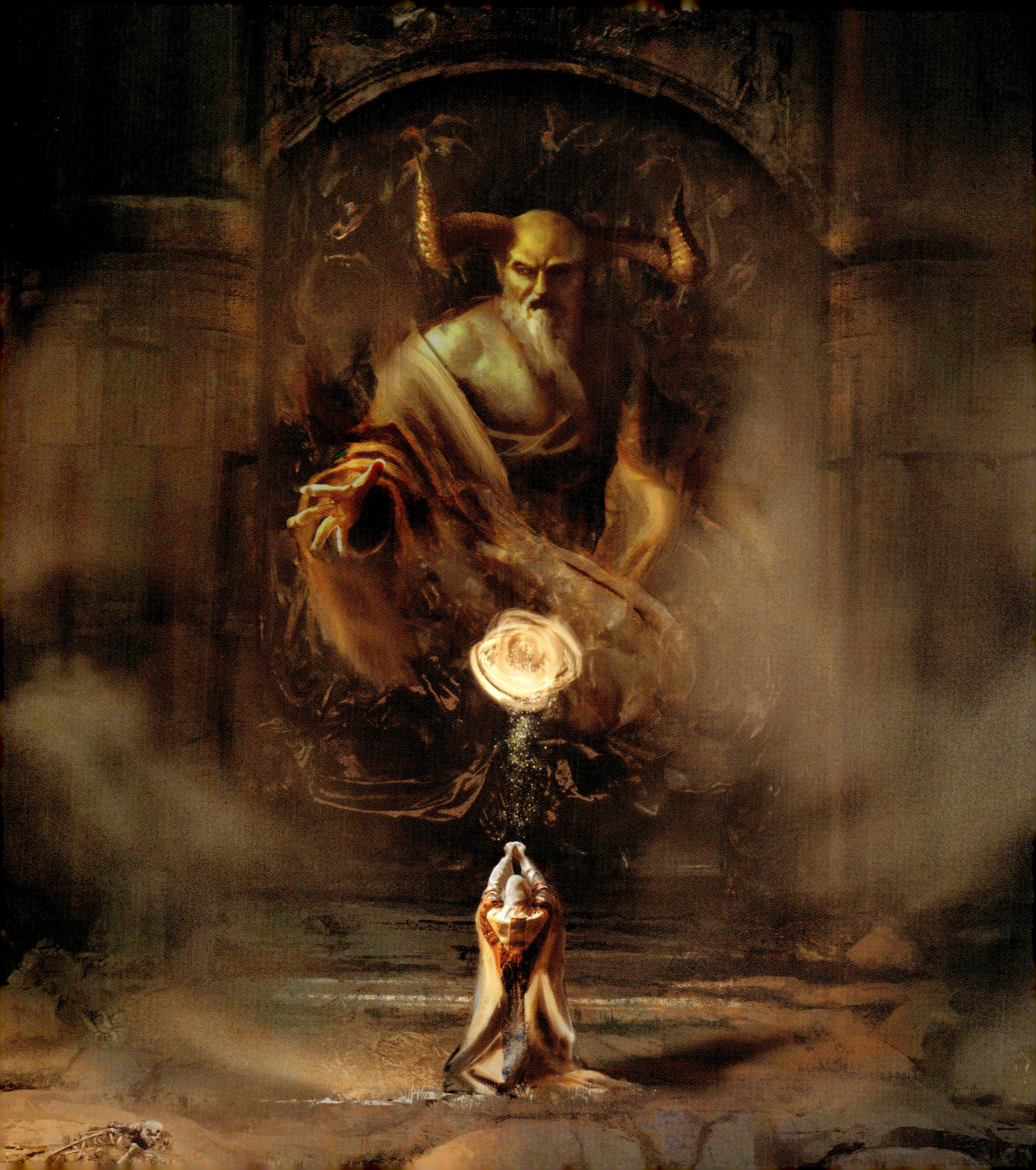

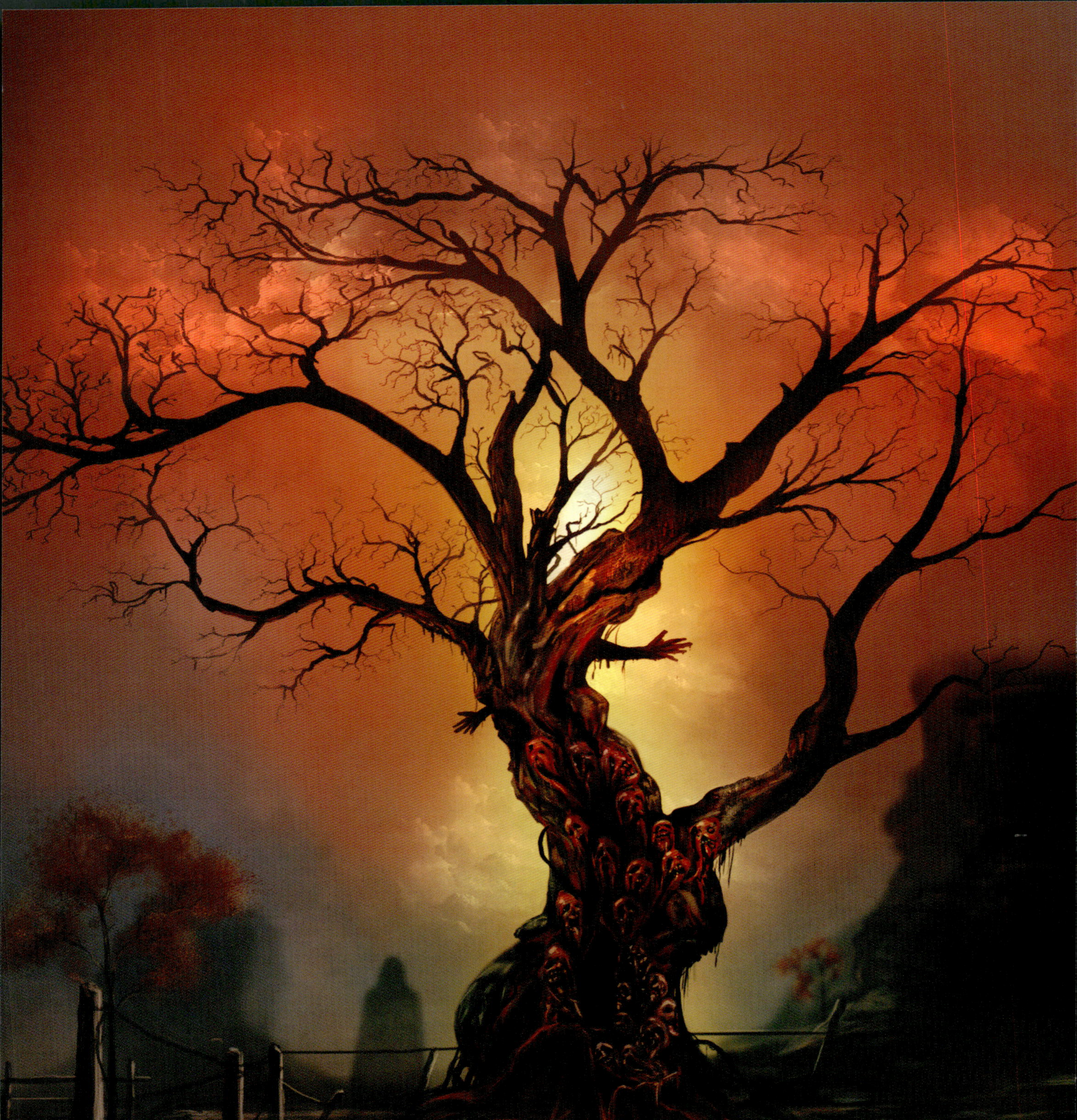

'Riot and revel, blood-food and foulness, eternal twilight and nightmare and the screams of the dead and the not-dead and the chant of the faithful.'

'I Cthulhu'

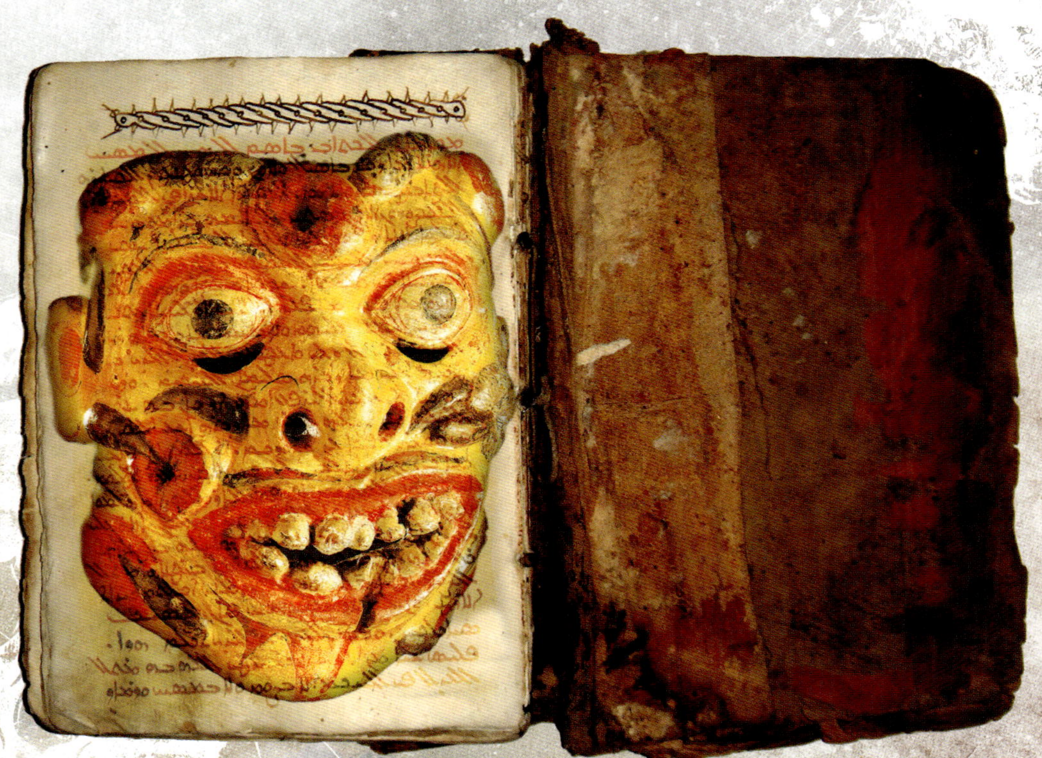

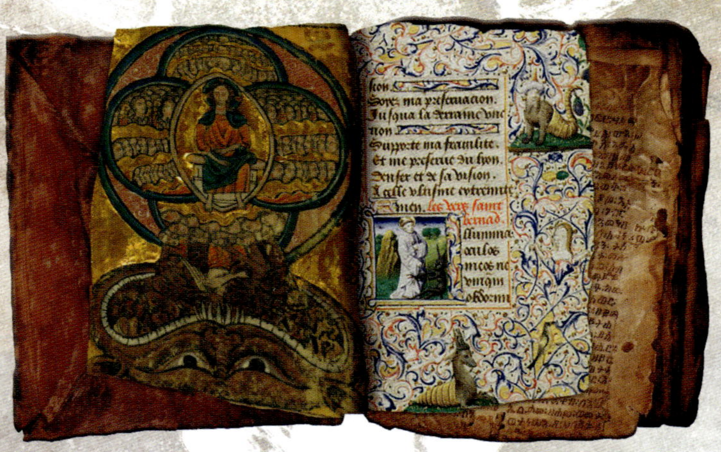

Invoking the Dark Arts

After H.R. Giger's original *Necronomicon* paintings, Alan Moore (b. 1953) could be said to be one of the most well-known and influential artists inspired by Lovecraft.

The Courtyard (2003) and ***Neonomicon*** (2011) graphic novels have won numerous awards and are regarded as some of the most disturbing and authentic representations of Lovecraft's world and his Cthulhu mythos; ***Neonomicon*** was even taken off the shelves at a library in South Carolina after a 14-year-old's mother complained about her daughter borrowing it.

H.R. Giger's Necronomicon

Swiss surrealist artist H.R. Giger is synonymous with the word 'Necronomicon'. He produced astounding, often monochromatic nightmarish dreamscapes, and indeed he released his very own ***Necronomicon*** (1978). But these weren't just made-up words and a poorly crafted leather cover; Giger's ***Necronomicon*** was an artistic tribute to the creatures, scriptures and spells in the original book of the dead. The unique and beautiful structure he gave to these creatures made for incredibly compelling yet disturbing views – just what Lovecraft would have wanted!

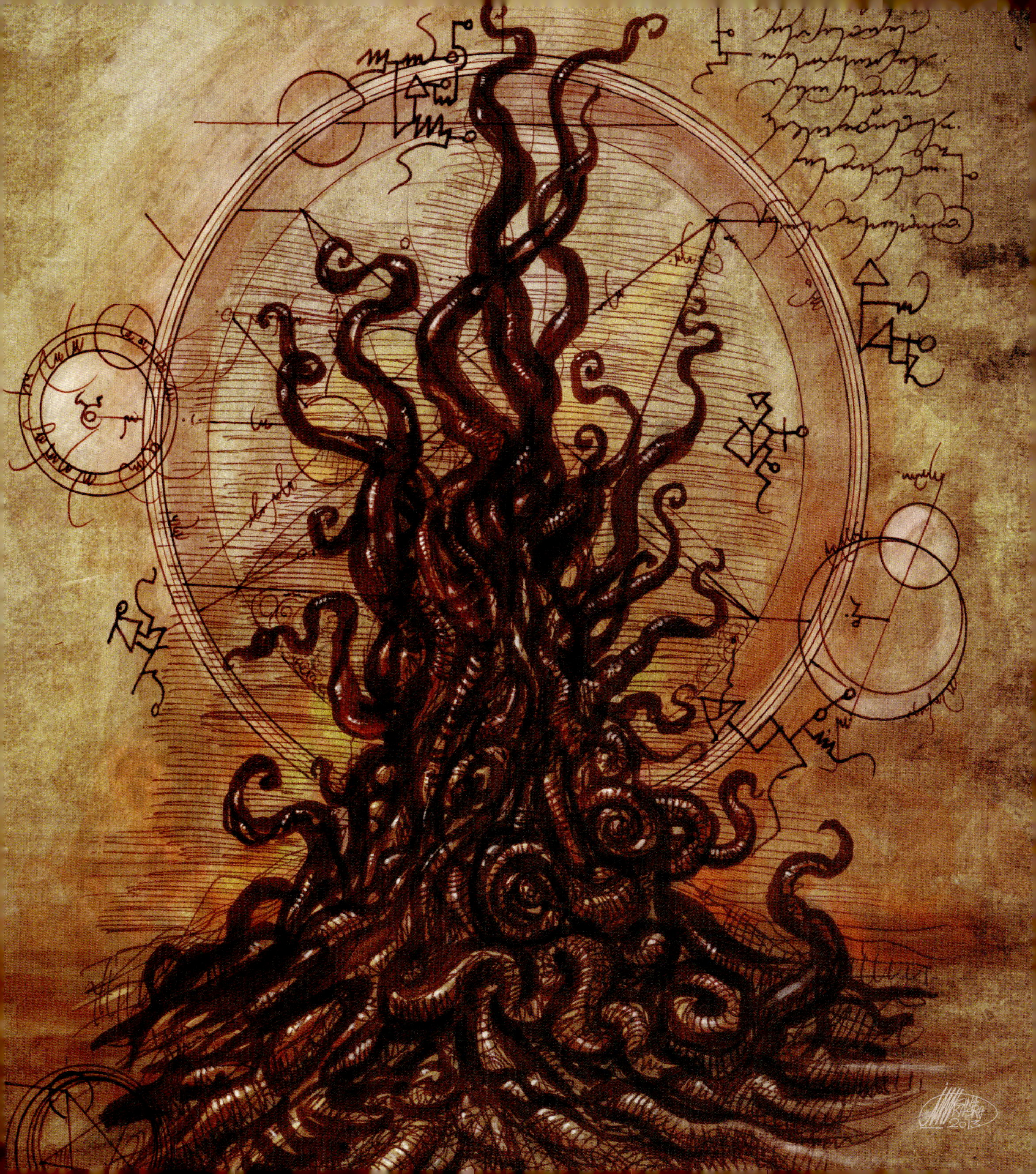

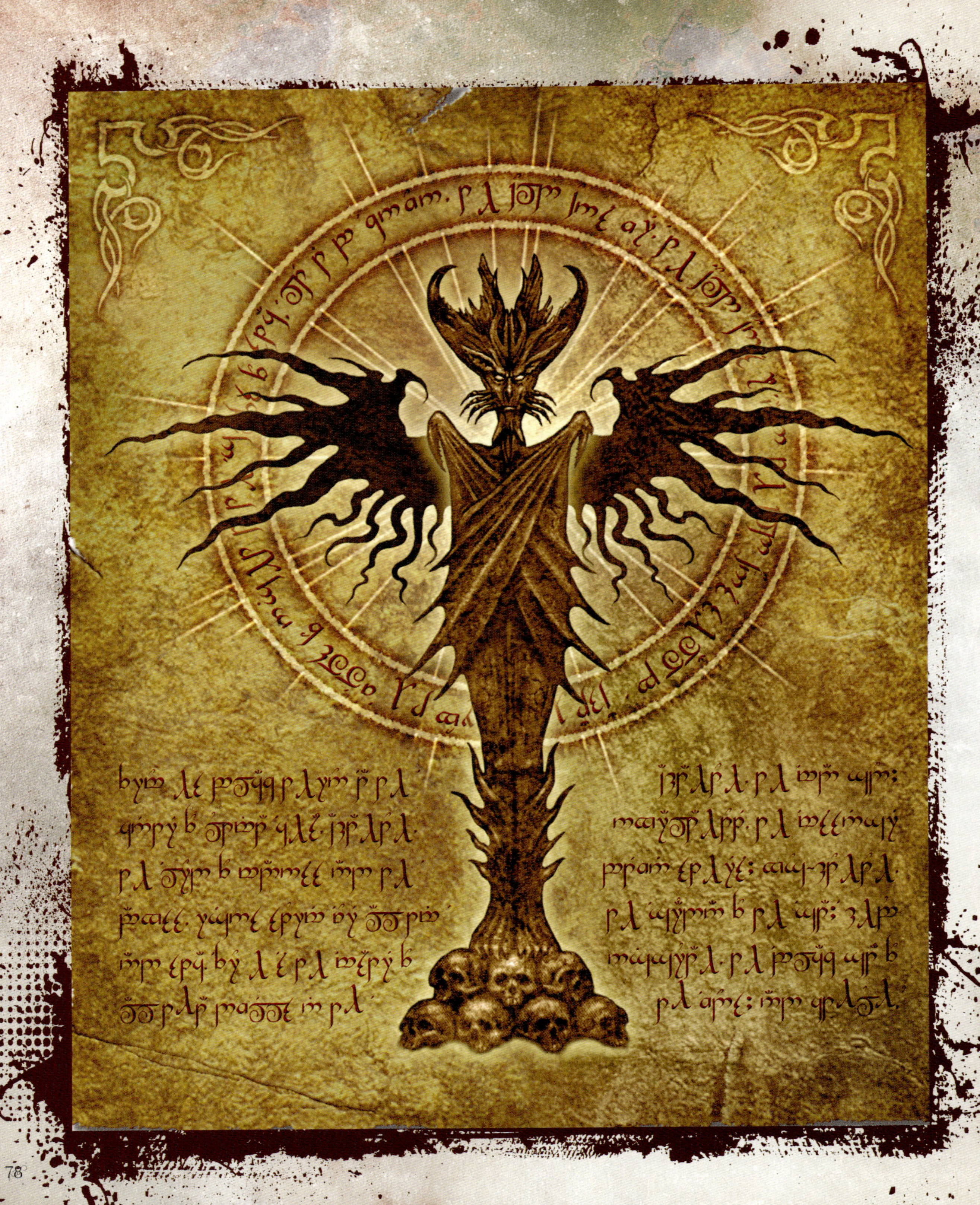

The success of the book ensured Giger became a cult phenomenon. In 1986, he created cover motifs for Sony's first laser discs; 1988 saw the artist produce slipcase motifs for books by Timothy Leary (1920–96), Aleister Crowley (1875–1947) and, of course, for the original weirdo H.P. Lovecraft. Giger even saw two bars – in Tokyo and in his hometown of Chur, Switzerland – built in his honour.

Nightmares

The two had more in common than Giger may have originally thought; Lovecraft was known to write down his dreams religiously – after all, the fictional author and name for the ***Necronomicon*** did come to him in his sleep – whilst Giger has said that many of his paintings, apart from being inspired by Lovecraft's original ideas, were done as a way of banishing disturbing and nightmarish dreams. 'They were horrifying,' he says. 'But I found that when I made artwork about them, the dreams went away.'

The Courtyard

In ***The Courtyard*** there are plenty of thematic instances that allude to the horrific world that Lovecraft initially produced, brought together with Moore's iconic style; it's even more terrifying than one could ever imagine. ***The Courtyard*** tells the story of special federal agent, Aldo Sax, who is tracking down the motives for a series of brutal killings carried out by three separate individuals. One element all three killers have in common is a gibberish language, but any Lovecraft fan would spot that it's the

'We read much in Alhazred's Necronomicon about its properties, and about the relation of ghouls' souls to the objects it symbolised; and were disturbed by what we read.'

'The Hound'

'Aklo' rhetoric – a language that rewrites the mind of the user, so that the perception of the reality of the 'Great Old Ones' occurs.

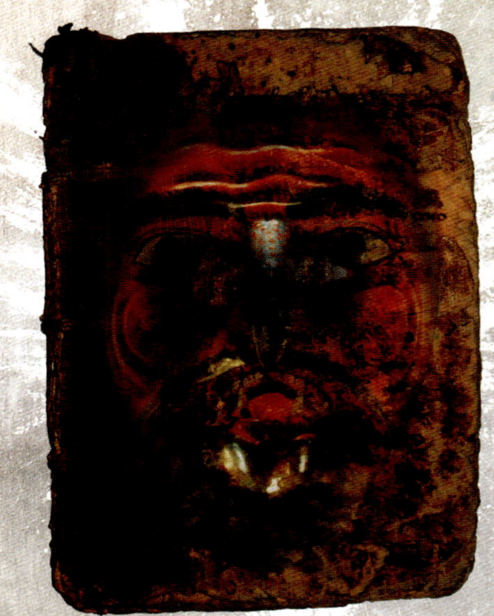

Neonomicon

Neonomicon continues the story, with FBI Agents Lamper and Brears visiting the now insane former agent Aldo Sax, who resides in a psychiatric hospital after committing two murders. This goes on to prove another Lovecraftian/ ***Necronomicon*** influence of decreased sanity after exposure to the book. They are now investigating a copycat killer and probe Sax for his motives and, of course, Sax speaks in 'gibberish'.

The Fishmen

The story continues with heavy focus on disturbing sexual paraphernalia, with Lamper killed by cultists and Brears raped and impregnated by a 'fishman'; this evil alludes to the fish-like nature of the 'Old Ones', as well as Lovecraft's fear of the water. It could also complement H.R. Giger's ***Necronomicon*** inspired ***Alien***, in which the sexual aspects of the creature are included to spark a natural and internal fear in us. Months later, Brears visits Sax again and is surprised that she can now understand his 'gibberish' as Aklo, the language of these fishmen. Upon realizing the events in Lovecraft's fiction are very real, she concludes that the future apocalypse will be heralded by the birth of her child – the one and only Cthulhu.

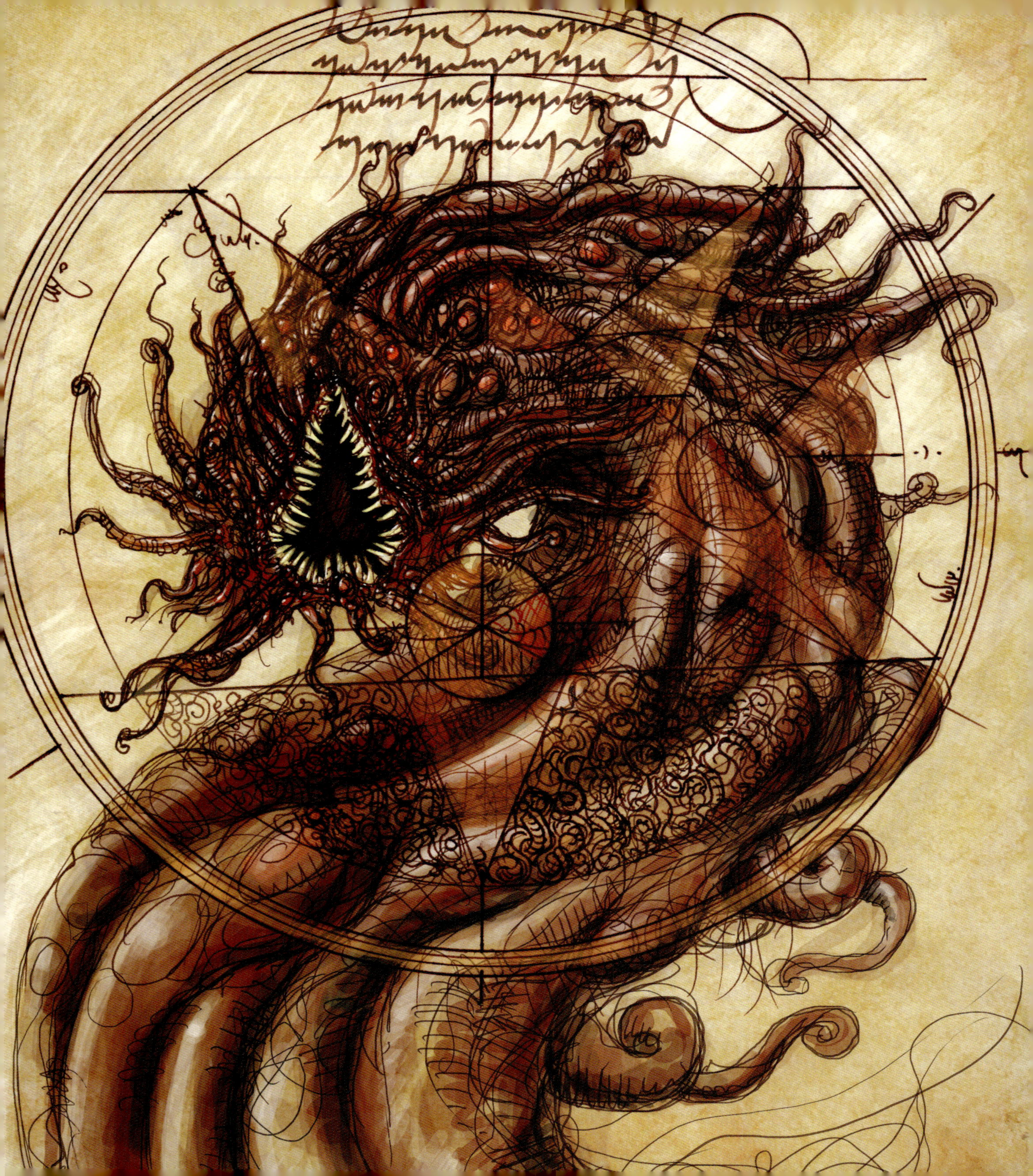

The Art of Neonomicon

The artwork within both stories was crafted by Jacen Burrows (b. 1972), who also worked with Moore on his ***Yuggoth Cultures and Other Growths*** publication (2003). Burrows' style is incredibly detailed and fits perfectly with the disturbing nature of the story, with the creatures showcasing an aesthetic that succinctly complements Lovecraft's descriptions of the ***Necronomicon's*** creatures. Drawing the book in four horizontal length panels per page created a movie-like display, with the gallery at the end of the graphic novel showcasing Burrows's ability to capture the horrifying world of Lovecraft unlike any other contemporary.

Dave Oliver

Based in Newcastle-Upon-Tyne, Dave Oliver works for a small game developer company and is inspired by the likes of Robert Bloch as well as all things Lovecraft. In ***Fugue*** (***see*** page 33), he takes inspiration from 'The Outsider' by H.P. Lovecraft, with the quote 'I know always that I am an outsider; a stranger in this century and among those who are still men.' 'I am hounded by the persistent suspicion that I have seen something like this before,' he says of his creation. 'Once lodged in my memory, it has lurked about in the recesses until I poured it forth.' Basing the face on his own, Oliver says that the artwork is a self-portrait of sorts. The Lovecraftian and especially Cthulhu inspiration can also be seen in his ***Loss*** (***see*** page 36) and ***Aephemeridae*** (***see*** pages 96–97) creations – there's no denying those tentacles.

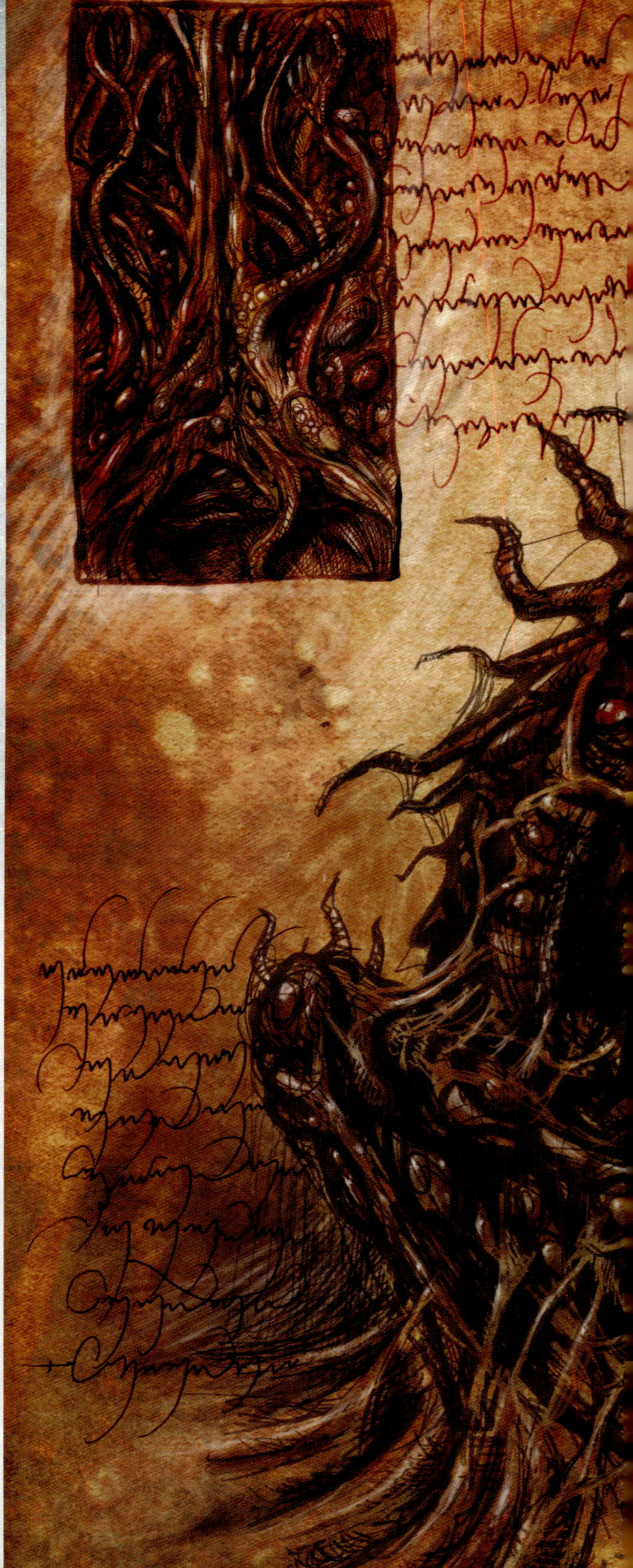

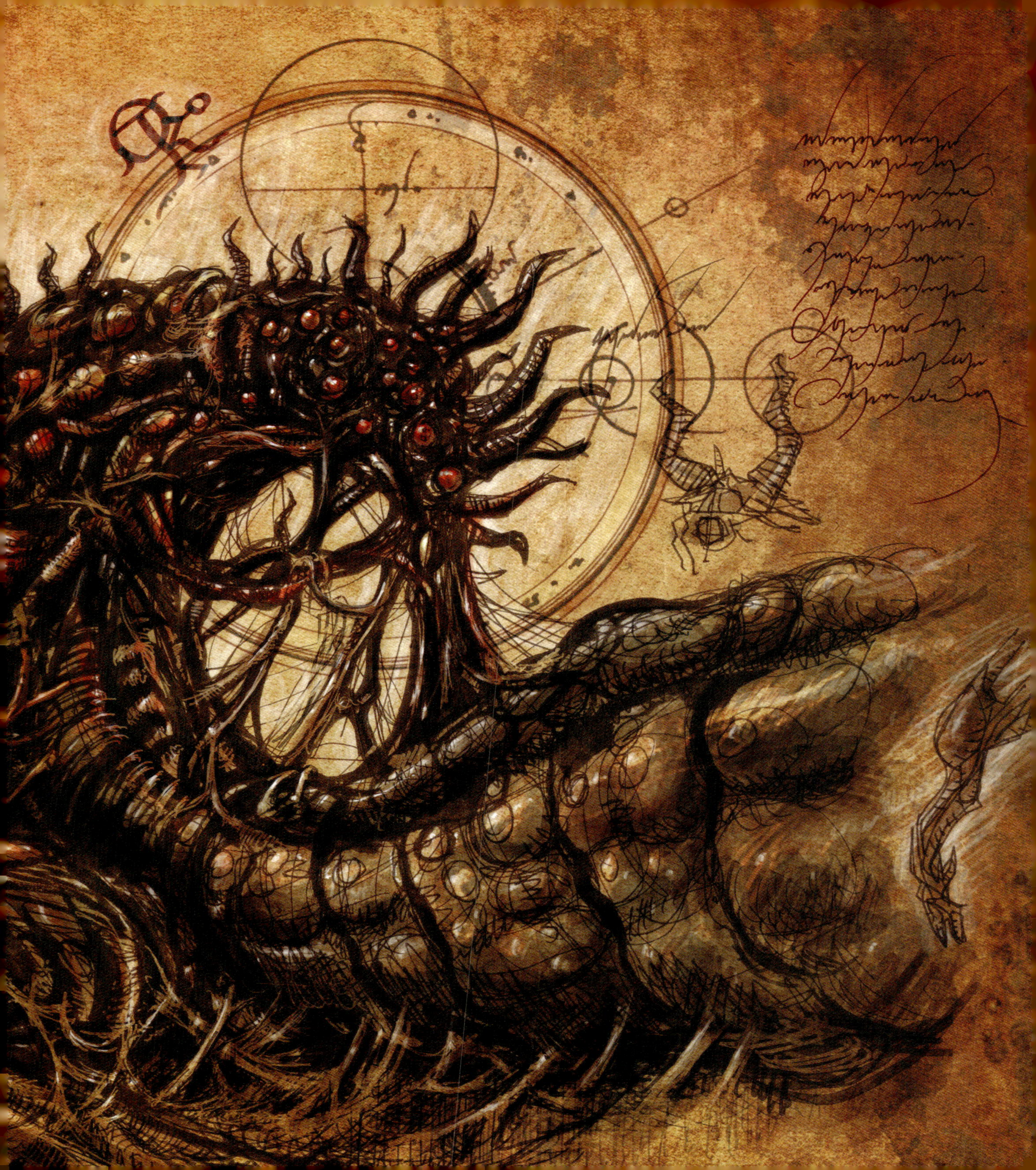

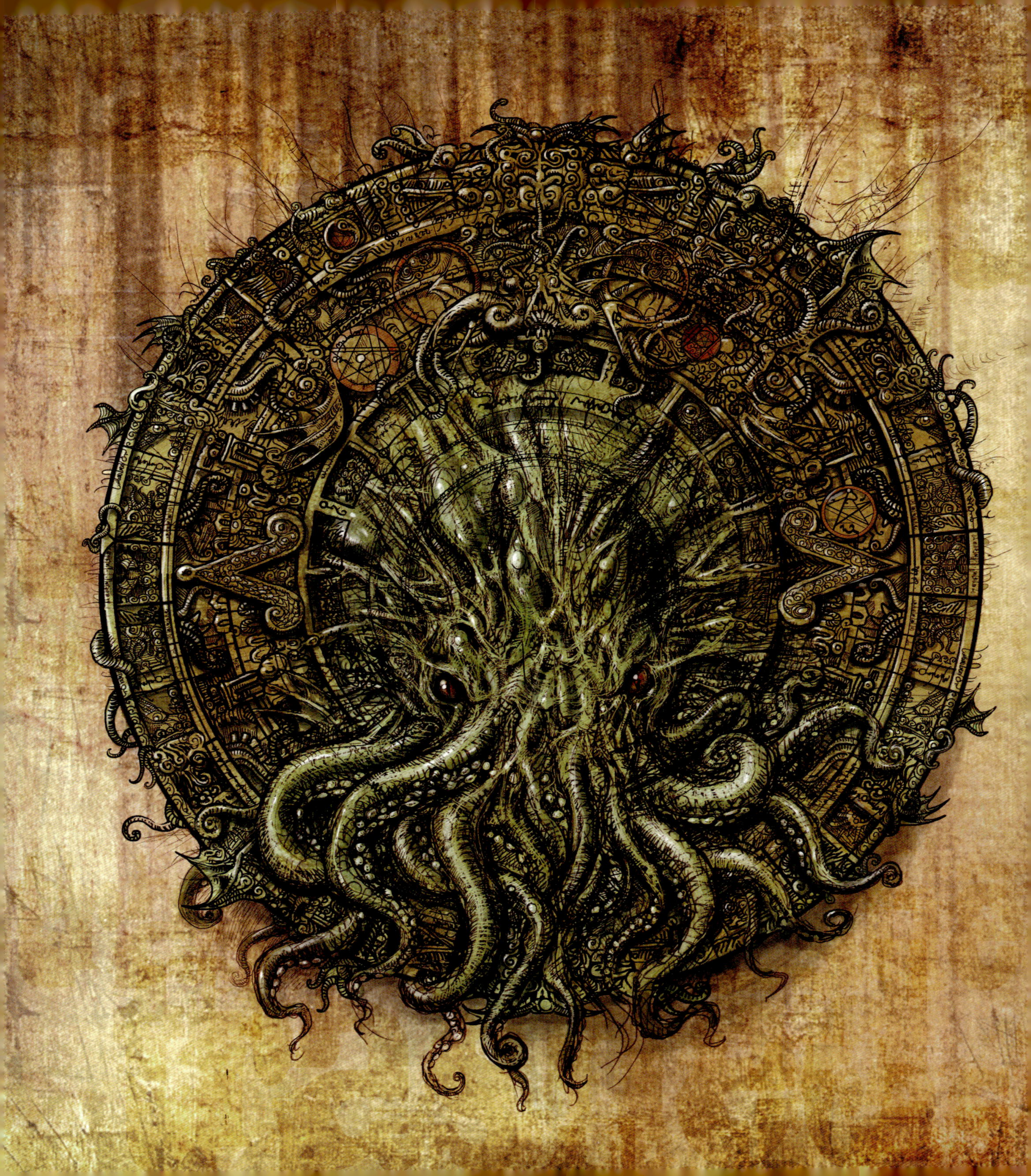

François Launet

François Launet, also known as Goomi, works as a 3D supervisor for the company Illumination-Macguff, and also as a freelance illustrator for many different projects. He cites H.P. Lovecraft as one of his main influences, and loves to use a mixture of techniques, such as digital painting, 3D, ink drawing, acrylic on canvas, photographs, airbrush or calligraphy. After many years of serious illustrations and paintings, he also created a humourous webcomic about the Old Ones, the gods created by Lovecraft: The Unspeakable Vault (of Doom). Some of his fantastic artworks can be seen in this book, some of which are his spellbinding depictions of ancient arcane texts full of ancient beings and mysterious symbols (***see*** for example pages 77, 81, 83 and 84).

Jason Engle

Jason Engle (***see*** his artwork ***Vengeful***, page 39) has been creating art for the publishing and entertainment markets for over 14 years, contributing to a huge range of fantasy art books as well as being featured in magazines and publications across the world. 'At a very young age I knew that I wanted to be an artist, and pursued that goal with every free moment,' he explains. Using art itself as his teacher, Engle shunned the traditional artistic education, enabling him to work his way towards a fantasy portfolio inspired by the likes of Lovecraft and his protégées. Primarily working with pencil and matte drawings, Engle's

'As for seriously-written books on dark, occult, and supernatural themes – in all truth they don't amount to much. That is why it's more fun to invent mythical works like the Necronomicon and Book of Eibon.'

H.P. Lovecraft

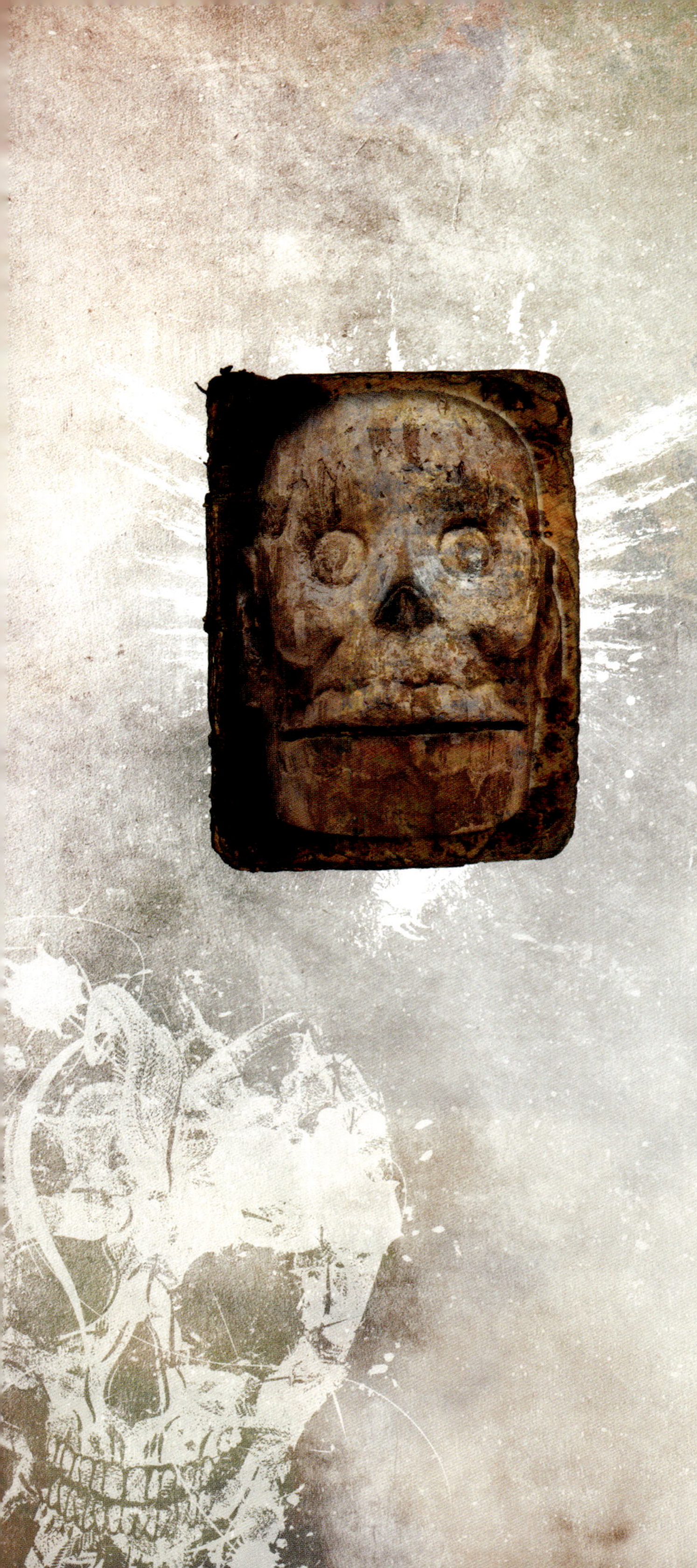

fascination with magic within his work brilliantly complements the otherworldly spell scripture within the pages of the ***Necronomicon***.

Joseph Vargo

Since the early 1990s, the name Joseph Vargo has been synonymous with gothic fantasy. Vargo's chilling, mist-shrouded world of forlorn ghosts, brooding vampires, living gargoyles and other creatures of the night have earned him an immense and loyal following. His artwork ***The Dark Gods*** (***see*** page 15), for example, is perfectly Lovecraft- and Gigeresque, capturing the ancient power of dark beings, and their thirst for blood. As if he wasn't cool enough, Vargo is also a horror writer as well as a noted composer and musician, earning worldwide acclaim with his band Nox Arcana. In 2004, Nox Arcana released ***Necronomicon***, a dark intrumental album based on Lovecraft's works, as a tribute to the Cthulhu Mythos. The band resurrected the Lovecraftian theme again in 2009 with ***Blackthorn Asylum***, which is based upon Lovecraft's story 'From Beyond'.

'Sometimes people only see horrible, terrible things in my paintings.'

H.R. Giger

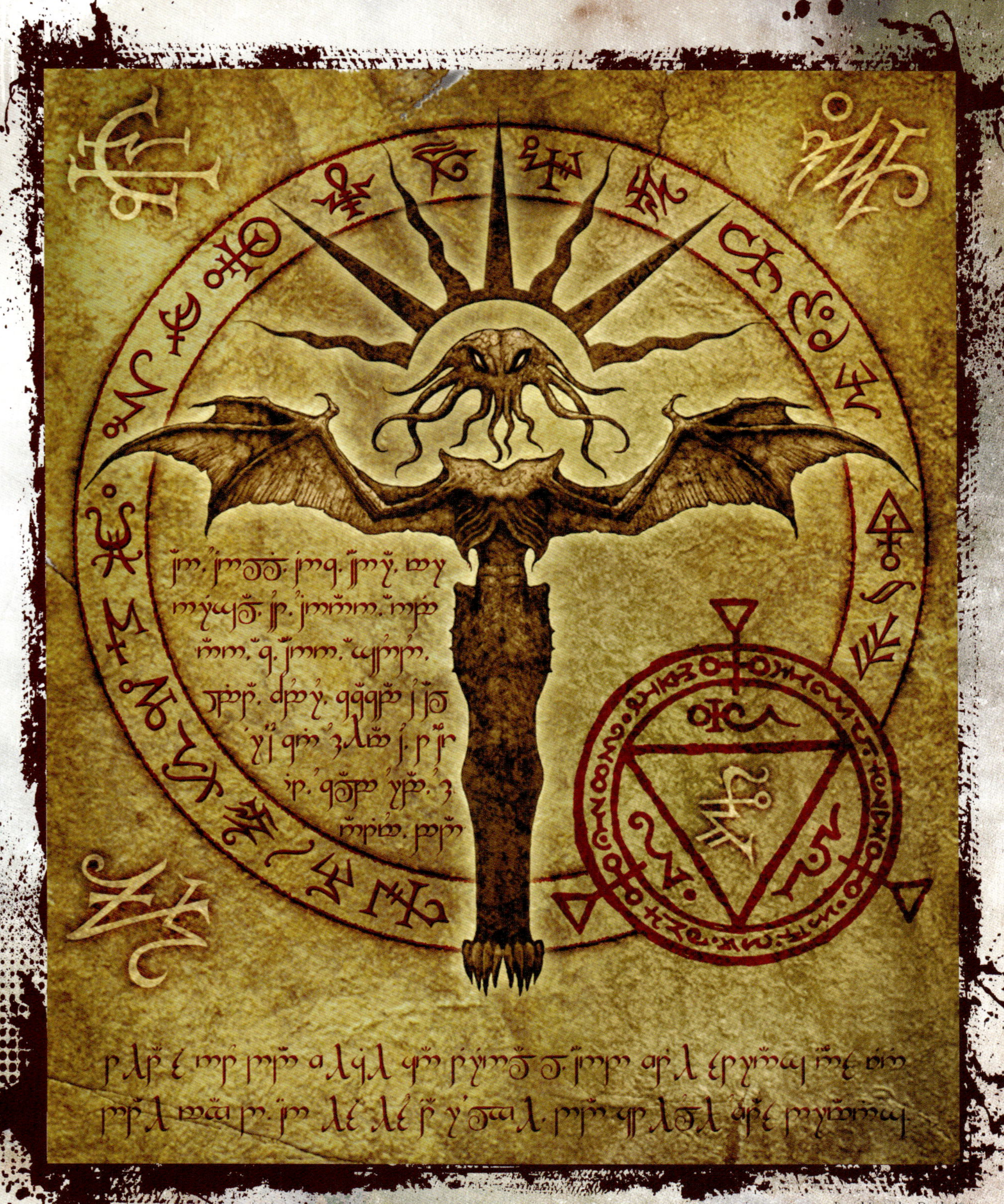

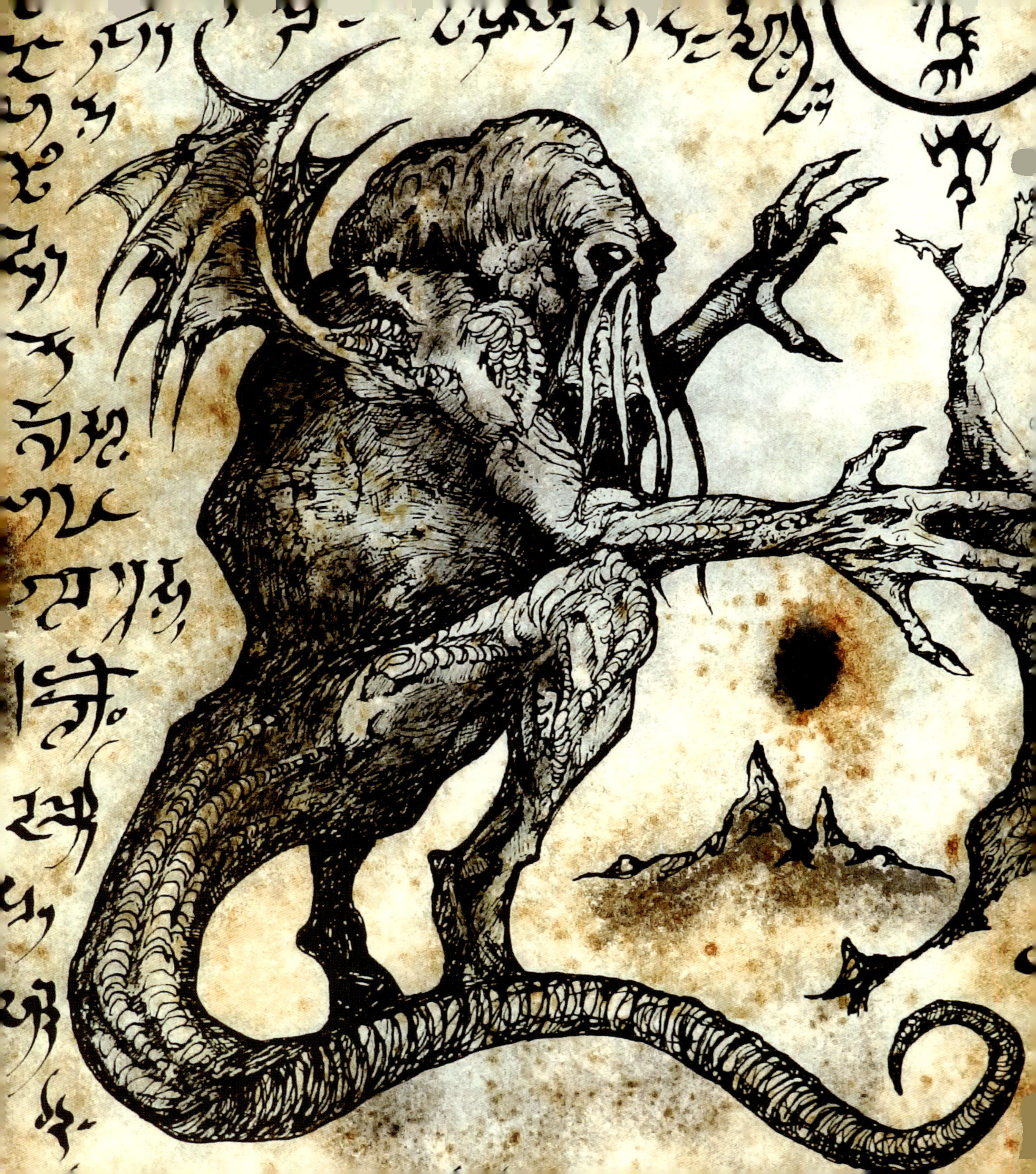

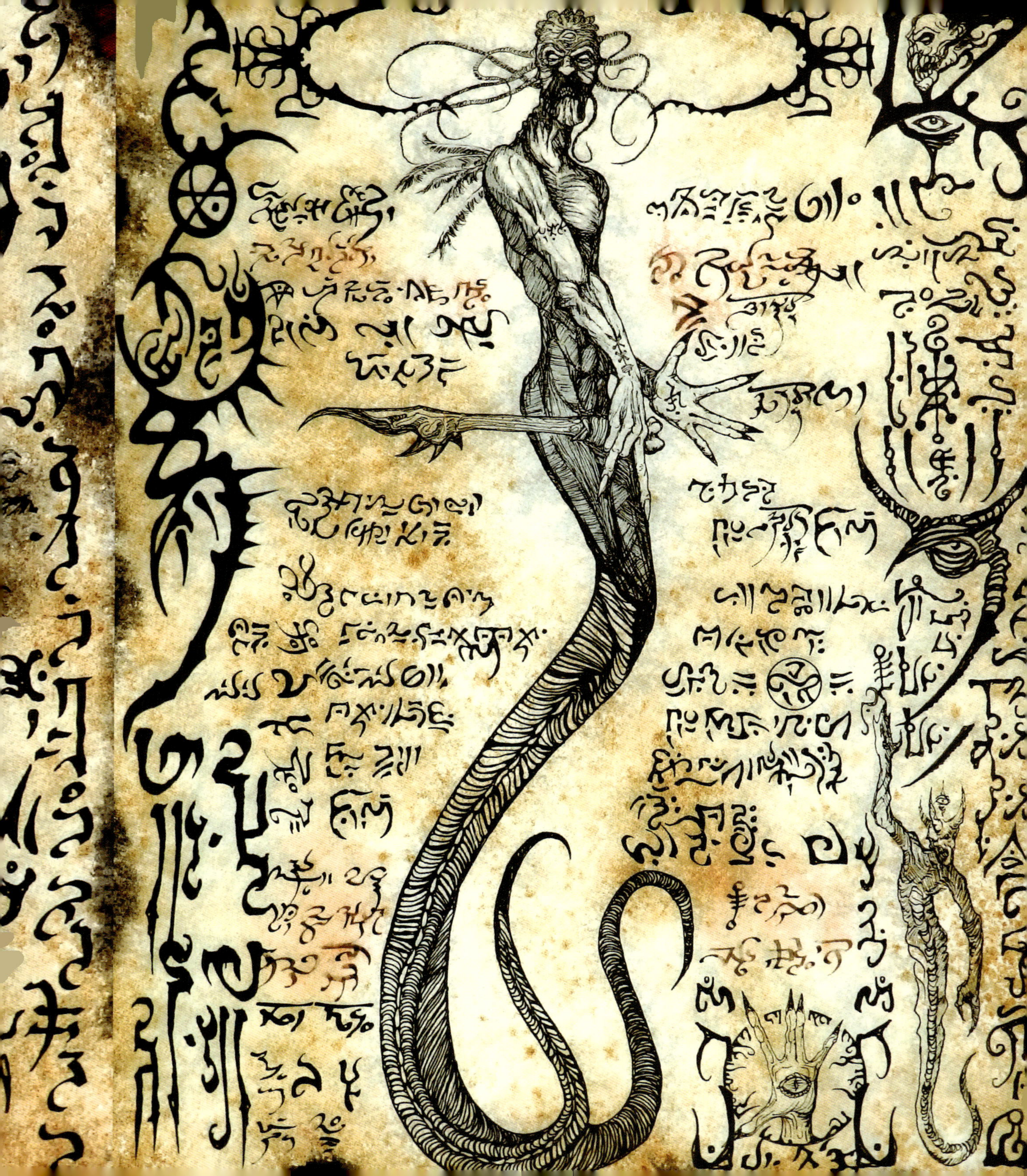

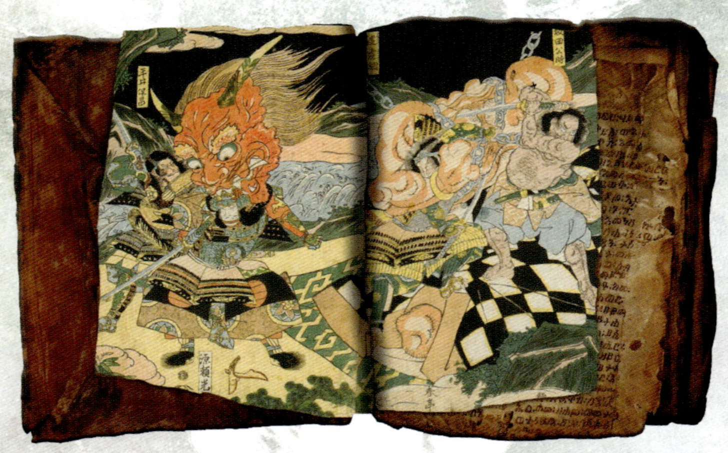

All Hell Breaks Loose onto the Screen

Of course, the pages of the *Necronomicon* are ripe for the picking when it comes to on-screen gore, psychological horror and TV thrillers. The endless possibilities of demonic creatures and otherworldly gods are simply screaming out for the silver screen treatment. Thankfully, directors and writers across the world quickly jumped on the Lovecraft bandwagon and began interpreting the stories, ideologies and sinister spells to create their own ***Necronomicon***-inspired tales.

The 'Evil Dead' Trilogy

This is an obvious one. Sam Raimi and his 'Evil Dead' series is the go-to example when it comes to showcasing the ***Necronomicon*** on the big screen. First found in the cabin in the original film ***The Evil Dead*** (1981), the ***Necronomicon*** is actually depicted as the 'Naturom Demonto', which sees the naïve group summon all kinds of evil lurking in the woods. It's easy to see why it became the cult phenomenon that it is today – with two sequels, it's one of horror's finest trilogies and we all have H.P. Lovecraft and his ***Necronomicon*** to thank for their inspiration.

The Army of Darkness

By the third 'Evil Dead' film – ***Army of Darkness*** (1992) – the 'Naturom Demonto' had evolved

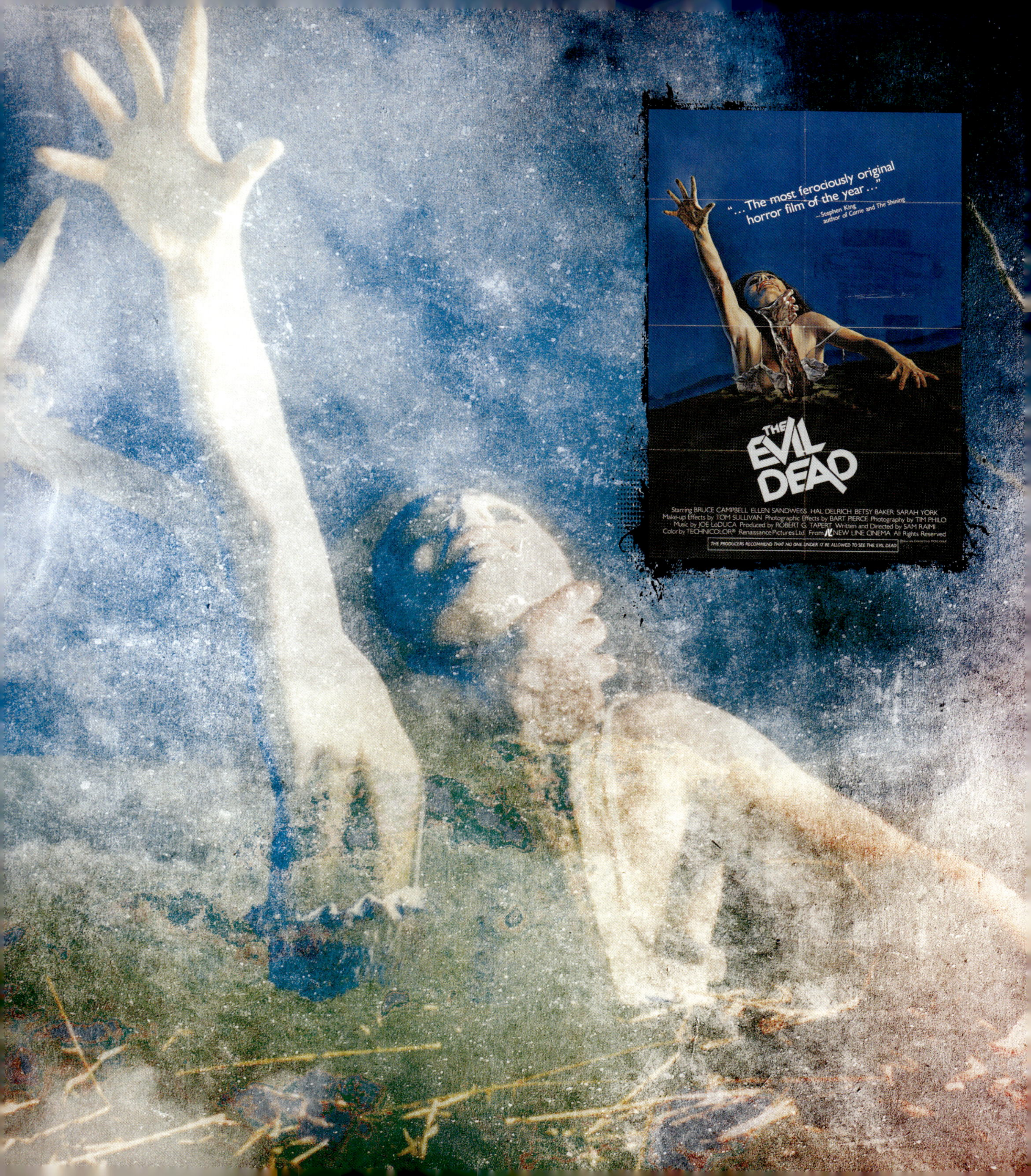
"... The most ferociously original horror film of the year ..."
—Stephen King author of Carrie and The Shining
THE EVIL DEAD
Starring BRUCE CAMPBELL ELLEN SANDWEISS HAL DELRICH BETSY BAKER SARAH YORK
Make-up Effects by TOM SULLIVAN Photographic Effects by BART PIERCE Photography by TIM PHILO
Music by JOE LoDUCA Produced by ROBERT G. TAPERT Written and Directed by SAM RAIMI
Color by TECHNICOLOR® Renaissance Pictures Ltd. From NEW LINE CINEMA All Rights Reserved
THE PRODUCERS RECOMMEND THAT NO ONE UNDER 17 BE ALLOWED TO SEE THE EVIL DEAD

into the ***Necronomicon***. Raimi clearly took inspiration from Lovecraft's description of the book's aesthetics; bound in human flesh and inked in ancient dried blood, in the final film the ***Necronomicon*** actually comes complete with a face … and a biting one at that. Whilst it might not be the exact depiction of Lovecraft's original, it still reigns supreme as one of the most iconic representations of the ***Necronomicon*** – and a hilarious homage, in true Sam Raimi style.

Sam Raimi

With all three films packed full of Raimi's now iconic satirical and often in-your-face humour, the director loved to quote other movies within his work; the chant that Ash utters in the third instalment (that he, of course, doesn't quite get right) is in fact, from ***The Day the Earth Stood Still*** (1951). Just like Lovecraft and his circle of Cthulhu mythos and ***Necronomicon*** writers, horror and science fiction writers, directors and film-makers continued to influence each other. The 'Evil Dead's' ***Book of the Dead*** is pretty much the perfect homage to the original evil scripture. In 2013 a loose continuation of the 'Evil Dead' franchise followed, which although not directed by Raimi, was still produced by him. The 'Naturom Demonto' makes a return, harking back to the original 1981 ***Evil Dead*** movie.

Necronomicon: Book of the Dead

In 1993, three directors attempted to put together a film that would cleverly combine three separate works by

Combine os elementos de
água e fogo para atrair
a ... forma ingodanta
dos Demônios 165

Quod factur Modo uno
dirimeretur Corpus Hominis
sacrificandum est ut animae
uno serviatur

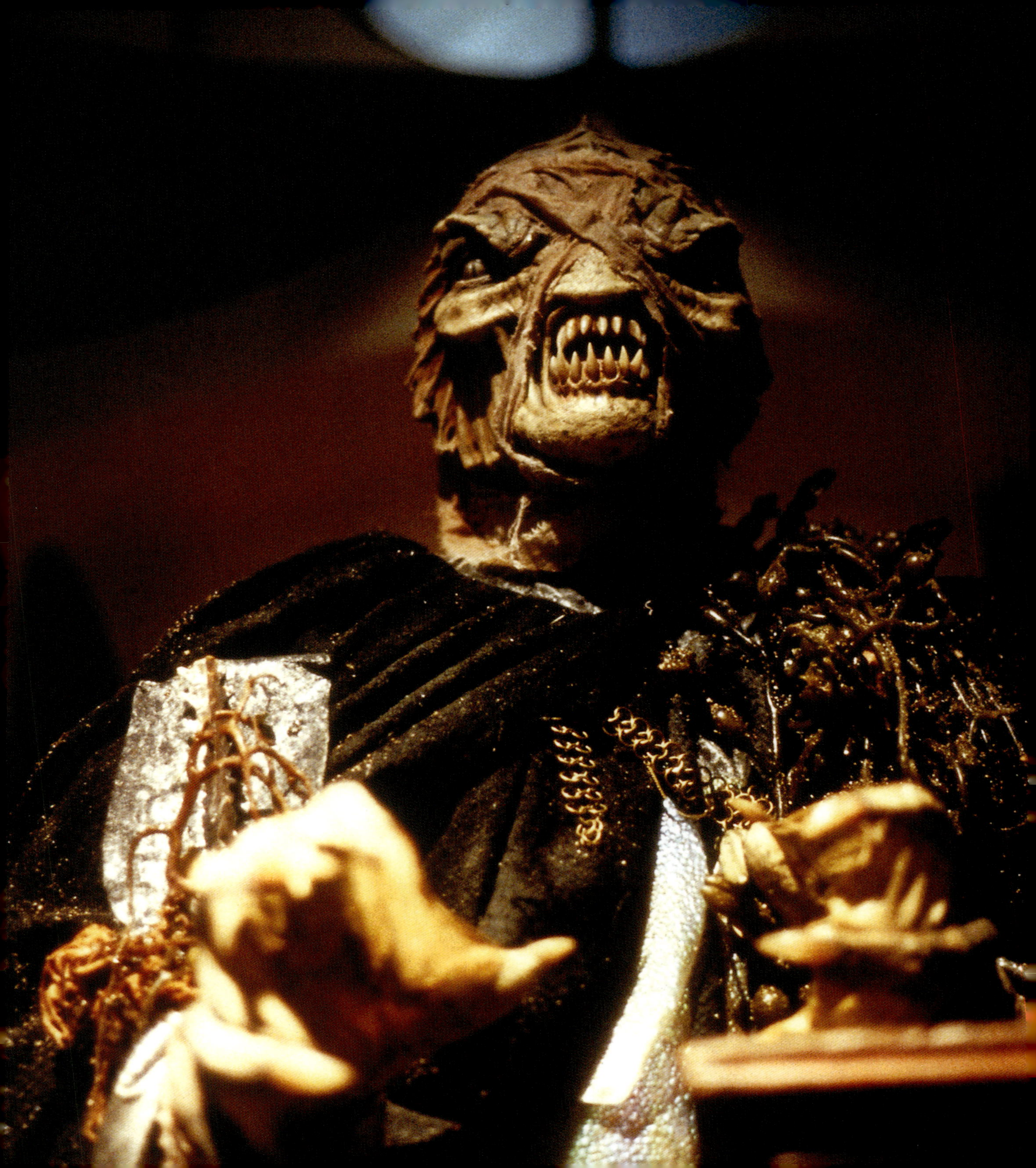

H.P. Lovecraft – these included 'The Rats in the Walls' (1924), ***The Case of Charles Dexter Ward*** (1941) and 'The Call of Cthulhu' (1928). Whilst most of the reviews are less than favourable, the three directors Christopher Gans (b. 1960), Shusuke Kaneko (b. 1955) and ***Re-Animator*** (1985) producer Brian Yuzna (b. 1949) did their best in creating a homage to Lovecraft and his ***Necronomicon***.

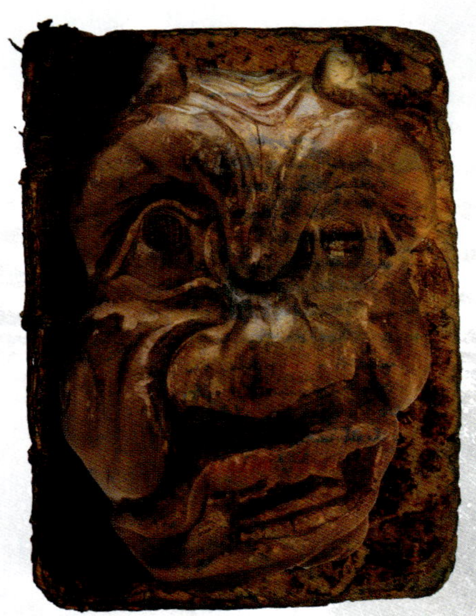

The Pages Unfold

Featuring Jeffrey Combs (b. 1954) as Lovecraft himself, the character goes in search of the book during the 1930s, finding it guarded by monks in an old library. After getting his hands on the ***Necronomicon***, he copies a range of stories from it which then unfold during the three short films. Of course the real H.P. Lovecraft constantly told his peers of the fictional creation of the book, so it would have been interesting to get his take on this particular depiction. ***Necronomicon: Book of the Dead*** isn't quite up there with the greats but its obvious devotion to Lovecraft and the ***Necronomicon*** makes for an enjoyable watch.

The Dunwich Horror

Before the 'Evil Dead' series in the 1980s, the ***Necronomicon*** film and the 'Friday 13th' series in the 1990s, there was 'The Dunwich Horror' (1970). Certainly flawed in its execution, director Daniel Haller (b. 1926) had fun with Lovecraft's world, telling the tale of the half-human, half-monster Wilbur Whateley, who's hell-bent on getting his hands on the dreaded ***Necronomicon***. Unfortunately, it's

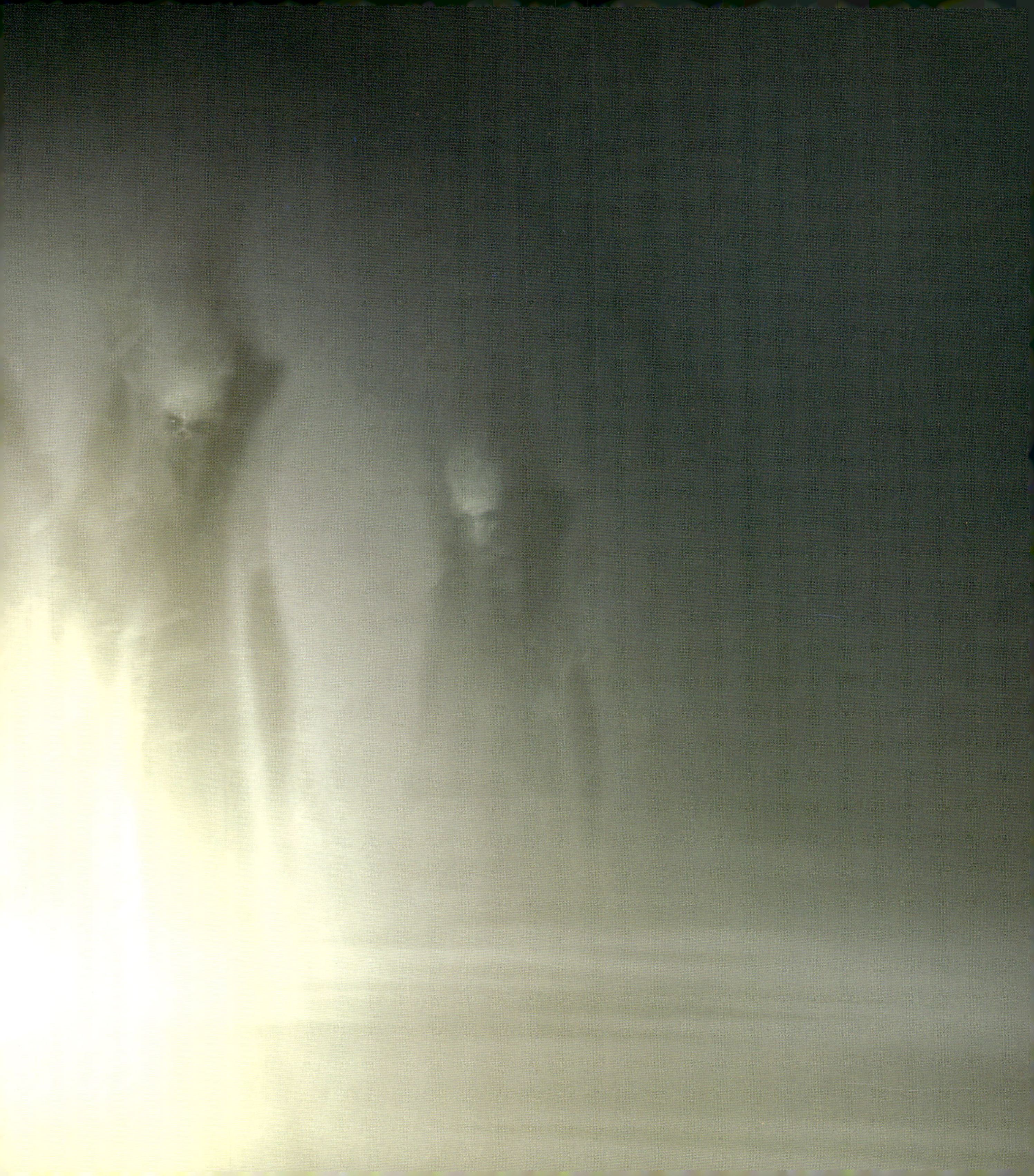

housed in the Miskatonic and safeguarded by Professor Armitage, which makes for quite a struggle between the two.

Doused in a late 1960s psychedelic LSD-like vision, the film hasn't dated too well. 'Come back old ones. Princes of Darkness. Repossess the Earth,' utters Whateley, as he urges those pesky otherworldly creatures back into our Earthly realms. Not quite the thought-out scripture chants that Lovecraft preferred, but it'll do the trick!

The Final Friday

Whilst the plots of some films revolved around the ***Necronomicon***, plenty of others paid homage in a more simple and subtle manner. With the success of the 'Evil Dead' series, horror audiences across the world were now able to recognize the importance and evil intentions of the book without too much explanation.

An example of the ***Necronomicon*** is featured in the final 'Friday' movie, ***Jason Goes to Hell: The Final Friday*** (1993). The film-makers revealed during the commentary part of the DVD that the book used in the film is the very same prop used in the 'Evil Dead's' ***Army of Darkness***. There's no real reference to it during the film and no one actually picks it up – it's merely placed in a crate labelled 'Arctic Expedition', which also acts as a nice nod to the arctic environments of Lovecraft's ***At the Mountains of Madness***, though there's no real proof of this. Some fans of the film believe it was placed there to hint at the Voorhee family's evil intentions; that they may have used it to

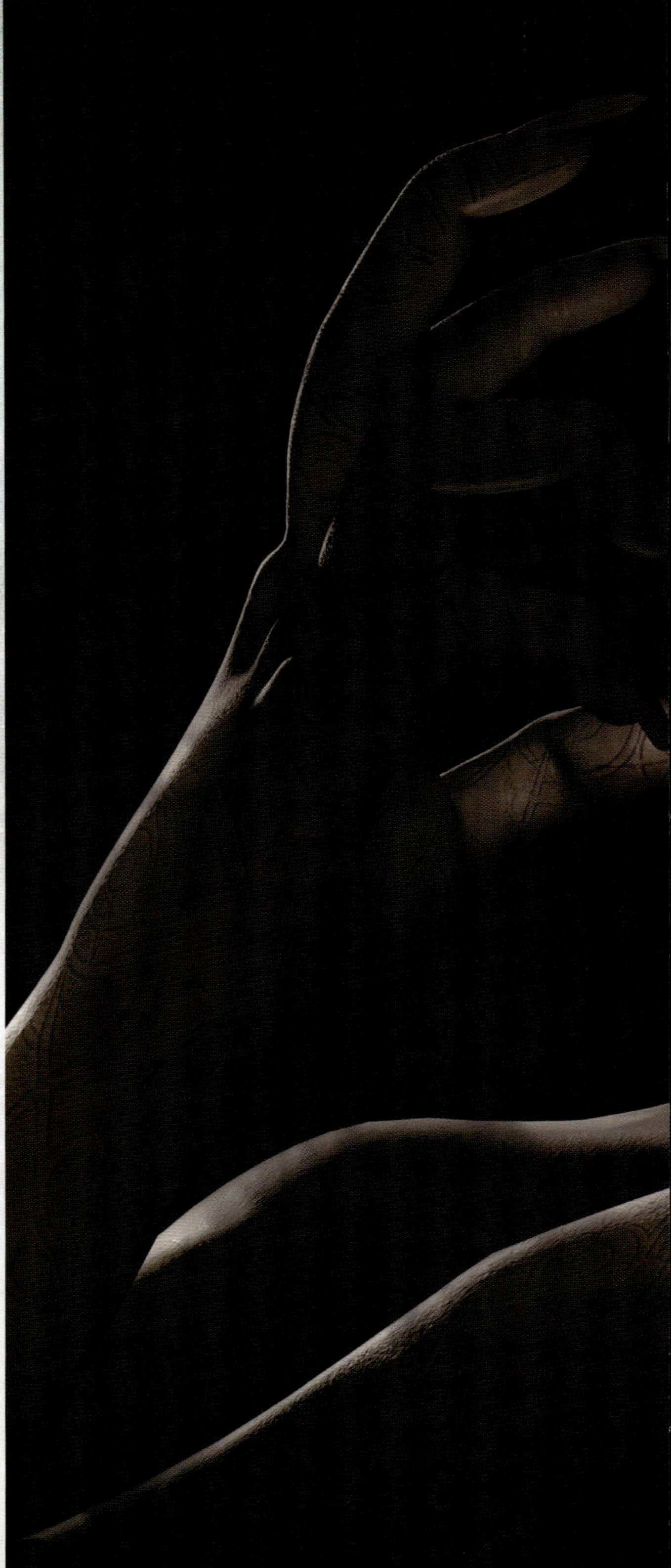

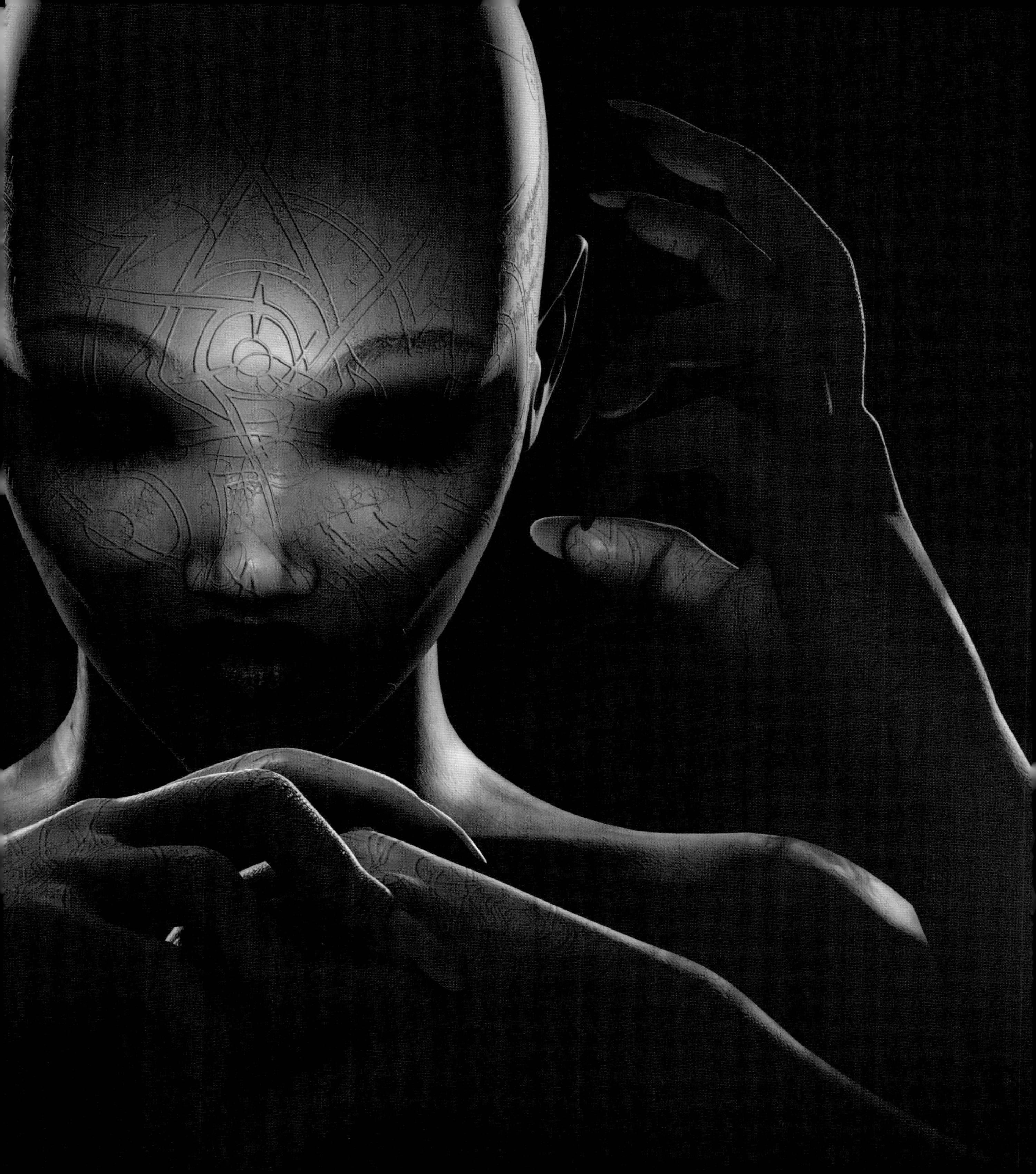

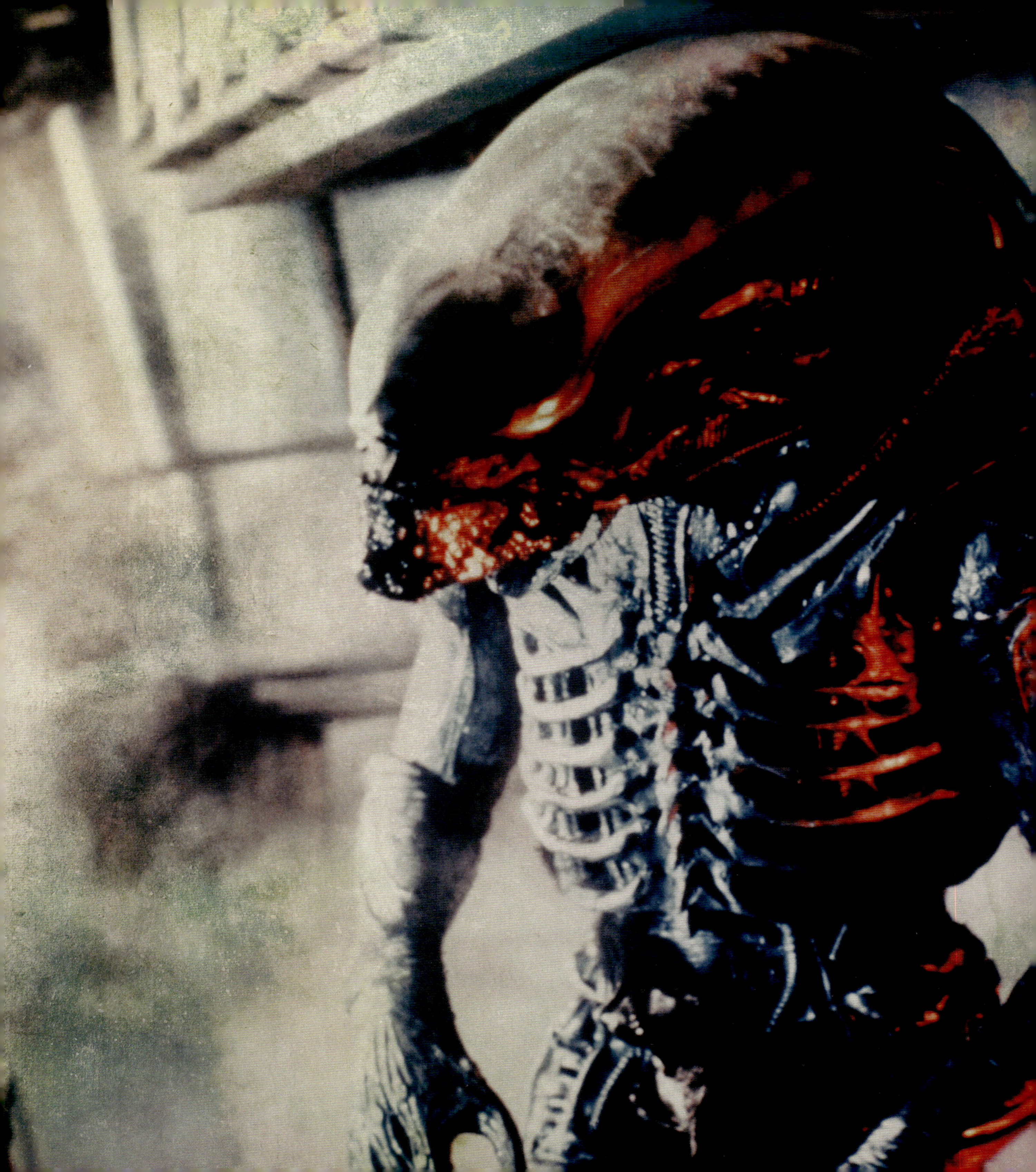

summon a dark being. Nevertheless, it's another nice example of horror film-makers complementing each other, especially during the late 1980s and early 1990s.

How Alien Came To Be

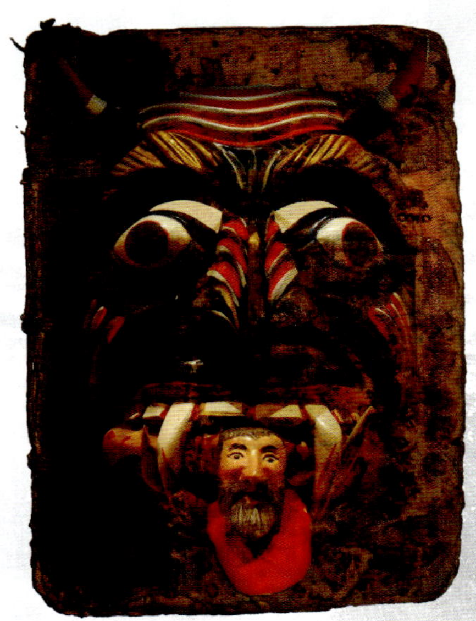

Certainly one of the most iconic movie monsters ever created, H.R. Giger's ***Alien*** is a pop culture phenomenon in its own right. As already mentioned, before he conceived the sci-fi masterpiece, Giger made his love of H.P. Lovecraft clearer than ever by releasing his own ***Necronomicon***. We have the ***Necronomicon*** to thank for Giger's involvement with Ridley Scott (b. 1937) and the ***Alien*** franchise (1979–92). Scott spotted the 1976 ***Necronom IV*** print and knew immediately that Giger was the artist to bring his intergalactic visions to life. Aggressive yet sexual with an undeniable beauty, Giger's alien was the perfect creature to disturb, entertain and above all, terrify the audience.

As with the 'Great Old Ones' of the original ***Necronomicon***, Lovecraft manages to scare his readers by portraying these creatures that remind us mere humans of how insignificant and weak we actually are. By reflecting hints of ourselves and Earthly creatures within his monsters – i.e. the octopus-like features of Cthulhu, teamed with a human-like body – we can recognize its immediate evil. Giger's alien was also human-like but with an armour that gave it full protection, with no obvious eyes and laced with sexuality to further disturb the viewer. There's no denying that the only thing to ever influence

such a disturbing, nightmarish creation would be none other than Lovecraft's ***Necronomicon***.

The Necronomicon in TV

It wasn't just the big screen that got a taste of the ***Necronomicon***; TV series, movies and lengthy dramas also featured small homages and obvious inspirations throughout the years. ***Cast a Deadly Spell*** was an HBO TV movie that tackled the ***Necronomicon*** head on, with a questionable yet fun, satirical approach to both the horror and detective genres.

Portraying H.P. Lovecraft as uptight Detective Harry Philip Lovecraft, the TV movie takes place in 1948, where magic – particularly black magic – is the norm. Lovecraft refuses to use magic for 'personal reasons' and is hired by a mysterious man to find a stolen book. What book, you ask? The ***Necronomicon***, of course. Holding the key to taking over the world and releasing the 'Old Ones', the tongue-in-cheek showcase of old school gangster tomfoolery and Lovecraft in-jokes definitely make this one an enjoyable watch.

Necronomicon and HBO

It seems HBO held onto their love for the ***Necronomicon*** after their TV movie, with nods to Lovecraft in a range of shows – most notably, 2014's ***True Detective***. The show is part influenced by R.W. Chambers' fictional play 'The King in Yellow', which has many similarities to Lovecraft's

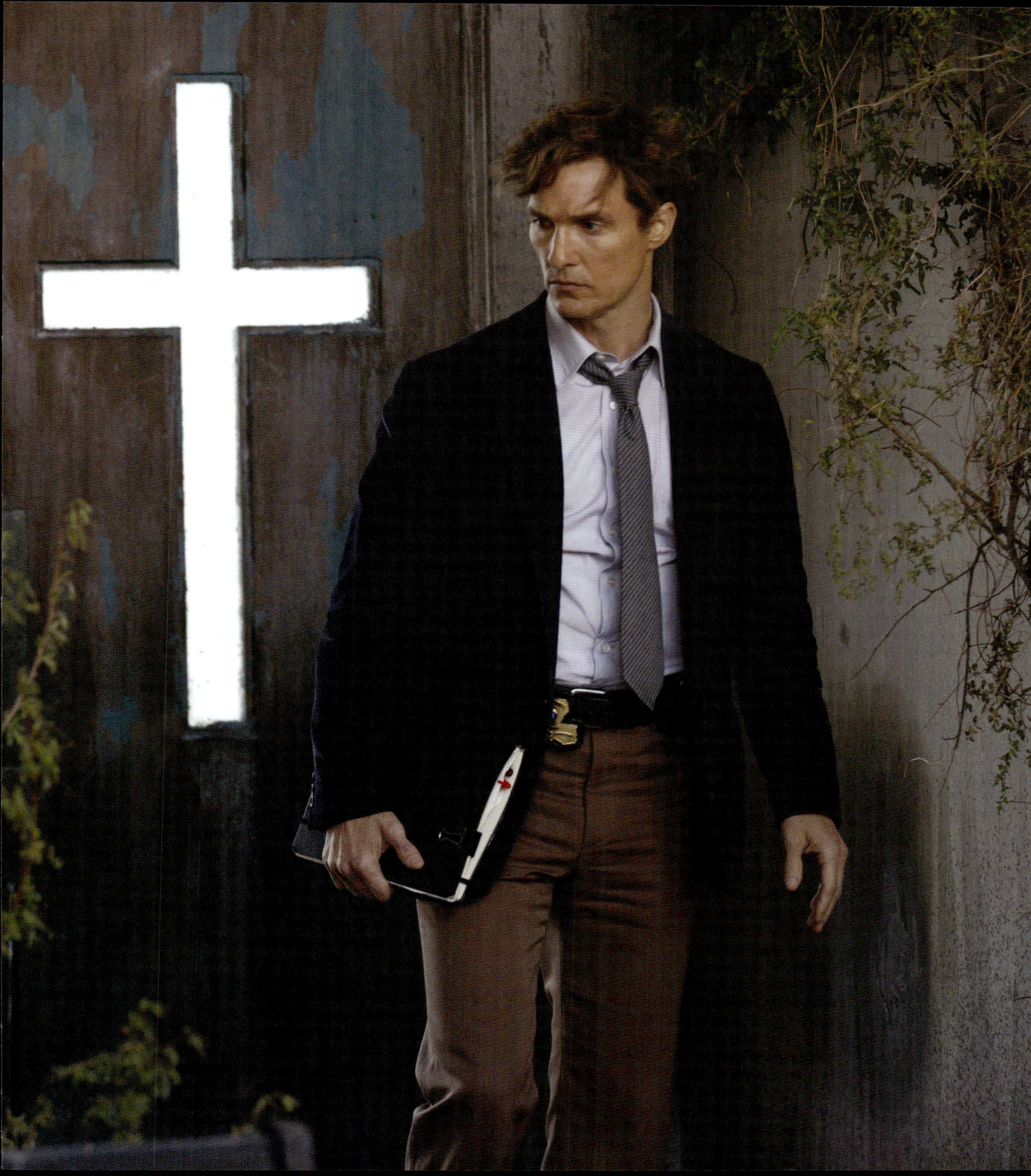

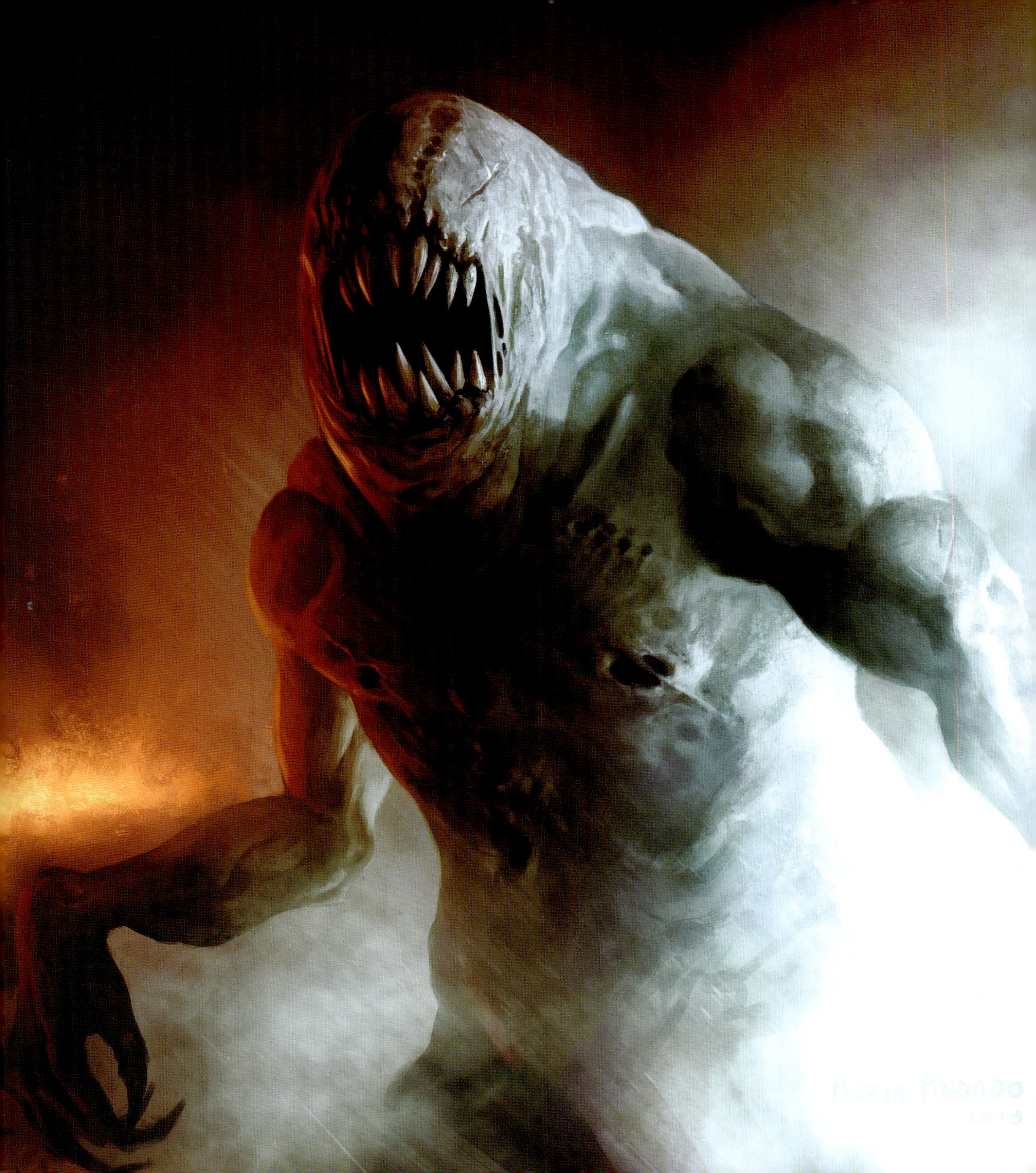
BORJA PINDADO
2013

Necronomicon. The play, said to render its readers mad, plays a pretty big part during the series, which features plenty of Weird Fiction nuggets that only hardcore Weird Fiction fans would spot.

'We shall see that at which dogs howl in the dark, and that at which cats prick up their ears after midnight.'

'From Beyond'

A Modern Classic

The play is first mentioned during episode two, when Rust Cohle uncovers the journal of the ritualistically murdered former prostitute. 'I closed my eyes and saw the King in Yellow moving through the forest,' he reads aloud. 'The King's children are marked. They became his angels.' The tone of the show changed instantly, as this brand of horror is rarely showcased on modern television; Lovecraft and Chambers fans were in for a treat.

It Was All Yellow

There are also regular hints of yellow throughout the show – from Cohle's apartment to the illegal warehouse rave, it seems the show's creators used the colour to represent the character's collapse into insanity and decadence. There are also glimpses of black stars – on paper and on characters themselves – which is an ode to Act I, Scene II of 'The King in Yellow' – 'Strange is the night where black stars rise.'

The thematic similarities between both plots showcase their characters' descent, after realizing the incomprehensible, horrific and terrifying truths of the universe. With Lovecraft filling out his own aspects concerning 'The King in Yellow' for his **Necronomicon** and Cthulhu mythos, **True Detective** complements both the original short story and Lovecraft's 'cosmic universe'. Describing the universe as 'a certain atmosphere of breathless and unexplainable dread of outer, unknown forces,' this 'dread' can be felt throughout the show; from the subtle hints of birds flying in a spiral formation, to the ramblings of Rust, there's certainly something supernatural going on.

Monster

One particular quote from Matthew McConaughey's character, Rust Cohle, that is particularly Lovecraftian comes during episode 3 – 'To realize that all your life, you know, all you love, all you hate, all your memory, all your pain – it was all the same thing. It was all the same dream, a dream you had inside a locked room, a dream about being a person. And like a lot of dreams … there's a monster at the end of it.' Could this 'monster' be part of Lovecraft's ***Necronomicon*** universe? Who knows? But there's certainly something about it that complements Lovecraft's 'anti-future' of human beings – our earthly fear of the outside.

House M.D. and the Necronomicon

Another incredibly popular show that decided to pay homage to the ***Necronomicon*** is Fox's ***House M.D.*** (2004–12). Whilst it only features in one episode, it's still a nice little tribute to the original book of the dead. Taking place during 2010's season 6, episode 17, House and his team of doctors tackle the case of Sir William the 'Knight' who lives in a closed-off community that bases its existence on the

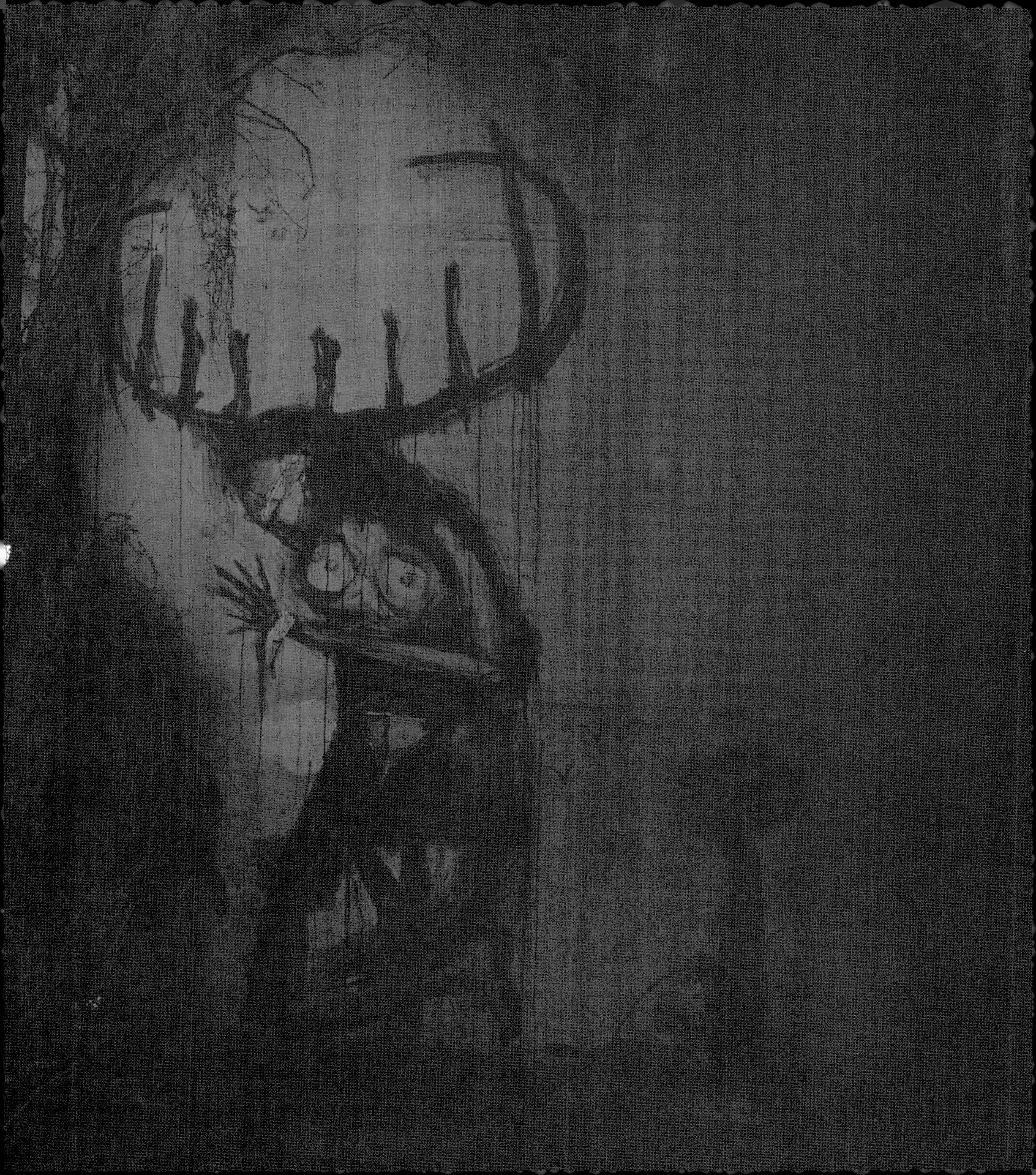

ideals of the High Renaissance; the team go in search of the cause of William's collapse.

Witchcraft

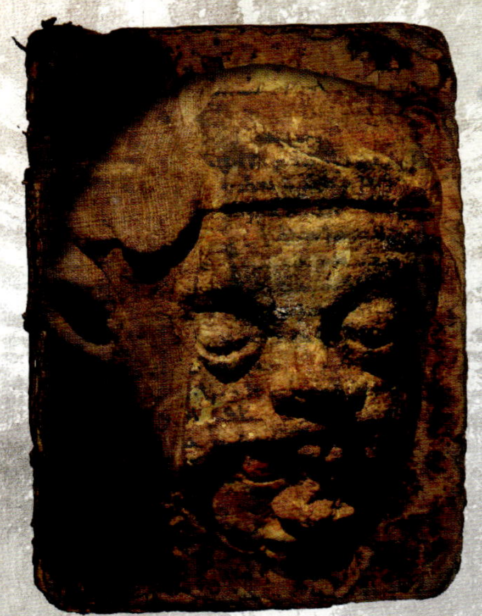

As his health rapidly deteriorates, two doctors uncover a hidden room at William's apartment. Filled with the usual knick-knacks you'd associate with a supernatural enthusiast, they stumble upon a copy of the ***Necronomicon***. The book's aesthetics sadly don't conform to the traditional bound in human flesh and inked in blood approach; instead, there's a simple, satanic symbol etched on the front cover with the ***Necronomicon*** title showcased across the front.

Sadly, that's pretty much all there is to say about its influence – the team mainly call William a 'witch', debating whether he's summoned some sort of evil magic that has made him ill. Turns out it was just steroid abuse, which is certainly a far less interesting take. Although the title 'Knight Fall' – apart from the literal depiction in the episode – could be a nice ode to darkness taking over the Earth once the 'Old Ones' come along, that's kind of clutching at straws.

Cartoons

The ***Necronomicon*** isn't merely for fans of serious drama or horror movies. Its influence has gone on to inspire a few well-known cartoons, with the book further establishing itself as a go-to plot enhancer. Ever heard of a little show called ***The Simpsons*** (1989)? Well, as it turns out, creator

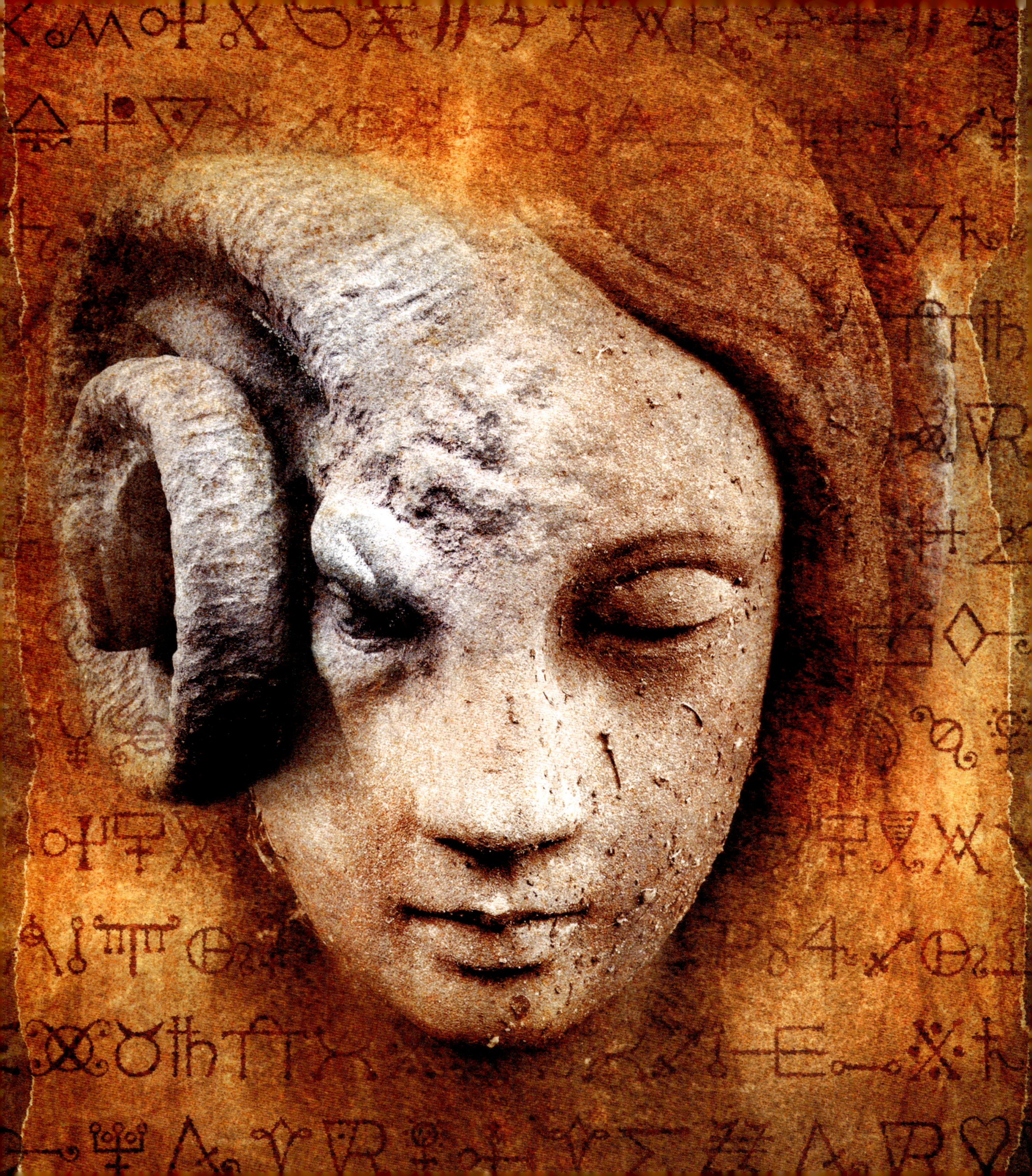

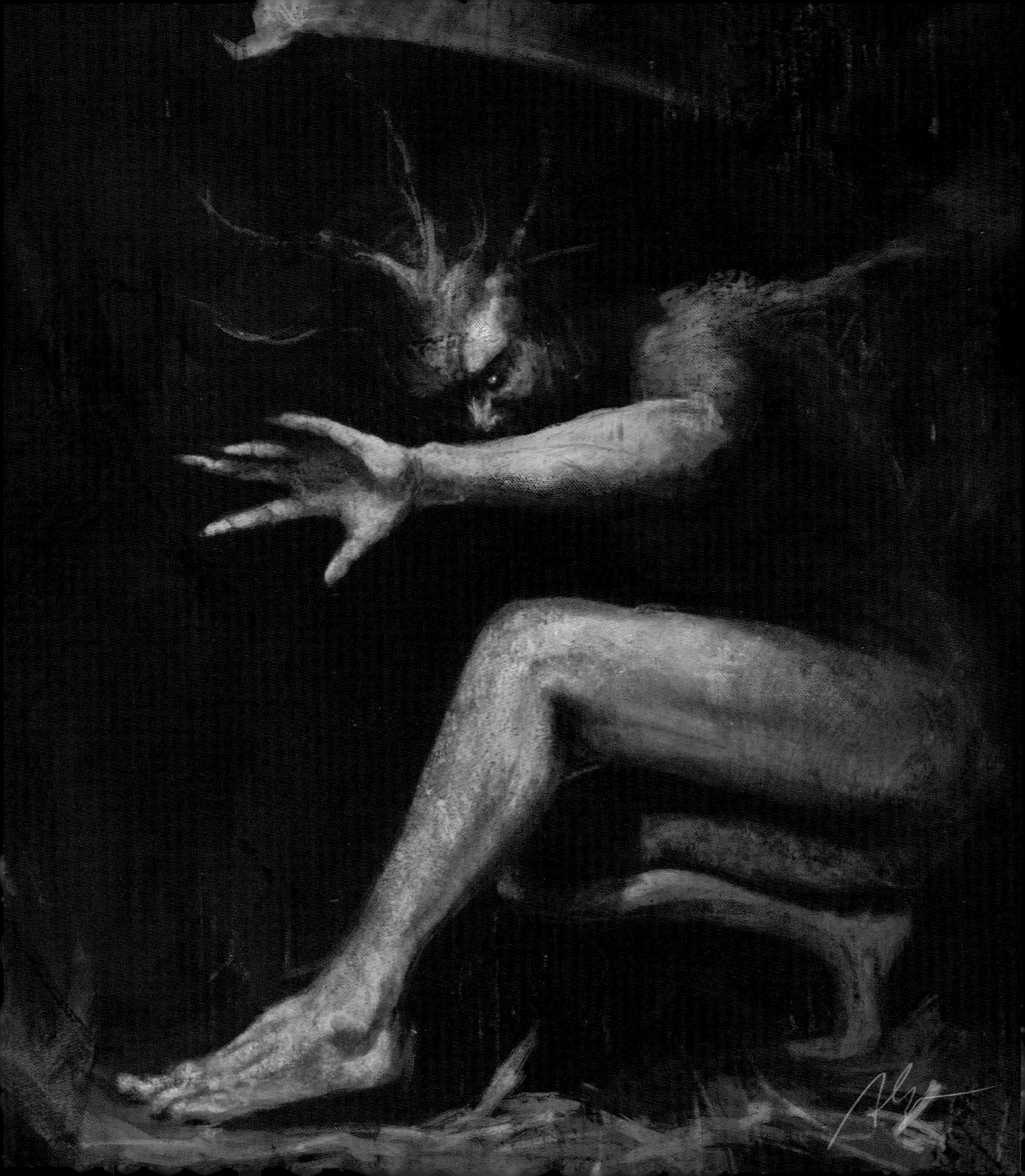

Matt Groening (b. 1954) is a pretty big Lovecraft fan and decided to poke fun at America's Republican Party using the ***Necronomicon***.

Modern Satire

In season 13, episode 7, the show opens at the headquarters of the Springfield Republican Party – a castle-like building which would fit nicely into just about any Lovecraft novel – where Mr Burns, the Rich Texan, Dracula, Ralph Nader and Krusty the Clown all discuss what unmitigated evil the party can take part in this week. After they've all revealed their ideas, Mr Burns declares that Bob Dole will read from the ***Necronomicon***. Dressed in a sinister-looking robe, he utters a ***Necronomicon*** scripture in Latin before the segment comes to an abrupt end. In typical Simpsons' style, it's a hilarious take on the Lovecraft classic – and devilishly naughty to attribute the ultimate evil to the Republican Party.

'The process of delving into the black abyss is to me the keenest form of fascination.'

H.P. Lovecraft

Superheroes

It isn't just ***The Simpsons*** that has included the ***Necronomicon*** in their animations. In 2005, ***Justice League*** featured it in the episode 'The Balance'. Wonder Woman is sent by the god Hermes to help free Hades from the clutches of a practitioner of dark magic, Felix Faust; an interest that ultimately cost him his university teaching job as well as his soul.

Wonder Woman and Hawkgirl venture into Hades' library, where Hawkgirl picks up a book that closely resembles the

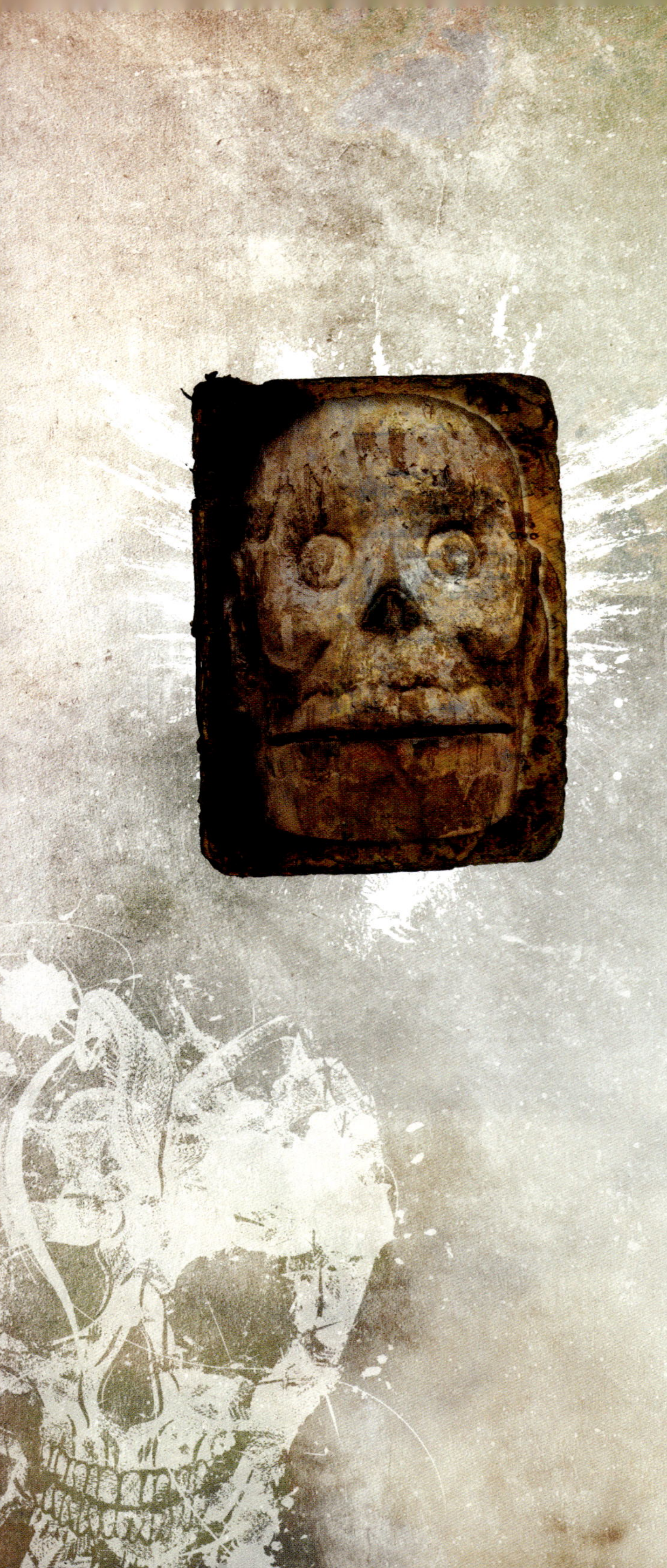

Necronomicon during the 'Evil Dead' era – evil face and all. They eventually find Faust in Hades's library, where he speaks of the book's contents: 'The lost scrolls of Herculaneum, Merlin's juvenilia, Pierre Menard's ***Don Quixote***.... Dark tomes that make the ***Necronomicon*** look like a children's book.' The library itself is a nice ode to Lovecraft and could even be a nod to the author's descriptions of the books whereabouts – often guarded in museums or old libraries.

Ghostbusters and Beyond

The ***Necronomicon*** also makes appearances in ***Aqua Teen Hunger Force*** (2000), season 3, episode 4, in which Frylock almost hands Meatwad the ***Necronomicon*** instead of the ***Bible*** – another, quite literal, example of the 'good vs. evil' approach. In season 1, episode 12 of ***The Grim Adventures of Billy and Mandy*** (2001–07), Billy steals Grim's – the show's take on the Grim Reaper – 'bad book' which is later revealed as the ***Necronomicon***. Unfortunately, as it has fallen into the wrong hands, Billy accidentally starts an apocalypse by summoning Yog-Sothoth – the all-knowing, all-seeing Outer-God. You'll be pleased to know that Mandy, Grim and Hoss Delgado manage to stop the end of the world.

Comic Importance

The Ghostbusters and the ***Necronomicon*** collide in an episode of ***The Real Ghostbusters*** (1986–91). In season 2, episode 32 'The Collect Call of Cathulhu', the

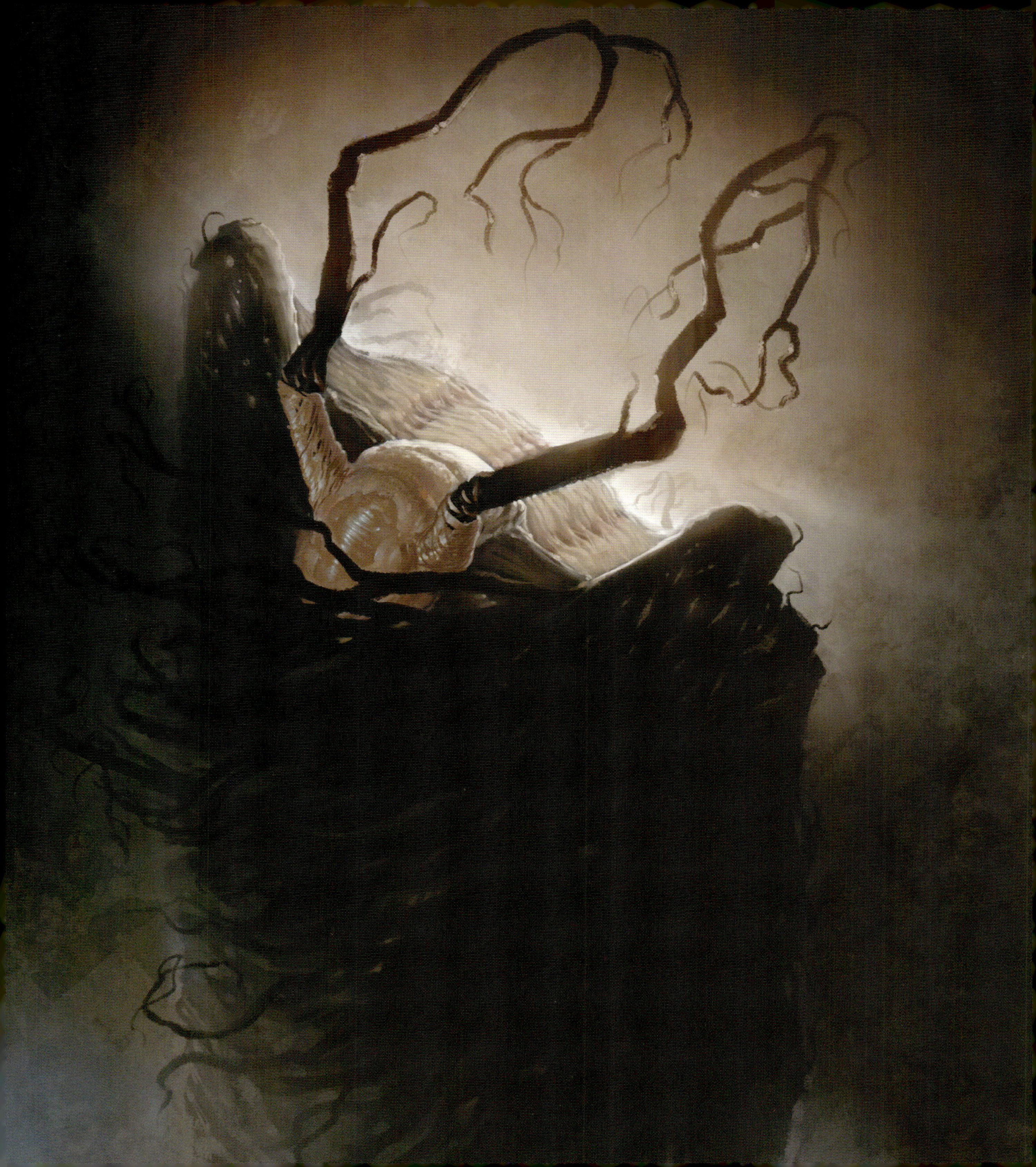

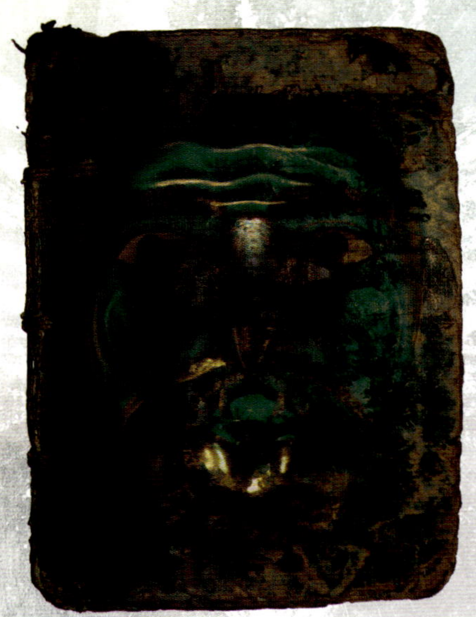

Necronomicon is stolen from a public library after Ashton decides to put the book on display. Ashton passes the book off as just being a bunch of 'spooks', which, of course, is proven very wrong in the duration of the episode. The Ghostbusters find themselves fighting otherworldly creatures in the sewers – a nice touch considering many of the monsters within the ***Necronomicon*** allude to Lovecraft's fear of the water – as well as chasing down cults and using comic books to help them complete their mission. Whoever tells you comic books are a waste of time, should take a long hard look at the life lessons of this episode.

'Consume the darkness between the dimensions! Cross the gulf with a single stride! Here on this threshold is placed a gift. This is my gift. Come forth and receive it! Stars align!'

Cast a Deadly Spell

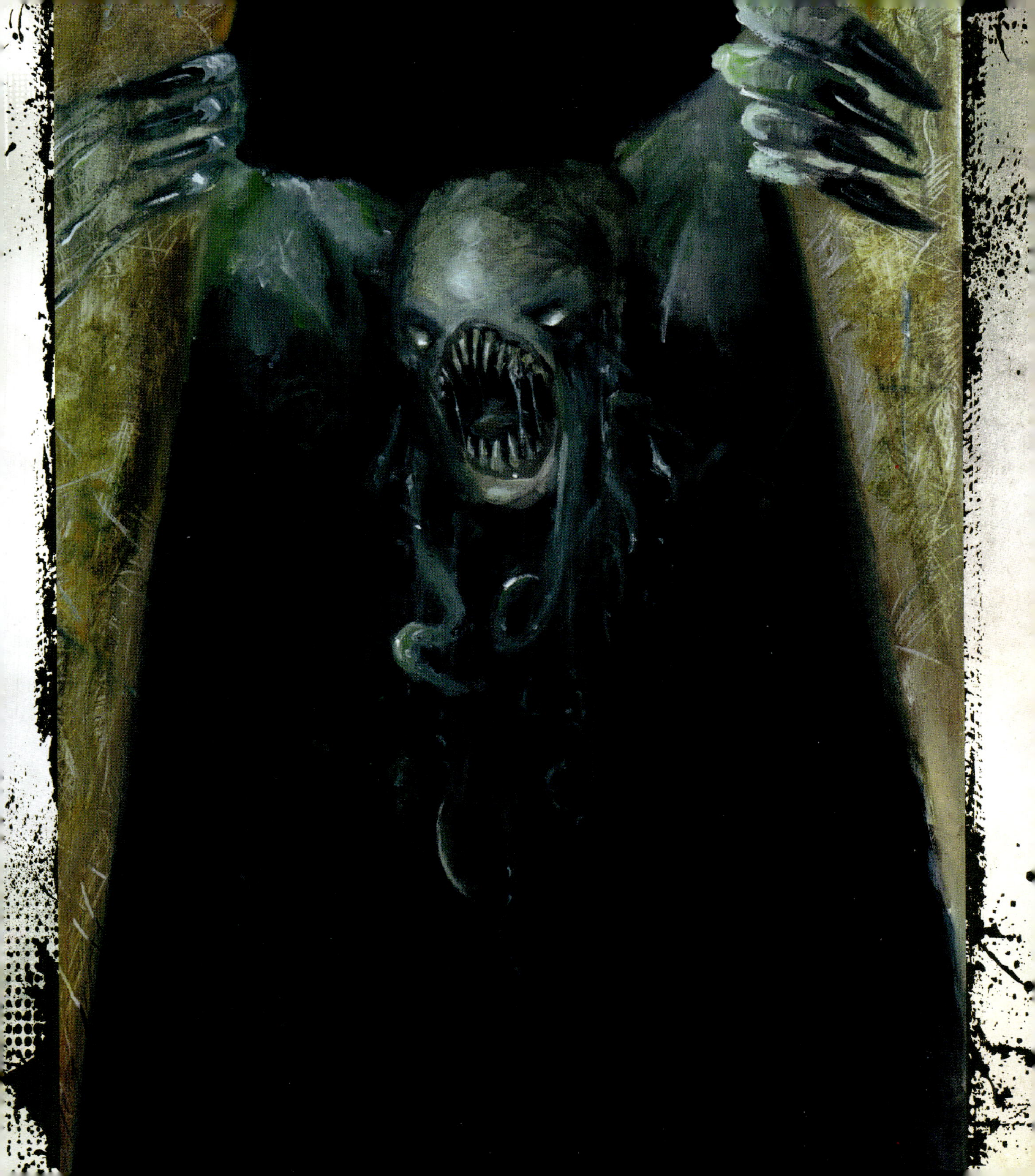

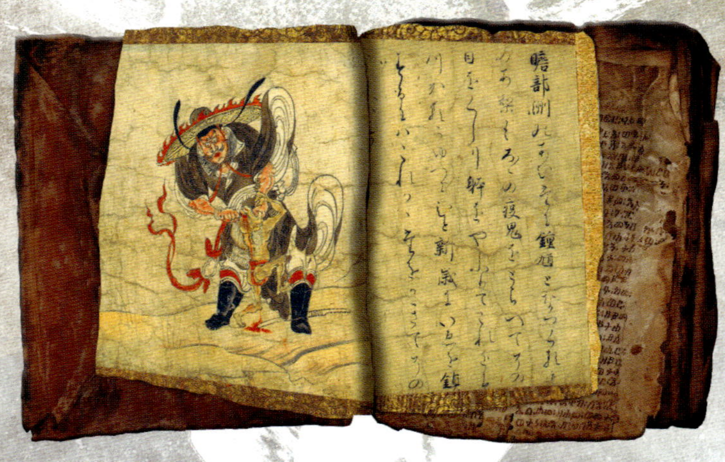

Playing a Deadly Game

Any avid Lovecraft fan would probably love to get their hands on the *Necronomicon*. Whilst this isn't actually possible, you can always settle for the next best thing – video games. By now, most game developers and writers have realized the book's infiltration of pop culture, so can easily slip it into just about any plot without much explanation.

Max Payne

In 2001, the 'Max Payne' franchise decided to add a little more evil to their story with the subtle inclusion of the ***Necronomicon***. Listing Cthulhu as one of the beings invoked by mob boss and all-round baddie Jack Lupino, Max Payne heads over to Ragna Rock where Lupino is residing in his perverse church, which showcases a terrifying mix of pretty much every occult thing going, with a big emphasis on Norse mythology. The place is littered with ancient texts, of course – most notably paperback editions of the ***Necronomicon***.

This is just another example of pop culture outlets using the ***Necronomicon*** to represent evil – whether it be in atmosphere, environment or, in this case, a particular character.

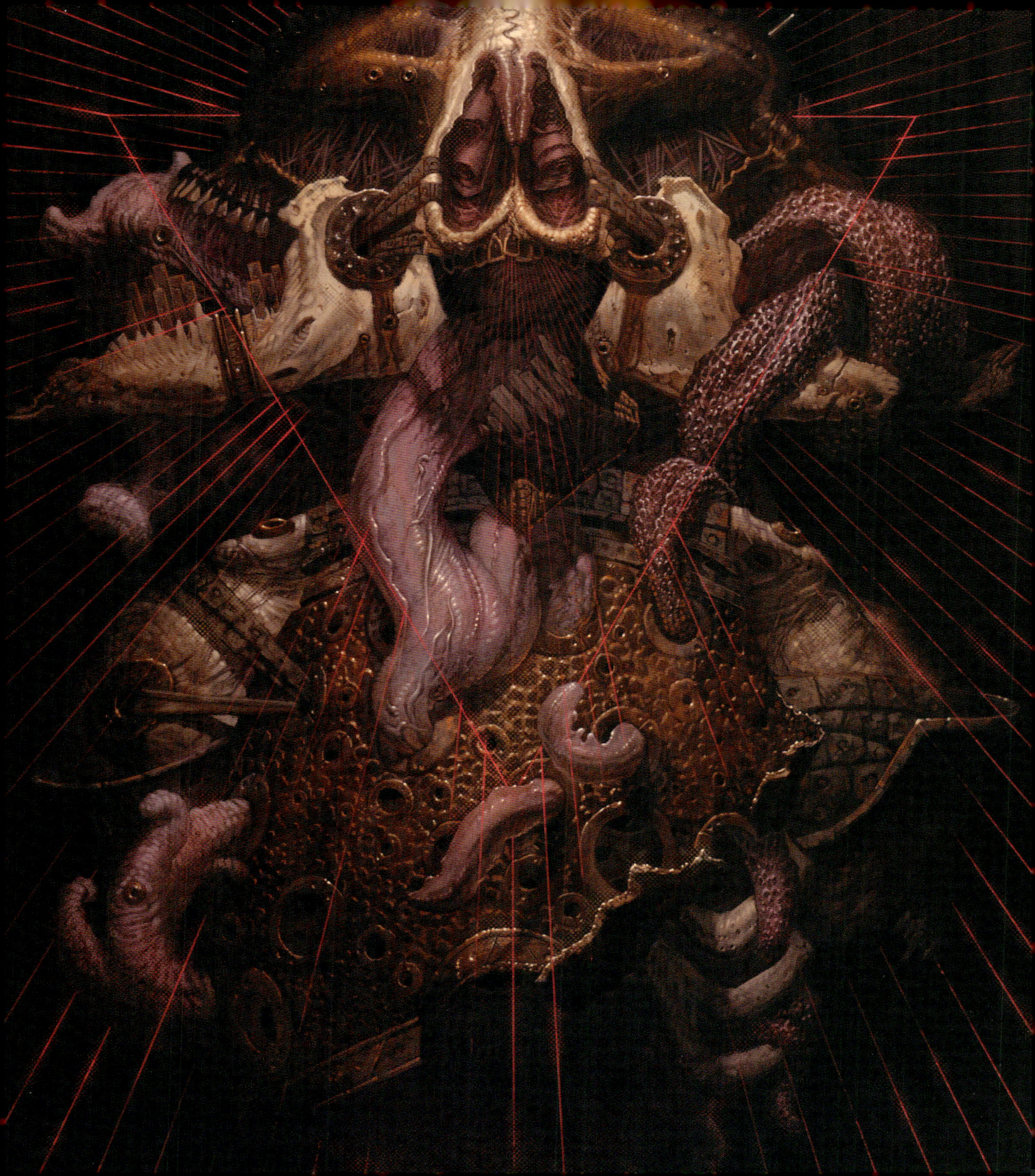

Tales of Phantasia

In 1995, the first game in Namco Tales Studio's 'Tales' series used the ***Necronomicon*** as an actual weapon for the character of Claus, a 29-year-old professor whose studies in magic earned him fame for being able to use spells naturally whilst still being a human. Claus's default weapon is the ***Necronomicon***, which allows him to summon elemental spirits to fight his enemies – and we all know that the spirits of the 'Old Ones' would be pretty detrimental to just about anyone.

Tales of Symphonia

The book makes another appearance in the fifth instalment of the 'Tales' series – 2003's ***The Tales of Symphonia***. Abyssion, an optional boss related to the Devil's Arms side quest, uses the ***Necronomicon*** along with the arms to revive the power of the Dark Lord Nebilim in his own body. This could relate to the ***Necronomicon's*** ability to rid its readers of their souls – much like Faust in the TV show 'Justice League'. In this game, however, the party do manage to kill him and, just to make sure nothing bad continues to happen, Genis Sage uses his Fireball weapon to destroy the ***Necronomicon*** for good.

Defense of the Ancients

The year 2003 also saw the release of online battle arena ***Defense of the Ancients*** – part of the video game ***Warcraft III: Reign of Chaos*** and its expansion, ***Warcraft III: The Frozen Throne***. Based on the 'Aeon for Strife' map for StarCraft, the game uses the ***Necronomicon*** to summon 'Warriors' and 'Archers' that can fight for you for 40 seconds; their strengths and abilities increase as the ***Necronomicon*** increases in level. Only specific heroes have the ability to use spells to summon minions, but the ***Necronomicon*** allows other heroes to summon them too.

Eternal Darkness: Sanity's Requiem

Silicon Knights released psychological horror action adventure game ***Eternal Darkness: Sanity's Requiem*** in 2002. With those kinds of genres thrown into the mix, there was only one place to look for inspiration – H.P. Lovecraft and his ***Necronomicon***. As the ***Necronomicon*** states, if the 'Old Ones' were to be summoned, our Earthly world

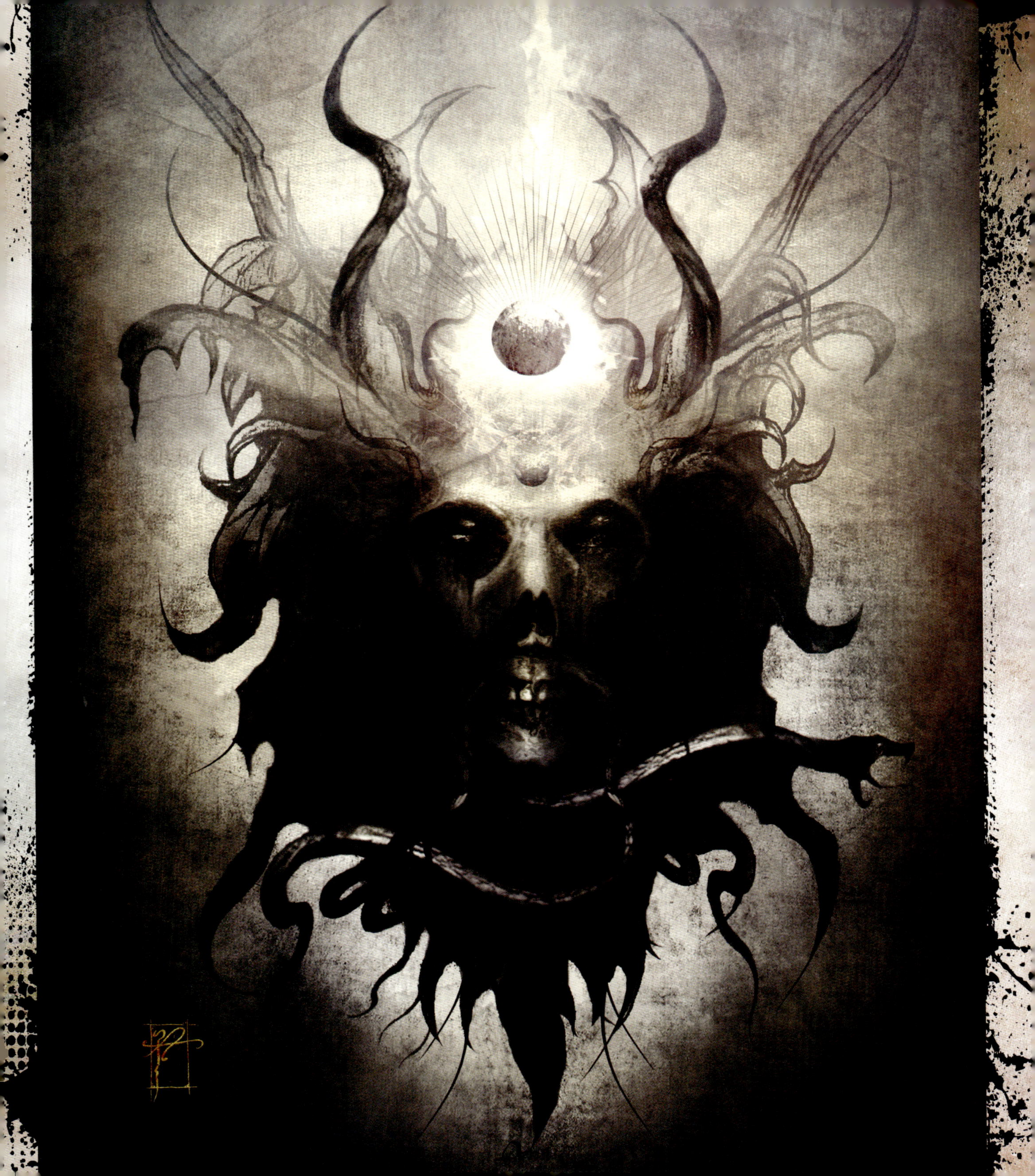

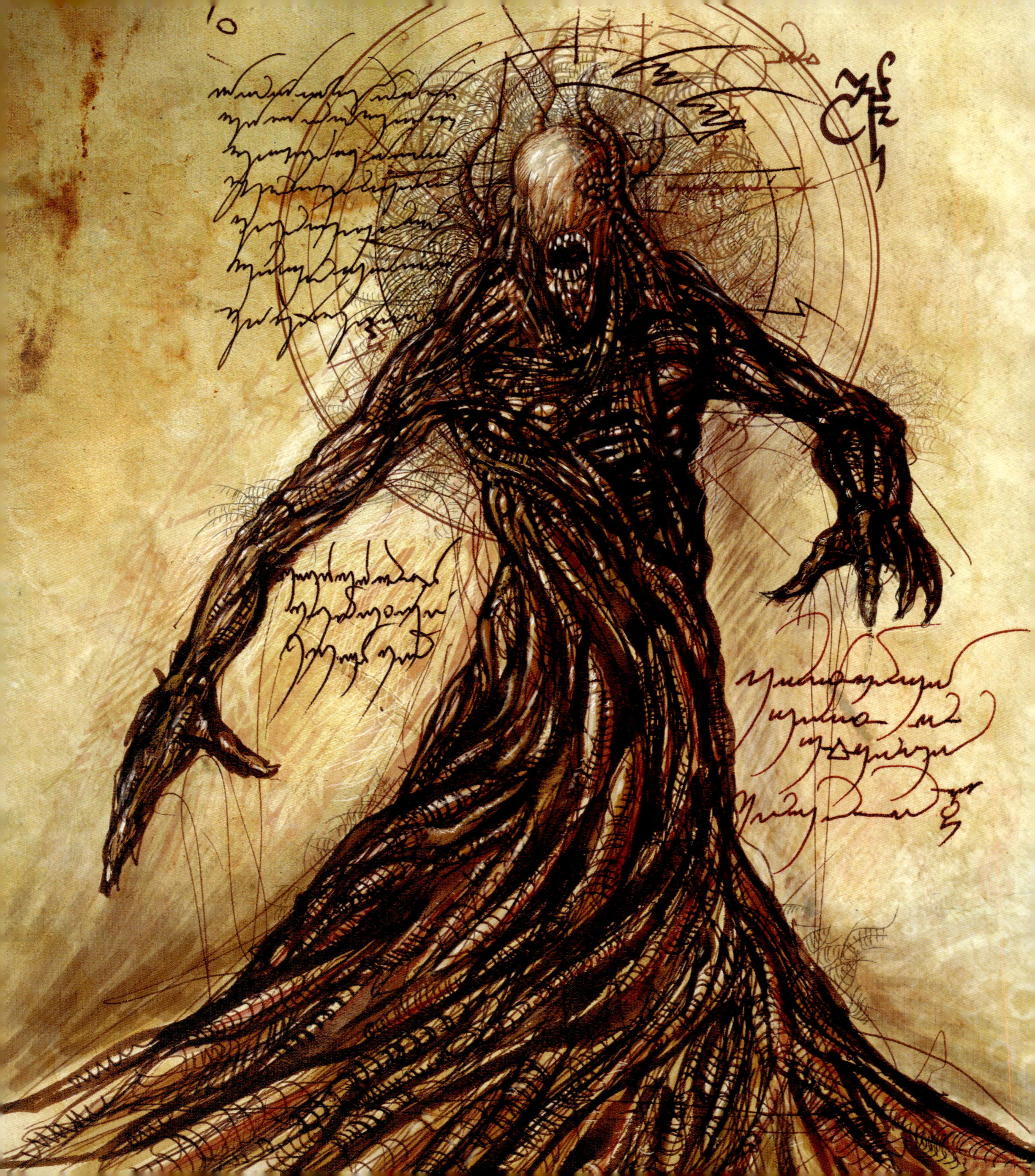

would be plunged into eternal darkness – the developers and writers focused particularly on this aspect.

The ***Tome of Eternal Darkness*** is an obvious ode to the ***Necronomicon***, with the Ancient Ones featured in the game representing Lovecraft's 'Great Old Ones'. The Ancient Mantorok, who lives underground and waits is also a clear homage to the great Cthulhu, who lies dreaming in the sunken city.

Story Within a Story

However, the game doesn't just take inspiration from the ***Necronomicon***; it also touches on many thematic aspects of traditional Lovecraft stories – with further hints to ***The King in Yellow***. As the game's protagonists are exposed to horrific sights, their sanity level starts to decrease; much like that of the characters who encounter the ***Necronomicon*** and the fictional play 'The King in Yellow'. The game's story in general is told in a similar way to Lovecraft's 'The Call of Cthulhu' – with the story-within-a-story the most recognizable aspect. ***Eternal Darkness: Sanity's Requiem*** went on to win the Satellite Award for Most Innovative Story Design, so it just goes to show that Lovecraft continues to have quite the impact.

'It was all the same dream. A dream that you had inside a locked room. A dream about being a person. And like a lot of dreams there's a monster at the end of it.'

True Detective

Further Your Arcane Knowledge

There are so many books and websites around to help you delve further into the darkness of the ***Necronomicon*** – if you dare, of course! As well as those below, you should also check out the fantastic fiction discussed throughout the main text.

Books

***At the Mountains of Madness: A Graphic Novel* illustrated by I.N.J. Culbard:** This, along with the other titles in the graphic novel series, truly captures the essence of Lovecraft with beautiful and often harrowing drawings.

Clive Barker's A–Z of Horror: This TV series and accompanying book studies some of the most inspiring horror creations, including those of Lovecraft and H.R. Giger.

***H.P. Lovecraft: A Comprehensive Bibliography* by S.T. Joshi:** This gives a great, in-depth look at Lovecraft's stories, exploring thematic similarities as well as the history of the man himself.

Necronomicon: The Best Weird Tales of H.P. Lovecraft: A compendium of Lovecraft's work.

New Tales of the Cthulhu Mythos: An anthology of fiction edited by Ramsey Campbell.

Websites

10 Things You Should Know about H.P. Lovecraft:
theguardian.com/books/2014/aug/20/ten-things-you-should-know-about-hp-lovecraft
To celebrate Lovecraft's birthday, *The Guardian* put together this neat little list of unknown gems about our favourite author.

August Derleth Society:
derleth.org
The Society is dedicated to promoting Derleth's work and preserving his memory.

How Stuff Works: How the *Necronomicon* Works:
entertainment.howstuffworks.com/arts/literature/necronomicon.htm
Jonathan Strickland put together this great all-round guide to the ***Necronomicon***. In another article, he tackles Cthulhu

The H.P. Lovecraft Archive:
hplovecraft.com/
A fantastic resource all about the man himself, where you can learn about his life, his work and his fictional universe.

H.R. Giger's offical website:
hrgiger.com
Many of Giger's phenomenal artworks can be viewed here, as well as information about his life and his work on ***Alien***.

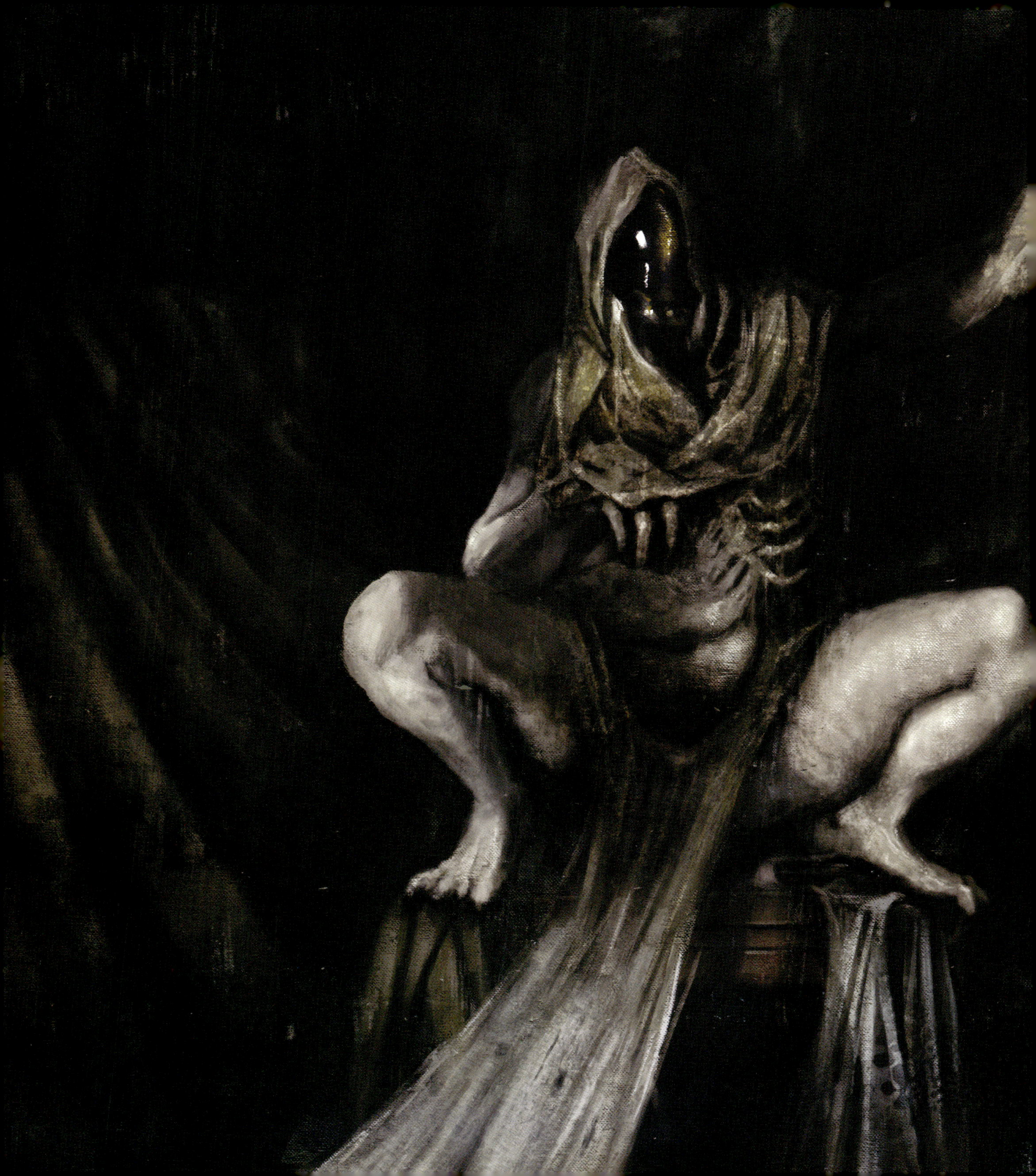

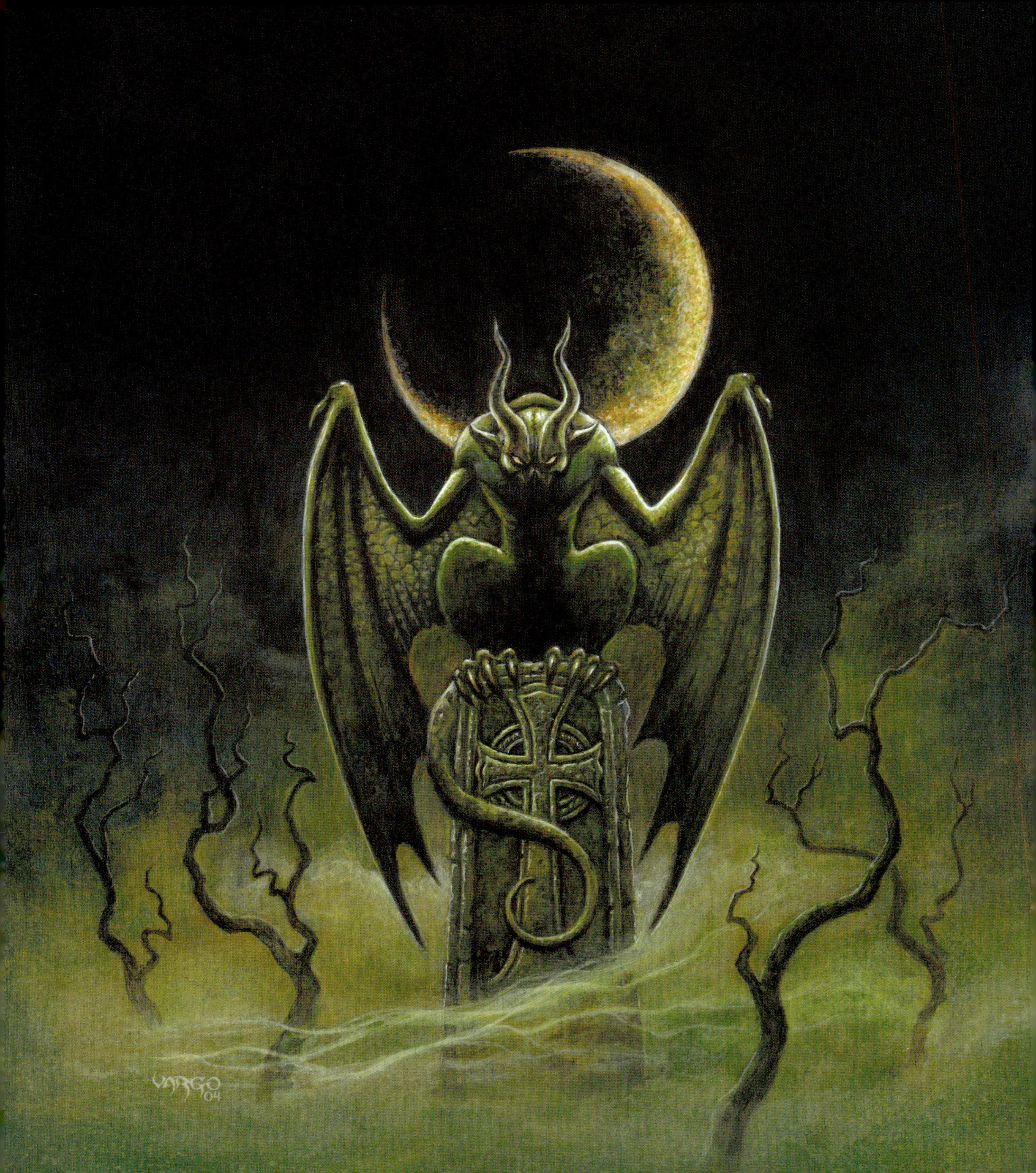
VARGO
'04

The *Necronomicon* Anti-FAQ:

digital-brilliance.com/necron/necron.htm

A scholarly collection of frequently asked questions written by the book's fictional author Abdul Alhazred.

***Necronomicon* Playing Cards:**

ebay.com/itm/1-Deck-NEW-BICYCLE-MYTHOS-NECRONOMICON-Playing-Cards-Limited-Edition-/111120402585

Funded back in 2012 on Kickstarter, these playing cards are a great way of exploring the creatures lurking within the pages of the ***Necronomicon***.

The NetherReal:

netherreal.de

A detailed website which includes amongst its treasures the Cthulhu Lexicon,an online encyclopedia of creatures, places and artifacts from the Cthulhu Mythos.

OpenCulture: Free Lovecraft audio books:

openculture.com/2014/10/h-p-lovecrafts-classic-horror-stories-free-online.html

OpenCulture has brought together the best in Lovecraft audio books and has put them in a handy little playlist for you to enjoy.

Selected Authors of Supernatural Horror:

http://alangullette.com/lit/horror.htm

Featuring biographies, photographs and links to other resources on not only H.P. Lovecraft but also authors such as Algernon Blackwood, Arthur Machen and Edgar Allan Poe.

Sacred Texts:

sacred-texts.com/nec

This handy website tells you all about the history of the ***Necronomicon***, as well as linking to a number of Lovecraft stories.

Stuff You Should Know: Is the *Necronomicon* real?:

stuffyoushouldknow.com/podcasts/is-the-necronomicon-real

This podcast brings together three die-hard Lovecraft fans, where they discuss pretty much everything to do with the ***Necronomicon*** and its origins in just under half-an-hour.

Quotation Credits

The quotes throughout the book are given brief attributions. Fuller credit information can be found here: 16: 'The Festival' (first published in January 1925 ***Weird Tales***) by H.P. Lovecraft; 30, 37: 'The Dunwich Horror' (first published in April 1929 **Weird Tales**) by H.P. Lovecraft; 44: ***The Burrowers Beneath*** (1974) by Brian Lumley; 58: ***Army of Darkness*** (1992), said by the character Ash Williams (played by Bruce Campbell); 72: 'The Silver Key' (first published in January 1929 ***Weird Tales***) by H.P. Lovecraft; 75: 'I Cthluhu' (1986) by Neil Gaiman; 79: 'The Hound' (first published in February 1924 ***Weird Tales***) by H.P. Lovecraft; 85: From a letter to Willis Conover (July 29, 1936) by H.P. Lovecraft; 86: attributed to H.R. Giger; 111: attributed to by H.P. Lovecraft; 114: ***Cast a Deadly Spell*** (1991), said by the character Amos Hackshaw (played by David Warner); 121: ***True Detective*** (2014–), said by the character Rust Cohle (played by Matthew McConaughey).

Acknowledgements

Biographies

Sammy Maine (Author)

Sammy Maine is a writer who has lent her skills to the likes of *Computer Arts*, *SFX* magazine and *Imagine FX*. When she's not penning her thoughts about design and art, she's attending gigs and pretending that music journalism is a career that still exists. Born in America and growing up in Turkey, London and Northampton, she now resides in Bristol.

S.T. Joshi (Foreword)

S.T. Joshi is a leading authority on H.P. Lovecraft, as well as other writers mostly in the realms of supernatural and fantasy fiction. He is the author of *The Weird Tale* (1990), *The Modern Weird Tale* (2001), and *Unutterable Horror: A History of Supernatural Fiction* (2012). His award-winning biography *H. P. Lovecraft: A Life* (1996) was later expanded as *I Am Providence: The Life and Times of H. P. Lovecraft* (2010).

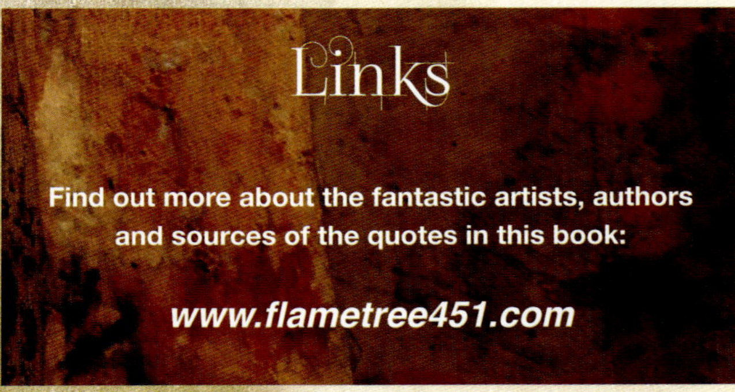

Links

Find out more about the fantastic artists, authors and sources of the quotes in this book:

www.flametree451.com

Picture Credits

The Artists

Special thanks to all the artists who have contributed artwork for this book:

© 2015 **Marcelo Orsi Blanco** All Rights Reserved 1 & 63; © **Dave Oliver** 3 & 33 & 33, 36, 41, 42, 49, 96–97; © **Joseph Vargo** (www.josephvargo.com) 4, 9 & 128, 12, 15, 17, 31, 78, 87, 124; © **Bryan Reagan** 6, 88, 89, 127; Artwork by/© **ComtesseDionaea**/FURORART.deviantART.com, Model: **Silvia Alessandrini**/silvietepes.deviantART.com 11; Artwork by/© **ComtesseDionaea**/FURORART.deviantART.com, Model: **Candace Nirvana**, Model Photographer: **Marcus J. Ranum** 21; Artwork by/© **ComtesseDionaea**/FUROR ART.deviantART.com, Model: **Miss Souls**, Model Photographer: **Tom Lanzrath** 23; © **Francois Launet** 18–19, 22, 25, 26, 77, 81, 83, 84, 120; © **Gwabryel** 24, 115; © **Dan Verkys** 28–29, 53, 60; © **Borja Pindado** 35, 45, 46, 104; © **Jason Engle** 39; © **Camille Alquier** 47, 64, 68, 73, 110, 123; © **Bastien Grivet** 50; **Sanskarans** (Sandeep karunakaran); © SANS Entertainment 55; © A**lexander Levett** 56; © **Pasi Juhola** 59; © **absumaniac** 67; © **Matthew G. Lewis** 113, 117; © **Robert W. Cook** (Norot) 119.

Other Picture sources

Courtesy of/© **Photoshot** (and the following): 94; **LFI** 91; **Metropolitan Filmexport** 93; **1979 20th Century Fox/LFI** 100; **HBO / DR Photo JIm Bridges** 103, 107.

Courtesy of/© **Shutterstock** and the following: **breaker213** 74; **Heartland Arts** 71, 109; **DarkGeometryStudios** 99.

All recurring decorations are courtesy of public domain/ Wikimedia Commons.

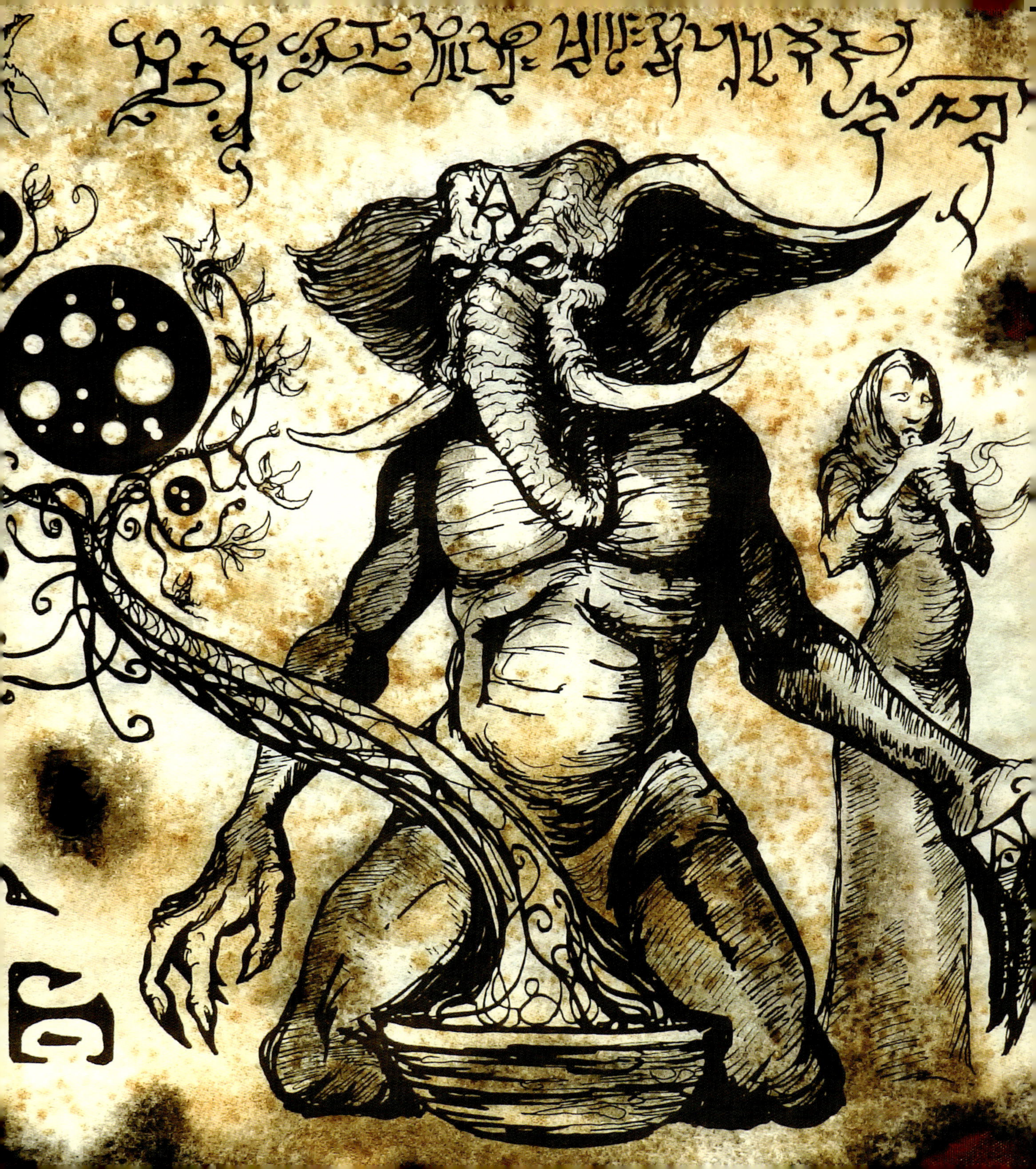

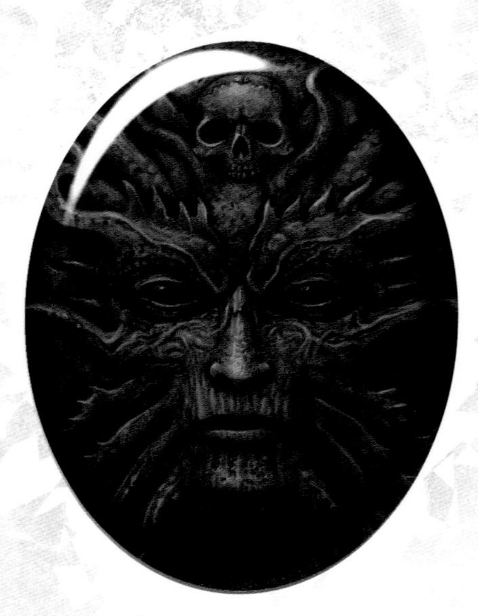